Homo Psyche

T0386119

Homo Psyche

On Queer Theory and Erotophobia

GILA ASHTOR

Fordham University Press

NEW YORK   2021

Fordham University Press has no responsibility for the persistence or accuracy
of URLs for external or third-party Internet websites referred to in this
publication and does not guarantee that any content on such websites is,
or will remain, accurate or appropriate.

Fordham University Press also publishes its books in a variety of electronic
formats. Some content that appears in print may not be available
in electronic books.

Visit us online at www.fordhampress.com.

Library of Congress Cataloging-in-Publication Data

Names: Ashtor, Gila, author.
Title: Homo psyche : on queer theory and erotophobia / Gila Ashtor.
Description: New York : Fordham University Press, 2021. | Includes
    bibliographical references and index.
Identifiers: LCCN 2021014280 | ISBN 9780823294169 (hardback) | ISBN
    9780823294152 (paperback) | ISBN 9780823294176 (epub)
Subjects: LCSH: Homosexuality—Psychological aspects. | Queer theory. |
    Erotophobia.
Classification: LCC HQ76.25 .A84 2021 | DDC 306.7601—dc23
LC record available at https://lccn.loc.gov/2021014280

Printed in the United States of America

23 22 21   5 4 3 2 1

First edition

CONTENTS

Contents

Homo Psyche

Introduction
Homo Psyche: On Queer Theory
and Erotophobia

Queer Theory's "Self-Critical" Turn

Can queer theory be *erotophobic*? This project proceeds from the per-plexing observation that for all of its political agita, rhetorical virtuosity, and intellectual restlessness, queer theory conforms to a model of erotic life that is *psychologically* conservative and narrow. Even after several decades of combative, dazzling, irreverent queer critical thought, the field remains far from grasping that sexuality's radical potential lies in its being understood as "exogenous, intersubjective and intrusive."[1] This predica-ment is especially bewildering because, in designating sexuality its pri-mary object of study, queer criticism has always attested to the primacy of sex and sexuality to any future paradigm of radical thought. Having taken the complexity of desire from the margins to the center of close reading, insisted on the subject's multiplicity and on the value (for criticism and for life) of non-conforming, non-normative attachment, queer theory has avowed the seriousness of sex as a privileged site for philosophical and politico-ethical speculation, even judging others according to how well or poorly they integrated insights about sexuality into their analytics. And yet, this book shows that to the extent theorizing sexuality aspires to a rigorous reformulation of prevailing ideology, and to the degree queer studies provides a set of conceptual elaborations beyond its own perfor-mative gestures, the practical-philosophical promises of queer theory remain unfulfilled.

The scope of the following critique is avowedly comprehensive even as it recognizes that the self-reflexivity of queer discourse can make it seem inured to large-scale criticism of this kind. At once grandiose and fatalistic, judgmental and self-deprecating, queer theory often gives the impression that it undefensively anticipates critique. Indeed, in the nearly three decades since Eve Kosofsky Sedgwick declared that "an understanding of virtually any aspect of modern Western culture must be, not merely incomplete, but damaged in its central substance to the degree that it does not incorporate a critical analysis of modern homo/heterosexual defini-tion,"[2] queer studies has rarely shied away from deconstructing its own premises. As a field, it has demonstrated a remarkable appetite for ques-tioning its most basic conceptual coordinates, which, as a discursive strategy, has worked to solidify its status as the vanguard of cutting-edge theory. Declaring itself "a category in the process of formation,"[3] queer theory has proudly insisted on the instability of its own aims and objects. Indeed, this deliberate willingness to transcend any particular object or identity, what Annamarie Jagose has called "its definitional indetermi-nacy, its elasticity," is "part of queer's semantic clout, part of its political efficacy." The professed detachment toward any particular object or iden-tification has seemingly served queer theory quite well; in the second decade of the twenty-first century, queer studies has expanded its hori-zons to include trans and disability studies, queer of color critique, affect studies, postcolonial critique, and animal studies in rich and heteroge-neous ways that build on and adapt many of the field's earliest, and more limited, presuppositions. As Jack Halberstam has recently said in relation to studying "wildness" through a queer theoretical lens, "In my chapter on falconry in *Wild Things*, I discuss the writer T. H. White through Helen Macdonald's brilliant rendering of him. . . . She is fairly confident that he is a closeted gay man, but I am not sure. I mean, he's not obviously having relationships with men; he'd like to have relationships with boys, but that's not an option. He's into flagellation, sadomasochism, and hawks. What kind of desire is that? As Macdonald points out, the words White uses are fairy, fey, and ferox—and this vocabulary offers a very different geometry of desire, one that runs through the ferox and not the closet, through the binary of domestic/wild and not secret/known."[4]

Even amidst all this self-transformation, queer theory is often explic-itly iconoclastic, as if maintaining low expectations is the only attitude conducive to indeterminacy. In a remark that captures this sentiment well, Michael Warner has said that in the field's early days, "most of us were using the term in those years with not entirely straight faces."[5] This same attitude of amusement, self-mockery, and skepticism is evident across a range of work in which queer theorists exhibit eagerness to puncture their own lofty, rainbow-colored dreams. As early as 1994, Teresa de Lauretis—who is credited with coining "queer theory" in a 1990 conference by the same name—rejected the term as a marketing strategy and by 2011, Janet Halley and Andrew Parker opened their edited collection, *After Sex? On Writing Since Queer Theory*, by asking, "What has queer theory become now that it has a past?"[6] While announcing its own futility may be a defense against shame or future disappointment (it doesn't shock or sting as much if whatever you could say about me, I've already said about me first), in recent years this preternatural interest in examining the limits of its organizing claims has resulted in what Heather Love has called, a "crisis for the field of queer studies."[7] As a reflection of this "crisis," the past decade of queer scholarship can be characterized by the "self-critical" turn in queer studies: Whereas the first generation of queer critique could still locate revolutionary potential in the indefinable, open-ended, infinitely mobile horizon of anti-identitarian identity, a new generation of work demands that queerness be problematized, contextualized, and deconstructed in an urgent effort to examine what underlying ideological conditions produce a *queerness* that is surprisingly complicit with existing politico-ethical norms.[8] Therefore, whereas early queer theory was shaped by an activist and antihomophobic discourse that secured its identity in the defiant repudiation of social-sexual norms, a growing body of second-generation queer scholarship continues to persuasively show how queerness converges with, and reproduces, the imperialist political structures it defined itself against. Concepts such as homonormativity (Duggan), homonationalism (Puar), and queer liberalism (Eng) draw a direct connection between the field's present-day complicity with oppressive national and transnational regimes and the unrecognized ideological foundations of its theoretical canon.

As many theorists have observed, the political landscape has changed dramatically in the two decades since queer theory emerged. The assimilation of gays and lesbians into the cultural, legal, and social mainstream has complicated the field's early identification of sexual non-normativity with political subversion, provoking urgent debate about the conceptual viability of the homosexual as a "revolutionary agent, or as the harbinger of a new era" (Love, 2017). As David Eng, J. Halberstam, and Jose Esteban Munoz observed in their 2005 field intervention, "What's Queer About Queer Studies Now?," "While in prior decades gays and lesbians sustained a radical critique of family and marriage, today many members of these groups have largely abandoned such critical positions, demanding access to the nuclear family and its associated rights, recognitions, and privileges from the state. That such queer liberalism comes at a historical moment of extreme right-wing nationalist politics should give us immediate pause."[9] Eng, Halberstam, and Munoz's call for a "continuing critique" locates its urgency in the pervasive sense, shared by scholars across a broad interdisciplinary spectrum, that, in spite of its proclaimed radicalism, the tools that currently make up the queer theoretical canon are consistently failing to disrupt established positions and ideologies. This concern with the future of the field and challenge to its dominant rhetorical and intellectual tropes contribute to the momentum generated by a younger generation of queer scholars who are actively confronting the limits of queer epistemology and methodology.

For many practitioners, the current de facto reliance on negativity, and its associated interpretive strategies, is a malignant deformation of critique that effectively delimits the field's subjects/objects of study, affective range, critical processes, and theoretical findings. In a deep and provocative elaboration of these themes, Michael Snediker's *Queer Optimism* (2009) demonstrates how the field's overinvestment in negative affects and correlative condescension toward positive ones has effectively estranged queer studies from the actual subjects it purports to explain by insisting on tropes that are drastically at odds with complex queer experience.[10] In several recent books, Mari Ruti has also focused on the impotence of a negative modality, which, she argues, prioritizes its own aesthetics of coolness and brutality at the expense of ethical considerations. As Ruti has recently observed in her book-length conversation with political theorist Amy Allen, "I have chafed against some of the more excessive features of progressive theory, such as its semi-automatic celebration of the annihilation of the subject and its by now almost ritualistic rejection of everything that even hints at agency, autonomy, or normative justice. I of course understand the historical reasons for the refutation of these tropes, which have to do with the ways in which progressive theory has positioned itself in opposition to everything that's associated with the Enlightenment, because there's no question that the ideals of the Enlightenment can't be dissociated from problematic notions of self-transparency, sovereignty, rationality, and mastery. . . . Nevertheless, I've been uncomfortable with critical-theoretical models that valorize desubjectivation and the pulverization of the subject. . . . I'm also suspicious of these models because their fetishization has become the default position in my field."[11]

In 2015, a decade after Eng, Halberstam, and Munoz's intervention, Robyn Wiegman and Elizabeth Wilson issued another major challenge, this time drawing attention to how the field's "attachment to a politics of oppositionality (against, against, against)" reduces normativity's complexity to a simplistic operation of power that queer critics can then heroically negate and reprimand.[12] The forceful critique of how an entrenched "antinormativity" actually bolsters, rather than challenges, the operation of a "repressive hypothesis" takes place within a broader conversation about the "negativity" of contemporary literary studies.[13] Bruno Latour's much-cited essay in *Critical Inquiry* entitled "Why Has Critique Run Out of Steam? From Matters of Fact to Matters of Concern" (2004) figures prominently as an inspiration for the rich arsenal of alternative reading styles that are fashioned explicitly against the "thought styles" and "critical moods" of contemporary theory.[14] As Elizabeth Anker and Rita Felski have described of the "post-critical" turn, "It is no longer feasible, in short, to assume that critique is synonymous with leftist resistance. . . . Indeed, the shift away from suspicion may conceivably inspire a more nuanced vision of how political change comes about" (9).[15] According to this view, queer theory's reflexive and entrenched position of "negativity" inadvertently replicates the very imaginative and ethical rigidities it means to subvert. Felski points toward "a growing sense that our intellectual life is out of kilter, that scholars in the humanities are far more fluent in nay-saying than yay-saying, and that eternal vigilance, unchecked by alternatives, can easily lapse into the complacent cadences of auto-pilot argument" (9).

If the provocative field interventions of Eng, Halberstam, and Munoz in "What's Queer about Queer Studies Now?" (2005) and Wiegman and Wilson in "What Is Queer Theory without Antinormativity?" (2015) mark two major moments within the last decade of the field's "self-critical" turn, there have been many significant critiques that have operationalized and extended these insights by focusing on some of the field's most entrenched, but otherwise routinely unanalyzed, features.[16] The publication of Kadji Amin's *Disturbing Attachments* (2017) marks a key moment in the increasing formalization of this up-and-coming scholarship. Directed explicitly against the field's received perception of itself as "endlessly open-ended, polyvalent, and reattachable,"[17] Amin calls for a "heuristic of deidealization" that interrogates "the worrisome harmony between *queer*'s much trumpeted mobility, flexibility, adaptability, and portability and the demands for accelerated obsolescence and flexible and mobile labor that characterize late capitalism" (182). Amin's call for a critical engagement with queer studies' unacknowledged ideologies builds upon a steady development of scholarly projects that see in the field's default affective tropes and methodologies a debilitating threat to its cogency as a radical, critical discourse. Joseph Fischel's recent analysis of the field's default attitudes toward "sexual harm" challenges queer studies to develop a more sophisticated model for the relationship between subjectivity and the Law.[18] And writing at the intersection of queer theory and literary studies, Heather Love draws attention to the violence that enables the "queer" to be the "subversive intellectual" who—anti- and inter-disciplinary—has no natural home. By showing, instead, that "the radicalism of the queer break with academic norms" is actually "a familiar form of disciplinary rivalry" (77), Love argues that queer theory requires a more complicated relationship to the "empirical premises and methodological protocols of the social sciences."[19] What distinguishes the recent "self-critical" turn in contemporary queer studies from the usual tradition of relentless self-reflexivity is the scope of these emerging critiques and the applications of a deconstructive method on the field's axiomatic foundations.

These groundbreaking analyses by practitioners in critical race theory, literary and disability studies, and transgender and affect studies, and an abiding concern of many established critics with the practical utility of a queer analytic to grasp the complexity of contemporary life, conduce to a new generation of "self-critical" scholarship that is organized by the shared contention that *queer* no longer guarantees a reliable theoretical purchase on sexual transgression, radical politics, or critical thought. These analyses reflect the urgent demand for scholarship that problematizes the ideological assumptions and conceptual axioms of contemporary queer studies. However, and despite the widespread disappointment with existing modes of analysis, there has, as yet, been no scholarly study that effectively links this "self-critical" turn in second generation queer studies with the "post-critical" turn in the humanities at large. In particular, and despite the pervasiveness and popularity of recent calls to deconstruct the ideological foundations of contemporary queer thought, no study has as yet considered or in any way investigated the singular role of *psychology* in shaping the field's conceptual impasses and politico-ethical limitations. My own study is engaged with these proliferating debates, but rather than discrediting queer negativity for its hypercriticality, for its supposedly being *too* negative, I will show how the performance of a critical attachment to negativity actually works in yet another way that has, so far, gone entirely unnoticed: to protect and enable a core *positive* and *un*critical relation to normative and erotophobic psychological conventions.

Metapsychology refers to "the aggregate of a priori principles that must be in place at the outset for the initiation of analytic interpretation as such."[20] According to Laplanche, "Metapsychology is not the theory of clinical work. It is the theory of the human being insofar as he is affected by an unconscious. A theory, therefore, of the unconscious, of its nature, its genesis, its returns, its effects etc."[21] An analysis that focuses on the metapsychological dimension of queer theorizations will demonstrate why, in spite of how bold and emancipatory key queer formulations might initially seem, the field maintains an uninterrogated reliance on erotophobic psychological conventions that ultimately reproduces an erotophobic relationship to sexuality. Furthermore, it is only by distinguishing political ideology from metapsychology that it becomes possible to observe how, for example, a "queer" position that is "politically" antinormative could be nevertheless "psychologically" erotophobic. Joining the recent demand for scholarship that critiques queer studies' presumptive "antinormativity" (Wiegman and Wilson, 2015), institutional methodology (Love, 2016), "philosophical foundations" (Huffer, 2010), "strategic history" (North, 2017) and "affective genealogy" (Amin, 2017), *Homo Psyche* introduces metapsychology as a new dimension of analysis that zeroes in on the underlying psychological assumptions that determine contemporary critical thought. Such an intervention deepens current debates about the future of queer studies by demonstrating how the field's systematic neglect of metapsychology as a necessary and independent realm of ideology ultimately enforces the complicity of queer studies with psychological conventions that are fundamentally erotophobic and therefore inimical to queer theory's critical, radical, and ethical project.

Through the development of metapsychology as a distinctive analytic, this study illustrates how every discourse of sexuality is shaped by a set of psychological claims that, though determinative, remain routinely untheorized. An organizing hypothesis of *Homo Psyche* speculates that the total absence of any critical attention to the complicity of certain psychological tropes with an erotophobic ideology reflects the field-wide conflation of all psychology with dominant, and what Laplanche will call "Ptolemaic," psychoanalysis. This absolute equivalence of all psychological explanation with the paradigm of traditional psychoanalysis polarizes the field into those who either accept (and apply) or reject (and dismiss) psychoanalysis *tout court*. Unfortunately, such a rudimentary configuration of the field prevents a more sophisticated appraisal of how and in what ways particular psychological ideas reproduce erotophobic conventions. One major aim of this book is to demonstrate that by relying on psychoanalysis as a stable guarantor of sexual radicalism, queer theorizations apply Freudian/Lacanian positions without interrogating in what ways these metapsychological systems are *themselves* complicit with an erotophobic ideology. *Homo Psyche* therefore introduces a break with the current configuration of traditional psychoanalysis as the presumptive and undisputed foundation for radical psycho-sexual theorizations. In order to elaborate one example of a critical alternative, I will introduce the innovations of French theoretician and psychoanalyst Jean Laplanche. Among metapsychological thinkers, Laplanche (1924–2012) is unique for noticing—and devoting the majority of his later career to demonstrating—that psychoanalysis was not immune to erotophobic conceptualizations that went against its own proclaimed commitment to the radicalism of unconscious sexuality. In order to rigorously articulate and defend the centrality of sexuality to psychic life, Laplanche insisted on "new foundations for psychoanalysis" that radically departed from existing Freudian and Lacanian models of the mind.

To particularize how the use of an erotophobic psychological paradigm delimits and ultimately derails queer theory's otherwise radical ambitions, this study conducts a purposive survey of six major theoretical concepts, through the lens of six eminent individual critics who represent exemplary, influential, and authoritative developments of them: Eve Sedgwick on "hermeneutics," Leo Bersani on "sex," Jane Gallop on "violation," Lee Edelman on "radicalism," Judith Butler on "gender," and Lauren Berlant on "relationality." Although these thinkers and themes do not exhaust the range of ideas at work in queer criticism, and although their positions are not at all uncontested, and while there are other topics that are constitutive and essential, my particular choices reflect what, in my assessment, constitute major ideas that have shaped and continue to be hugely influential in the field. Although these critics are heterogeneous, idiosyncratic, and sometimes controversial, I treat their writing as a window into the zeitgeist of queer theory, and I believe that taken together they provide a substantial view from which to "put to work" queer studies. "Putting to work" is a phrase Laplanche uses to describe his methodology for testing the viability and coherence of Freudian ideas that proceeds by stressing key elements of a theoretical paradigm to examine how it functions.

Therefore, while their fidelity to psychoanalysis affirms the "subject"-centricity of these thinkers, in sharp contrast to other strands of queer thought that draw on the anti-psychoanalytic critiques of Foucault and Deleuze to define queerness in direct opposition to "psychological man,"[22] it is one aim of this project to show that metapsychology refers to more than merely a theory of the "deep" subject's privileged interiority and pertains instead to any speculation about how change takes place; how relationality is structured; how gender, intimacy, and pleasure are inhabited; and how knowledge is transmitted and obtained. Therefore, metapsychology is endogenous to critique. As such, a metapsychological analysis that examines the underlying psychological ideology operating in a text distinguishes Theory of Mind (a category of claims) from one of its particular iterations (psychoanalysis). Advancing this methodological break for the first time provides queer theory with an evaluative process that has been elusive in preceding critical endeavors: a technique for marking precisely where, in politico-ethical arguments that promise an extreme repudiation of oppressive ideological norms, the uncritical dependence on normative psychological assumptions perpetuates erotophobic formulations that misrecognize the complexity of queer erotic lives and thereby prevent queer critique from elaborating a subversion of sexuality's status quo. *Homo Psyche*'s integration of scholarship on Laplanche, close readings of literary texts, and a comprehensive critique of contemporary queer theory will generate new and unexplored theoretical territory for the further development of queer studies.

Critical and Queer: The Relationship to Metapsychology

In a field so thoroughly invested in understanding how social and political phenomena impact individual experience, it is remarkable that as yet no single study has been devoted to evaluating the type of psychological theories on which nearly all of queer formulations depend. The total absence of any sustained critical encounter between queer theory and metapsychology is particularly surprising given the centrality of psychological theorizations to queer studies' most enduring formulations. *Homo Psyche* shows how the bifurcation of the field into those who either accept psychoanalysis (and therefore apply it uncritically) or those who reject it (and therefore dismiss it tout court) has resulted in the total neglect of metapsychology as a legitimate angle of critique. In the absence of such an appraisal, queer theorists rely on vague and often superficial notions of what constitutes a "radical" idea—which is usually, merely, determined by its proximity to the norm. This simplistic approach to radicalism and normativity has also meant that, instead of interrogating what "radical" sexuality means, queer theorists resort to the uncritical application of a psychoanalytic paradigm that seems congenial with an anti-normative agenda. In practical terms, this has meant that psychoanalysis is seen as useful to the extent it corroborates ideas that have already been advanced and popularized within the poststructuralist canon. Rather than thoroughly evaluating metapsychological presumptions, mainstream queer theory adopts Freud-Lacan wholesale,[23] as though their supposedly "radical" bona fides have cleared them for uncritical application. My study observes how the automatic conflation of any theory of mind with Freudian-Lacanian psychoanalysis is routine and uninterrogated in the field even as it has prevented queer studies from treating psychology as a discrete sphere of ideology that can be rigorously deconstructed.

Although arriving at the extreme opposite conclusion vis-à-vis the theoretical benefits of psychology, Lynne Huffer's *Mad for Foucault* (2010) issues a vigorous call for queer theory to start explicitly acknowledging the major role of psychoanalysis in queer formulations. Huffer writes, "Queer theory now has a history—as a body of work, as an academic field, as an analytical focus, as a mode of thinking—the time has come to submit queer theory to the kind of historical, genealogical critique Foucault spent his life attempting to practice."[24] Huffer traces the failures of contemporary critical theory to its continued dependence on psychoanalysis, going as far as to say that the psyche is the field's untreated "symptom" of a deeper problem with subjectivity. According to Huffer, queer theory needs to be rebuilt along non-Freudian/non-Lacanian lines in order to actualize Foucault's vision of erotic life. This argument repeats the field-wide tendency of equating all psychology with Freudian-Lacanian psychoanalysis, thereby leaving an abstract anti-psychology, or "subjectless" desire, as the only alternative basis for a new queer subjectivity. While possibly compelling in the abstract, Huffer's recourse to "subjectless" sexuality reproduces the incoherence of Foucault's position; as Joel Whitebook has shown in "Against Interiority: Foucault's Struggle with Psychoanalysis," Foucault's ambivalence toward the psychic subject forced him to propose alternative terms that lacked clarity and meaning, such as "bodies and pleasures," which "assume the character of pure, informed matter that can be voluntarily shaped and reshaped—constructed—without constraint."[25] Although Foucault "tries to indict psychoanalysis as a coconspirator in this 'game of truth,' which tries to force sexual nonidentity into a classificatory scheme" (336), his notion of raw pleasures being violated by the normative apparatus of sexuality (which can only be redeemed through aesthetic self-fashioning) falls into an interminable trap that pits monolithic identity versus a utopianism outside of nature. As Tim Dean has rightly observed, "without an appreciation of the unconscious, queer sexualities themselves become normalizing (paradoxical though that sounds), insofar as sexuality becomes wedded to identity."[26] While so much depends on how "the unconscious" is defined—and there are certainly flawed versions, which Foucauldians are correct in rejecting—efforts to dispense with subjectivity altogether lack conceptual and practical coherence. As feminist philosopher Rosi Braidotti observed about the relationship between the posthumanism of

Donna Haraway and psychoanalytic theories of subjectivity: "[Haraway] wants to invent a new discourse for the unconscious" and therefore "opposes the Oedipalized unconscious, and the binary structures that descend from the Oedipal family romance" but "one still needs at least some subject position: this need not be either unitary or exclusively anthropocentric, but it must be the site for political and ethical accountability, for collective imaginaries and shared aspirations."[27]

In many ways, Huffer's indictment of psychology (on the grounds that all psychology equals a regime of moralizing subjectivity) exemplifies queer theory's long-standing struggle with psychoanalysis. Tim Dean and Christopher Lane have called the field's relationship to psychoanalysis "adversarial,"[28] and in a recent collection of essays on the topic Noreen Giffney and Eve Watson observe that queer studies is "both reliant upon and suspicious of psychoanalysis as a clinical practice and discourse."[29] In a view shared by many, Giffney and Watson write that "theorists use psychoanalytic concepts to help them think about a variety of topics" while nevertheless expressing disinterest in the clinical setting and profound skepticism toward a vast array of psychoanalytic ideas (32–33). In their criticism of this situation, Dean and Lane explain that major thinkers such as "Butler and Sedgwick use psychoanalytic terminology and concepts in their work while maintaining a critical distance toward psychoanalysis in a way that often seems incoherent. With regard to psychoanalysis, these critics sometimes want to have their cake and eat it too."[30] While this distrust can credibly be traced to sociological factors— "psychoanalytic attitudes towards homosexuality as a 'developmental arrest' (Segal 1990, 253), bisexuality as an immature regression to fantasy (Rapoport 2009), and transsexuality as a marker of a psychotic structure (Millott 1990) have resulted in uneasy and suspicious reactions from those involved in sexuality studies (Dean and Lane 2001)"[31]—the tension between these discourses also exceeds these events and can be said to have as much, if not more, to do with the fact that, as an intellectual discourse, queer studies developed in direct opposition to some of the most basic tenets of metapsychology. For example, while clinical theory views the individual's striving for a coherent identity as an important developmental achievement, queer theorists treat identity as a sociocultural construct that needs to be vitiated, not affirmed. Additionally, whereas clinical theory is oriented toward alleviating suffering by exploring the patient's private fantasmatic life, the Marxist-Foucauldian tenets of queer theory typically treat "privacy" as one of capitalism's most malignant effects. Critical race theory has further shown the ways that psychoanalytic claims to universality belie their Eurocentric origins, thereby failing to provide an account of psychology that is genuinely representative.[32] Gilles Deleuze and Felix Guattari's *Anti-Oedipus* is of course exemplary of this tradition; aiming to discredit the Freudian metanarrative of the sovereign self, they treat the Oedipus complex as a construct, not a psychological "fact," and aim to depersonify desire so as to liberate it from its current status as merely imitating culture. According to Deleuze and Guattari, the Oedipal triangle is neither a universal psychological structure nor a coherent representation of psychic events but merely a reproduction of nuclear family dynamics that Freud failed to recognize as such.[33] The emancipatory energy of this position is unmistakable— overthrow the sovereign self! become desiring-machines!—and it remains a popular trope within queer theory, despite extensive accounts of its severe limitations.[34] Moreover, these attempts to discredit psychoanalysis as a viable explanatory paradigm on the grounds that theories like the "Oedipus complex" are flawed, mistakenly conflate metapsychology with the "mytho-symbolic." As Laplanche shows, metapsychology is the "hard kernel" of psychoanalysis (referring to the subject of "enlarged" sexuality) while at another level, the "mytho-symbolic" refers to theories that are fundamentally narrative, "helping to give form to a personal history that is clearly of crucial importance to the human being."[35] The "Oedipus complex" is exemplary of a "mytho-symbolic" construction because it derives from cultural surroundings and is not falsifiable. "Unfortunately," Laplanche writes, "Freud ended up regarding the sexual theories of children [the mytho-symbolic]—the apparatus best suited to repressing the unconscious—as the very kernel of the unconscious."[36] As a result, critical attempts to delegitimize psychoanalysis because of its more egregious "mytho-symbolic" constructions merely reproduce Freud's own tendencies to misunderstand and misapprehend the constitutive differences among levels of theorization. Many of Freud's "mytho-symbolic" constructions are undoubtedly wrong, but discarding metapsychological conceptualization in its entirety is brash, superficial, and detrimental.

Reflecting on the relationship between psychoanalysis and critical theory from a slightly different angle, political theorists Amy Allen and Brian O'Connor have recently observed that the popular half-in, half-out way of using psychoanalysis is problematic because it leaves contemporary theory unable to substantiate many of its foundational claims. They write, "Although philosophy might therefore be credited with orienting us toward these insights into the 'pathologies' of modern life, it could do little more than gesture at the psychological dimensions of those experiences. Why does the withholding of recognition damage those who experience it? Which are the human needs that are failed under those circumstances? What motivates individuals and social groups to struggle to achieve recognition that has been withheld from them?"[37] Allen and O'Connor acknowledge that while psychoanalysis—at least in its most dominant permutations—may have had certain ideas that were unpalatable to critical theory, over the course of a century it has greatly expanded its conceptual repertoire such that it "offers a theoretically rich and highly developed set of reflections on philosophical anthropology that provides an important counterpoint to the tendencies toward excessive rationalism and moral idealism in critical theory" (12). To specify the pertinence of these reflections for queer theory, I would further note that, to the extent sexuality is *the* object of queer discourse, psychoanalysis represents more than just an "important counterpoint" but a necessary step in grounding the speculative aspirations of radical theory in a scrupulous understanding of biopsychical life. As Allen has written elsewhere, if we are interested "not only in diagnosing power relations in all their complexity but also in charting possible directions for social transformation, our analysis of power will have to tell us something about how subjection shapes not only our critical capacities but also our will and our desires. Not only that, but our account of autonomy will have to illuminate not just the possibilities for rational, critical reflexivity but also the prospects for reworking will and desire in a direction that motivates emancipatory self-transformation."[38]

This return of the "subject" in critical writing signals a growing awareness that, without a meaningful grasp of the forces that shape experiential life, anti-foundationalism invariably becomes hollow and ineffectual.[39] For this reason, critics within and adjacent to queer theory, such as Melanie Klein and D. W. Winnicott, have made efforts recently to draw on unfamiliar clinical paradigms as a vitalizing resource.[40] According to arguments made in this new work, the problem isn't psychology tout court, but the particular psychological theories of Freud and Lacan, which are insufficiently intersubjective and problematically oblivious to the role of attachment relationships in organizing emotional life. For many critics writing in this vein, queer theory's exclusive reliance on Freudian-Lacanian topologies is symptomatic of how hard it can be to take relationality seriously as a subject of critical reflection. As such, the answer to the Foucauldian critique of psychoanalysis isn't the total abandonment of a meaningful engagement with interior psychic life, but a reorientation toward alternative paradigms (object relations, intersubjective) that emphasize the subject's complex embodiment and embeddedness with others. In an essay that is emblematic of these efforts, Noelle McAfee explicates Winnicott's paper "Fear of Breakdown" in order to show how "collective identities are extensions of individual ones, in fact there is hardly such a thing as an individual identity, for 'identification,' whether external or internal, is always a social relation, a relation with another."[41]

The call to expand the psychoanalytic canon marks a major departure from how psychoanalysis has been traditionally conceived as necessarily limited to Freud and Lacan, and as such tracks with changes in how clinical and theoretical psychoanalysis has developed over the past several decades from a single, dominant Freudianism to a pluralism that recognizes a multiplicity of psychoanalytic paradigms to choose from.[42] Given psychoanalysis's notorious history of schisms and splits, the newfound environment of a "comparative psychoanalysis"[43] is welcome relief, enabling a range of different views to coexist peacefully as separate metapsychologies.

Queer Theory's "Ptolemaic" Tendencies

My book introduces Laplanche as a revolutionary psychological thinker who challenged established psychoanalytic doxa on the grounds it did not go far enough in elaborating the "realism of unconscious sexuality." In doing so, it can seem as though I am making the case for why—in the competitive marketplace of psychoanalytic models—he (and not Winnicott or Klein) offers a preferable metapsychology.[44] But while such a gesture is entirely compatible with discursive trends in both psychoanalysis and critical theory, I resist this approach on the grounds that it misapprehends the nature of Laplanche's intervention and avoids precisely the kind of confrontation with Freudian-Lacanian metapsychology that Laplanche sought to provoke. That is, whereas "pluralism" is the dominant mode of contemporary psychoanalysis, this approach—with its insistence on appreciating the hermeneutic value of diverse analytic paradigms—avoids any substantial engagement with scientifically necessary "first principles" and furthermore allows different models to be treated as equally true, regardless of the fact that most analytic paradigms merely disagree over which parts of subjective experience to highlight but lack comprehensive accounts of human motivation.[45] Moreover, this strategic "pluralism"—which most psychoanalysts celebrate as a symbol of how civilized post-Freudian psychoanalytic discourse has become—functions in yet another way that has gone undertheorized, which is to avoid challenging Freud's original language and formulations.[46]

In order to counter the harmonizing urge of so much recent psychoanalytic writing, I introduce Laplanche as a fierce critic of psychoanalytic doxa. Specifically, I show how Laplanche's meticulous close reading of Freud functions first and foremost as a "negative" metapsychology that aims to elucidate what we *cannot* say about the unconscious, and to illustrate all those ideas and tendencies within psychoanalysis that work *against* the elaboration of sexuality. To this end, Laplanche employs the metaphor of "Ptolemy" versus "Copernicus" to characterize the opposing movements at work in psychoanalytic formulations at all times. Using "centering" and "decentering" to track the movement of Freud's thinking toward and away from the radicalism of the unconscious, Laplanche contends that "if Freud is his own Copernicus, he is also his own Ptolemy."[47] As such, a *"rigorous metapsychology . . .* would be a metapsychology that certainly has its origins in Freud, but which, as the outcome of a working through, does not hesitate to make choices and propose important reconfigurations."[48] Addressing the role of his critical method in developing the foundations for a radical and rigorous metapsychology, Laplanche explains that "putting Freud to work means demonstrating in him what I call an *exigency*, the exigency of a discovery which impels him without always showing him the way, and which may therefore lead him into dead ends or goings-astray. It means following in his footsteps, accompanying him but also criticizing him, seeking other ways—but impelled by an exigency similar to his."[49] For Laplanche, the "exigency" that "impels" Freud is the "discovery" of unconscious sexuality. "There are two facets to the Freudian revolution in the radical decentering it offers," Laplanche explains. "The first is classical: the discovery of the unconscious, in so far as it is precisely *not* our center, as it is an 'excentric' center; the other facet, the seduction theory, is hidden but indispensable to the first for it maintains the unconscious in its alien-ness" (62). Determined to sustain the radicalism of sexuality's "decentering" as against Freudian theory's constant "self-centering and self-begetting," Laplanche insists on an attitude of *"faithful infidelity.* A fidelity with respect to reading and translation, restoring to Freud what he means—including his contradictions and his turning points; an infidelity with respect to the interpretation of Freud's *goings-astray*, in order to try to find what I call 'New Foundations for Psychoanalysis'" (285).

This prioritization of the *object* of psychoanalysis over and against Freud himself initiates a bold intervention that redirects the focus of metapsychology from Freud's particular ideas to the essential discovery of the "sexual" unconscious. From this vantage point, Laplanche reiterates that Freud makes an astonishing scientific discovery—"enlarged" sexuality—which can be defined in the follow way: "1. A sexuality that absolutely goes beyond genitality, and even beyond sexual difference; 2. A sexuality that is related to fantasy; 3. A sexuality that is extremely mobile as to its aim and object; and 4. (a point on which I myself lay great emphasis) a sexuality that has its own 'economic' regime in the Freudian sense of the term, its own principle of functioning, which is not a systematic tendency towards discharge, but a specific tendency towards the increase of tension and the pursuit of excitation. In short, it is a sexuality that exists before or beyond sex or the sexed, and which may perhaps encompass genitality but only under the very specific modality of the phallic."[50] According to Laplanche, Freud and his followers repeatedly conflate "instinct"-sexuality and "drive"-sexuality, leaving us totally unable to grasp the distinctive economy of "enlarged" sexuality.[51] If this were, say, chemistry instead of infantile sexuality, then we might expect the progress of science to proceed unproblematically, or at least that scientists would have little difficulty maintaining a consistent view of their object. But because discovering infantile sexuality is *unlike* discovering boron, then major obstacles arise in the endeavor to look *closely* at the object. Furthermore, and unlike Freud who repeatedly located resistance to his findings out there, in the general public of naïve and religious-minded readers, Laplanche asserts that from the outset, the biggest source of resistance comes not from outside but from Freud himself. It is *Freud* who struggles, and usually fails, to sustain the meaning of "enlarged" sexuality and therefore Freud himself who builds a theory that systematically turns its back on its own discovery. It is *Freud* who, in spite of advancing a theory of "enlarged" sexuality, then proceeds to develop an elaborate system that basically empties sexuality of its radical meaning, and *Freud* who systematically employs an array of rhetorical and conceptual tools to dilute, distort, and undo the force of his most original contributions.

In an effort to explain this confounding dynamic, Laplanche suggests that because the material of "enlarged" sexuality is so radical and provocative, Freud, who compared himself to Copernicus, in actuality couldn't help but also being his own Ptolemy. This view of Freud as both Ptolemy and Copernicus echoes a popular trope that there were "two Freuds"— the "good" one who discovers infantile sexuality and polymorphous perversity and the "bad" one who insists on a transcendental normativity—but it differs sharply from this familiar view by showing that the opposing tendencies of Ptolemy and Copernicus are not equally operational in Freud's theory such that a so-called "good"/radical Freud could be plucked from the "bad" one and made to stand alone, but instead that the revolutionary path of Copernicus is *not*-taken by Freud, and for the most part, *neutralized* by his most important formulations.

In a magisterial essay, "The Unfinished Copernican Revolution," Laplanche explains that, contrary to common sense assumptions, "the opposition between Ptolemy and Copernicus, geocentrism and heliocentrism is a simple, pedagogical one; but let us remember that a revolution is never as revolutionary as it thinks—it has its forerunners in the past, and what it offers as a new opening also carries with it possibilities for potential relapses."[52] Providing a summary of astronomical theory prior to Copernicus, Laplanche sets out to establish a theoretical landscape wherein "relapses" to pre-revolutionary theory are a potentially inevitable component of any revolution. While this may initially seem like a minor interpretive point, the implications are actually immense: First, it means that no revolutionary thinker, regardless of how self-conscious, is the final arbiter of his own theory's revolutionary qualities because that can only be determined by the field of possibilities a given theory opens up (this is in sharp contrast to Freud's insistence that "no one can know better than I what psychoanalysis is"[53]), and second, and related, that the success of a revolutionary theory is contingent on what it opens up and simplifies. Laplanche explains that a primary feature of the Ptolemaic system was its complete inability to explain the movements of stars; in a system "where the earth remains the center of reference," it was impossible to explain the movements of planets without complicated and elaborate recourse to a "whole series of accidental movements . . . movements which are always circular but displaced from the center, then displaced in relation to one another" (55). Observing that these highly mathematical hypotheses reflected the "ingenuity" of astronomers for fourteen centuries, Laplanche nevertheless reminds us that they all started out "from a basic hypothesis which is false," and that it is precisely this "false" origin that then demands such strenuous further elaboration: "The immediate result of heliocentrism, the perspective adopted by Copernicus, is an immense simplification. . . . The idea which seems banal to us today, that the earth is a planet in orbit like the others around the sun, does not make things simpler straight away: the circularity of the orbits means that a certain number of accidental hypotheses, epicycles and others, have to be retained. The way is open, however, to further progress towards unification; not only simplifications, but also an indefinite number of improvements: the system is no longer 'stuffed'; not only the physical closure of the world but also an epistemological closure has been surpassed" (55).

The metaphor of Copernicus is here meant to convey the extent to which heliocentrism represented a radical break from the geocentrism of early astronomy and, correlatively, how the "enlarged" sexuality of the unconscious ushers in a totalizing reversal in how we understand the fundamental organization of internal life: Instead of *ourselves* at the center of unconsciousness, it's actually *other* people that we revolve around. Indeed, for Laplanche, sexuality is such a powerful concept for reasons that are transgressive but rarely sensational; in other words, although there is a tendency in Freud's writing to equate the transgressiveness of sexuality with the superficial dimensions of sexual activity, in actuality, the deeper scandal of sexuality has to do with the fact that it violates our every effort at "self-begetting." Sexuality, as merely a repressed wish, is neither a revolutionary thought nor an idea that's particularly complex, and if this was all psychoanalysis could be said to reveal then its explanatory potential is demonstrably narrow. As Laplanche notes, "We can only smile at the ubiquitous claim that there exists a modern 'sexual freedom,' triumphant at last, and possibly even thanks to Freud himself."[54] If, however, sexuality can be "enlarged" beyond genitality and situated accordingly in the context of biopsychical development and relationality, it leads us away from the familiar illusions about our own independence and toward the discovery of the *other-in-us*. To wit, man is not only no longer the center of his own universe, but he is not even the primary source of his own sexuality.

As Laplanche will show, each individual is *preceded* by an adult, and this precedence, while seemingly banal, actually has staggering developmental consequences, one of which is that biopsychical development is now a process that fundamentally depends on an*other* human being. It is this immutable fact that sets each person on a psychological course that may *feel* private but is fundamentally oriented to the *other* person on whom one's own development depends. While each part of this logic will be extensively elaborated in great detail later, it is important for now to show that the central point Laplanche seeks to make is that there are two totally different versions of the story you could tell about sexuality: The first—and Ptolemaic version—is that the individual's psychic life is dominated by the repressed sexual wishes he feels toward his primary objects. The second—the Copernican version—is that the individual's psychic life develops in *relation* to the unconscious sexuality of his earliest objects. The Ptolemaic story locates the genesis of sexuality within each individual, and as such runs into considerable incoherence in its attempt to account for the *cause* of sexuality's origins. In sharp contrast the Copernican reformulation says that, in spite of how personal my sexuality *feels* to me, it actually comes at me, first, from another person. With this categorical distinction firmly in place, Laplanche becomes able to identify what constitutes the specifically "Copernican" discovery—which is the primacy of *otherness*-in-*me*—versus what merely seems revolutionary but is in reality yet another iteration of "Ptolemaic" ideology.

With this distinction in mind, it becomes possible to define "erotophobic" as the denial of "enlarged" sexuality that leads to and enforces the belief in psychic self-begetting. While linking autoaffection with the denial of difference echoes the major structuralist-poststructuralist critiques of logocentrism and the metaphysics of presence, Laplanche's elaboration of adult-infant seduction persuasively demonstrates why those attempts to affirm the primacy of otherness through analyses of linguistic mediation do not ultimately succeed because we are not afraid of "otherness" or "difference" in the abstract, but of *specific* others, as they live *in* us, and we avoid this awareness because of what it reveals about our own susceptibility to psycho-sexual distortion, our own unavoidable plasticity. Describing the importance of plasticity to any future conceptualization of the mind, Catherine Malabou has called for a new psychoanalysis that takes into account what neuroscience has taught us of mental development—namely, that affects are contingent on our particular, material environment and that traditional accounts of heteroaffection (poststructuralist, especially) simply do not go far enough in registering the possibilities of our self-estrangement. That is, neither Lacan nor Derrida can account for the kinds of impairments that result from our primordial affectivity because neither thinker has a paradigm that accurately reflects the degree to which our affectivity develops through a caretaking "other."[55] In sharp contrast to Freud's image of the timeless unconscious, where nothing is erased and every defensive maneuver has a "motive" that can, with persistence, be found, the brain of contemporary neuroscience is utterly contingent on complex activities within and outside of itself. In Malabou's words, "the cerebral unconscious, in diametrical opposition to the Freudian unconscious, is therefore fundamentally a destructible unconscious. This is why emotions and affects are exposed to their potential disappearance. Faced with a menacing event, the self, as we have seen, can detach itself from its own affects."[56]Although the broader metapsychological consequences of Laplanche's innovations are not the immediate subject of this book, it is important to observe that Laplanche is challenging many of the basic presuppositions of traditional psychoanalysis.

Laplanche's meticulous demonstrations of how an erotophobic sexuality haunts psychoanalysis from *within* its most fundamental and avowedly erotophilic conceptualizations provides an urgent opening in queer theory where psychoanalysis has either been rejected or deployed to corroborate popular poststructuralist tropes. Through close readings of six preeminent queer theoreticians, my book facilitates a timely encounter between the second generation of scholars who are critiquing canonical queer theory and first-generation practitioners whose pioneering work on queer subjectivity is engaged, often agonistically, with psychological concerns. Through the development of metapsychology as a new analytic, my analysis introduces a resource for exploring how erotophobic psychological tropes are currently underpinning the field's most ostensibly radical formulations. Bringing together a range of scholarly research in unprecedented ways, my book extends and deepens new directions of queer studies. Foucault's oft-cited call for "new relational modes" demonstrates why any radical ethical program hinges on transforming the existing paradigm of intimate and psychic life. And yet, an analysis of how the field thinks about essential questions pertaining to hermeneutics, sex, violation, radicalism, gender, and relationality reveals that what goes by the name of "negative" criticism invariably refers to the superficial and straightforward inversion of affective/symbolic norms. While extolling sexuality's dangerous dimensions might have initially functioned as an antidote to ideology's advertisements of procreative sex, today, the field's total reliance on negativity as *the* imprimatur of analytic credibility explains how "badness" functions as a style irrespective of whether deconstructive argumentation is successfully employed.[57] In fact, while recent critiques of negativity have impugned the performance of hypervigilant machismo, no one has yet drawn the link between the broad appeal of these conceptual tropes and their privileged capacity to sustain familiar, often intuitive and mostly *un*critical, ideas of truth and sexuality. As such, and much the same way as antinormative defiance enforces the norms it purports to critique, a metapsychological analysis will show that the "bad" sexuality at the dark heart of shattering, antirelationality, or the death drive ultimately reifies and reinforces the psychic career of an erotophobic sexuality.

Recent arguments engendered by queer studies' "self-critical" turn signal a persistent conviction that, in spite of its scandalous assertions and charismatic textual performances, contemporary queer theory has failed to produce coherent analyses of normativity, sexuality, relationality, and ethics that can function beyond the initial impulse to merely reject and dismantle existing knowledge and conventions. Sedgwick's seminal essay, "Paranoid Reading and Reparative Reading, Or, You're So Paranoid, You Probably Think This Essay Is About You" (1997),[58] anticipates this critique insofar as it links the field's viability as a radical method with the particular "theory of mind" it employs. Although Sedgwick's essay has been hugely influential for a diverse range of scholarly projects, I will show that her essay's insights into the determinative role of metapsychology have been uniformly undeveloped by practitioners in the field.[59] *Homo Psyche* builds upon Sedgwick's intuition that metapsychology is a dynamic dimension of critical theory that cannot be reduced to only one of its forms, namely "Ptolemaic" psychoanalysis. Through analysis that puts pressure on queer theory's use, and relation, to psychology, *Homo Psyche* identifies certain recurring critical tendencies: to conflate psychology with ideology, transform structuralist concepts into phenomenological tropes, treat the psyche as an abstraction rather than a dynamic and material reality, replace psychic complexity with positivist presumptions, and disavow the role of relationality in sexual life. Metapsychology is an independent scientific and theoretical realm that offers a singularly vital resource for approaching the contemporary moment in which the sources and causes of queer theory's impasses are the focus of sustained inquiry and intensive debate.

Overview of Chapters

In Chapter 1 on Eve Sedgwick and hermeneutics, "What 'Theory' Knew: Sedgwick, Queerness, Hermeneutics," I establish the coordinates of the field's relationship to interpretation and metapsychology. This first chapter will provide an extensive analysis of how psychology generally, and psychoanalysis specifically, has been featured in the development of queer studies. Lynne Huffer captures a sentiment shared by many who practice queer studies today when she observes that "psychoanalysis has proven to be a gilded sexual cage too glittering to be dismantled. If we take away the psyche, what is left us?"[60] Repudiating her own "previously unreflective use of psychoanalysis as a master code for deciphering the mysteries of the world" (187), Huffer insists that "queer theory's coupling of Freud with Foucault needs to be contested" because "queer theory's pervasive investment in a timeless psyche betrays the ahistoricism of performative conceptions of subjectivity" (129). Claiming that "when it stops spinning, queer Oedipus looks much like the old-fashioned model," Huffer mobilizes the Deleuzian critique of psychoanalysis to show that "today's psychoanalytic queer children are not orphans or prodigals; their sexual extravagances have failed to spin them out of the family orbit. . . . For as Foucault insists, the prodigal queer desire they claim in their 'innermost selves' can only be accessed through a psychoanalytic return to the family they thought they left behind" (128). Huffer's refusal to consider the fraught history between queer citizens and psychoanalysis as merely accidental or historically contingent but as, instead, exemplary of psychoanalysis's construction of "sexuality" as the "bad conscience" of the "internal" subject, formalizes the polarization in contemporary queer studies between those who believe that "queerness" requires a *better* psyche or *no* psyche at all. This chapter focuses on how Huffer's relegation of "stories" to the unique province of psychoanalysis misapprehends how hermeneutics has been, and continues to be, a vital site for the emergence of queer studies. In this vein, it becomes crucial to consider that in many accounts of the field's disciplinary history, it was Eve Sedgwick's determination to "read" literature differently that inaugurated a bracingly new and provocative method for approaching the place of sexuality in social and political life. Among her contemporaries, Sedgwick's influence on the field is by far the most extensively documented and reflected upon. In order to gain purchase on the question of the psyche's role in queerness, this chapter explores the construction of queer hermeneutics—and of queerness *as* hermeneutics—as one place where the dependence of interpretation on psychology is enacted in particularly urgent, sophisticated, and practical ways. If the distinctiveness of queer hermeneutics is secured by its agonistic relationship to knowledge, then what makes Sedgwick a particularly compelling figure with whom to explore the role of metapsychology in critical close reading is how relentlessly her virtuosic and field-defining interventions persistently prioritized an aesthetic appreciation of desire's multiplicity over concerns with its accessible meaning, maintaining throughout her analyses that desire was *most* charitably explicated the *less* it was assimilated into a preexisting interpretive frame. This essay focuses on tracking the impact for queer studies, of her particular attempt to develop "queerness" as a viable, antihomophobic hermeneutic. By introducing metapsychology as a method of analyzing the psychological foundations of contemporary queer theoretical formulations, this chapter endeavors to respond to Sedgwick's call for psychological explanations that could radically mitigate the erotophobic tendencies inherent in so many of the most established interpretive practices.

After establishing the historical and conceptual coordinates of queer studies' relationship to metapsychology, Chapter 2, "The Genealogy of Sex: Bersani, Laplanche, and Self-Shattering Sexuality," focuses on Bersani's idea of "shattering" sex as it has shaped queer studies' thinking on sex as a distinctively radical *psychic* event. Because Bersani develops his hugely influential ideas on sex and sexuality from an interpretation of Laplanche's early theories, this chapter offers an in-depth scholarly engagement with Bersani's oeuvre and examines the implications of his thinking for the development of queer studies. Indeed, the determination with which queer studies operationalizes an expanded definition of "queerness" that refers to activities and orientations beyond the category of explicitly "sexual" practices, in what Michael Warner describes as "a deliberately capacious way" that recognizes the "many ways people can find themselves at odds with straight culture,"[61] has had, as one of its results, the move away from sex as a serious object of sustained theoretical focus. In their volume, *After Sex?*, editors Janet Halley and Andrew Parker refer to this development when, in keeping with their title, they ask of queer theory, "does sexuality comprise its inside?" and "if so, then does queer theory have an outside?"[62] The considerable irony of "sexuality studies" losing interest in "sex" confirms what Leo Bersani has been saying for decades, that "there is a big secret about sex: most people don't like it."[63] Indeed, Bersani's prescience, combined with his own unwavering commitment to focusing on "sex" as a specific material practice and physical-psychological act, have made his work, and especially his formulation of "sex as shattering," the field's most developed meditation on this theme. Therefore, even while the recent collection of essays on Bersani's work begins by asking, "Is Leo Bersani a queer theorist?,"[64] it is precisely his unapologetic aloofness from recent trends in the field and lifelong interest in elaborating the specificity and non-metaphoricity of sex that has made his accounts of *what sex is* and *what it means* singularly influential. While recent criticism has playfully mocked[65] or directly challenged[66] the descriptive pitch of "shattering sex," Bersani's phenomenological account remains the most sophisticated effort to think about the impact of sex on subjectivity. As Mikko Tuhkanen has recently argued, Jean Laplanche's idea of *ebranlement* provides the conceptual foundations for Bersani's phenomenology of sex.[67] However, whereas Tuhkanen's essay follows Bersani's relationship to Laplanche through a close reading of Bersani's thought, I am interested in assessing the meaning of Bersani's differentiation from Laplanche for what it might elucidate about the particular theory of sexuality Bersani ultimately develops. Specifically, I focus on what it means for Bersani that the moment he decisively diverges from Laplanche is the same moment, in 1970, after the publication of *Life and Death in Psychoanalysis*, when Laplanche turns definitively against his own earlier thought in order to mount a rigorous and systematic reformulation of human sexuality. How does Bersani justify completely ignoring the implications of Laplanche's path-breaking, post-1970 critique? Especially since most of Laplanche's theoretical writing takes place after the 1970 text that Bersani depends upon? This chapter engages Laplanche's oeuvre directly in order to restore the context for Bersani's interpretive decisions, and thereby to explore the implications of Bersani's misreading and dismissal of Laplanche's radical psychoanalytic critique. Bersani's determination to advance his own idea of sexuality against the radical critique that Laplanche's work opens up restores the conflation of sex and sexuality and thereby belies the most radical feature of Laplanche's intervention: his demonstration of the incoherence of Freud's ideas about the genesis of sexuality. This chapter advances scholarship on Bersani and Laplanche and introduces Laplanche's ideas on "new foundations for psychoanalysis" to rethink "sex" within a radical metapsychology.

Moving from the historical analysis of Chapter 1, through Chapter 2's intensive scholarship, Chapter 3 uses a close reading of a literary text to explore how violation is conceptualized in popular queer interpretations of adult-child relationality, childhood sexuality, and the tension between sexual freedom and social norms. "Boundaries Are for Sissies: Violation in Jane Gallop and Henry James" interrogates the tension between protecting sexual freedom and developing a paradigm of sexual vulnerability. In keeping with its abiding commitment to "antinormativity," defiance, and "opposition to straight culture,"[68] contemporary queer studies consistently measures the rigor of its radical critiques by advertising their repudiation of the putative "lines" distinguishing the normal from not-normal in social-psychic life. Perhaps nowhere is the operation of this logic more vividly and vigorously defended than in the field's approach to childhood sexuality and in particular, questions pertaining to sexual innocence and violation. In his recent study of how "progressive theory" conceptualizes sexual harm and "consent," Joseph Fischel provocatively asks: "Are sex offenders the new queers?" (19).[69] Fischel describes his critical endeavor as "pushing back against certain strands of progressive scholarship and activism that either equate innocence with vulnerability and/or assume that narratives of innocence and vulnerability are only rhetorical maneuvers to preserve traditional gender and sexual norms" (15). Jane Gallop's *Feminist Accused of Sexual Harassment* (1997), a manifesto against the ideological underpinnings of sexual harassment laws and its deleterious assault on feminism and sexual freedom—through an account of her own real-life defense against accusations of sexual harassment by two graduate students—offers an early and sensational engagement with these questions. Gallop offers an exemplary performance of the contempt and incredulity Fischel attributes to "progressive theory" when in the name of sexuality's transcendental "truth" she insists on the fundamental nonsense of defining "boundaries" between appropriate versus inappropriate sex. Looking at the continuity between Gallop's exemplary text and more recent writing on childhood sexuality by Kevin Ohi, this chapter builds on Fischel's attempt to differentiate "innocence" from "vulnerability" and to reimagine the asymmetry between different sexual subjectivities. My analysis reads Gallop's text alongside Henry James's short story "The Pupil," in which a precocious young boy develops an intimate connection to his older male teacher, and then suddenly collapses and dies at the precise moment his mother transfers the boy over to his beloved teacher for permanent companionship and care. In addition to offering a sustained close reading of an undertheorized Jamesian masterpiece, this essay looks at how Jean Laplanche's "general theory of seduction" provides a new rubric for distinguishing the fantasy of childhood innocence from the reality of asymmetrical sexual development. Installing a meaningful difference in the sexuality of adults and children enables queer studies to approach "violation" as ethically and psychologically complex. Furthermore, by complicating the *straight*forward relationship of sexuality to structure, this chapter demonstrates how the reflexive repudiation of sexual "boundaries" perpetuates a simplistic, and ultimately erotophobic, conceptualization of sexuality.

Chapter 4, "Adults Only: Lee Edelman's *No Future* and the Limits of Queer Critique," evaluates the field's conceptualization of radicalism through a critical engagement with Edelman's hugely influential polemic. In her recent field intervention, *The Ethics of Opting Out: Queer Theory's Defiant Subjects*, Mari Ruti expresses "fatigue with the field's by now entirely habitual attempts to slay the sovereign subject of Enlightenment philosophy" and observes that "it is not an exaggeration to say that 'bad feelings,' broadly speaking, have become the 'good feelings' (or at least the useful feelings) of contemporary queer theory in the sense that they provide—whether through psychoanalysis, affect theory, or Foucauldian genealogies—a way to convey something about the contours of queer negativity" (2). This field-wide overinvestment in "queer negativity" has been most comprehensively analyzed by Robyn Wiegman and Elizabeth Wilson in their recent special issue of *differences*, "Queer Theory without Antinormativity" (May 2015), in which they problematize the viability of absolute negation and interpret the field's reflexive "antinormativity" as a debilitating threat to nuanced social analysis. They ask: "What might queer theory do if its allegiance to antinormativity was rendered less secure?," (1) and they observe that "antinormativity" systematically compromises the "critical force of queer inquiry."[70] The "child" occupies an exemplary status in these proliferating debates, as signifying, on the one hand, the rapid mainstreaming of gay and lesbian life and, on the other, the privileged emblem of ideological oppression. Lee Edelman's *No Future* provides the theoretical infrastructure for the political-ethical position that defines queer "antinormativity" as the repudiation of social norms, and calls, specifically, for defining radical queerness as that which says *No!* to the "Child." In a range of critical analyses, including, but not limited to, those by Ruti and Wiegman and Wilson, Edelman's polemic is singled-out as representing the radical ethical position that is technically and theoretically rigorous but otherwise practically, emotionally, and politically unsustainable. To complicate Edelman's equivalence of radicalism with negation, my own analysis introduces Laplanche's theorization of the adult-infant relationship to problematize the easy, and by now knee-jerk, association of the "child" with normative sexuality. Although Edelman grounds the psychological legitimacy of his critique of the "child" through his application of Lacan, a close reading of the metapsychology underpinning these claims will demonstrate that the popular formulation—Child=Social/Law and (therefore) Anti-Child=Queer Subject—fundamentally misreads Lacan's complex model of the relationship of the "Other" to "desire." In addition to how a rejection of the "Child" perpetuates a misreading of Lacan's complex ethical formulations, I also explore Laplanche's critique of Lacan, specifically, Laplanche's claim that conceptualizing the "child" in strictly linguistic terms rather than in the material and relational terms introduced by Laplanche's "general theory of seduction," ultimately functions to repress the realism of unconscious sexuality. This Laplanchian critique of Lacan will demonstrate why, in spite of how bold and allegedly extreme denouncing the "child" may seem, Edelman's attack on the figurative or hypothetical "child" actually *defends and perpetuates* an erotophobic relationship to sexuality.

Following the previous chapter's close engagement with a theoretical text, Chapter 5 shifts to a close reading of gender through Radclyffe Hall's landmark lesbian novel, *The Well of Loneliness* (1928). As Judith Butler's paradigm of gender "melancholia" structures a range of work in gender and sexuality studies today, this chapter, "Psychology as Ideology-Lite: Butler, and the Trouble with Gender Theory," examines the metapsychological foundations of Butler's theoretical claims in order to draw out the relationship she establishes between psychology and ideology. In *The Psychic Life of Power* (1997), Butler's determination to answer the question, "What is the psychic form that power takes?" leads her to announce that such a task "has been eschewed by writers in both Foucauldian and psychoanalytic orthodoxies" (3). Disclaiming any promise "of a grand synthesis," Butler nevertheless proceeds to offer what, in her diagnosis, Foucault's theory of power is lacking: a comprehensive "psychological" account of how the subject is formed in submission to power. Because, by her own estimation, a coherent theory of subjection requires a psychoanalytic theory of the subject, Butler's ambition to provide a better theory of power's "psychic life" stands or falls with her successful development of a "psychological" account of power. And yet, as my analysis of gender melancholia will show, Butler's use of psychology works to systematically deny any meaningful and practical distinction between "psychology" and "ideology." A close reading of Butler's "psychic" narrative of gender development demonstrates that despite acknowledging critical theory's dependence on the articulation of cogent psychological foundations, "psychology" has been systematically evacuated of its conceptual and practical utility as a distinctive analytic register and dynamic critical process. Taking Butler's relationship to psychoanalysis as exemplary, this chapter will show how, in contemporary queer studies, "psychology" is habitually treated as *ideology writ small*. To further particularize the consequences of Butler's gender performativity for the capacity of queer studies to approach sexuality and gender with psychological nuance and coherence, this chapter focuses on Hall's novel, which was banned upon publication in Britain, for its depiction of the female protagonist's sexual "inversion." The protagonist, who dresses mostly in male clothing and lives with her former teacher, Puddle, eventually falls in love with Mary, a beautiful woman, only to later violently sacrifice a future life with Mary and proclaim a life of loneliness, exclusion, and writing instead. Heather Love writes that, "with its inverted heroine and its tragic view of same-sex relations, *The Well* has repeatedly come into conflict with contemporary understandings of the meaning and shape of gay identity."[71] Surveying an extensive history of contentious critical reviews, Love concludes, "*The Well*, still known as the most famous and most widely read of lesbian novels, is also the novel most hated by lesbians themselves." Continuous with Love's determination to take seriously the novel's affective landscape of despair and desolation, my reading of *The Well*, and of how *The Well* has been historically read, will show that rather than a slow-motion depiction of gender melancholia, it is Butler's model of gender as melancholia that totalizingly obliterates the novel's complex psychic economy. Reading *The Well* from within Butler's (Freudian) frame leads to the simplistic, and false, alignment of romance as the emblem of a happy lesbian ending. That is, although critics feel betrayed by Stephen's choice to "sacrifice" Mary because it ostensibly confirms the Law's demand that lesbians die lonely and miserable, such a popular interpretation consistently fails to consider the *psychic* context of this violent, apocalyptic moment and how "loneliness" might actually signal a more radical sexual and ethical choice than existing theorizations imagine. Drawing on Jean Laplanche's ideas of gender as "assignment," this essay will show that while Butler offers a compelling account of the how the social expectation of heterosexuality gets reproduced with particular implications for the assumption of a "masculine" or "feminine" "identity," her paradigm cannot ultimately account for the development of "gender" as a psychic experience because it cannot consider the psyche as a distinctive register that is produced by particular relationships to differentiated and psychological others.

Finally, Chapter 6 explores the status of relationality in contemporary queer theory through a cluster of related close readings: Mary Gaitskill's novel *Two Girls, Fat and Thin*; Lauren Berlant's reading of Gaitskill's novel and meditation on her relationship to Sedgwick in "Two Girls, Fat and Thin"; and my own relationship to "two girls" as a student of queer theory and Berlant. Within contemporary queer and affect studies, Berlant's singular oeuvre identifies its particular critical position as a sustained resistance to the judgmental and pathologizing tropes of conventional ideology critique.[72] Interested in developing a mode of criticism that moves away "from the discourse of trauma" and toward more capacious and nuanced theoretical concepts for explaining the reality of "how most people live,"[73] Berlant's writing is marked by an indefatigable commitment to protecting the perplexing subtleties of psychic-social life from the critic's interpretive overreach, and she blames the critic's "habit of representing the intentional subject" as inevitably investing peoples' efforts to merely "stay afloat" as "overmeaningful." In "Two Girls, Fat and Thin," Berlant stages the juxtaposition between her own critical approach and the interpretive agenda of fellow theorist, Eve Sedgwick, through a close reading of Mary Gaitskill's novel of the same name.[74] The novel tells the story of two girls who, in different but formally similar ways, are each abused by those who are entrusted with loving them, embody their damaged psyches through an array of compulsive fixations, and in varying degrees of rage, lethargy, and disappointment negate psychic itineraries that promise either redemption or cure. Characterizing her own approach as "impersonal" and anti-biographical, in sharp contrast to Sedgwick's avowedly "personal" performances, Berlant uses the transformative relationship at the heart of the novel to substantiate her claim that a defense against claustrophobic hermeneutics requires emptying relational dyads of any meaningful psychological content, and to insisting instead that what underlies a relational dynamic between two people must be either determinable or "hav[e] nothing to do with anything substantive about each other." This chapter, "Two Girls²: Berlant + Sedgwick, Relational and Queer," explores my own relationship to Berlant as an additional iteration of "two girls" within which to challenge her conflation of biography with psychology and problematize her conceptualization of psychological interpretation as identical to pre-structuralist, psychoanalytic determinism. I develop Laplanche's theorization of "enigmatic signifiers" to complicate Berlant's bifurcation of psychology into either vulgar determinism versus a Lacanian "poetics of misrecognition." Specifically, through a close reading of the transformative relationship between the "two girls" of the novel, and the "two girls" of the essay, my analysis demonstrates that the anti-"personal" approach Berlant mobilizes as a defense of critical nuance leads to an impoverished conceptualization of subjectivity that uniformly fails to explain the psychological transformations that occur as a result of complex, intimate relationality. As an alternative to Berlant's Lacanian-inflected reading, I develop Laplanche's concept of "reactivation" to propose a theory of "textuality" that foregrounds relationality as the foundation of subjectivity.

"Putting" Queer Theory "to Work"

While a practice of sustained and deconstructive critique is one of *Homo Psyche*'s organizing ambitions, I resist the characterization of this project as somehow "simply" critical or antipathically "suspicious" even as the practice of pointing out limitations conduces naturally to a response of heightened vigilance. After all, to the extent vigilance signals an emotional attempt to anticipate, and thereby prevent, being shocked by an encounter with the limitations of one's self-knowledge, why—in the name of some vague interpretive goodwill—would criticism aspire to protect our *defenses* against learning? When vigilance aims to fortify our fragile certainty, why would we want a critical exercise that tiptoes around the anxiety of reading rather than one that asks us to modify our relation to not-knowing? Laplanche's methodology of "putting to work" Freudian ideas as involving, sometimes, using the "exigency" that propels the Freudian "discovery" even against Freud (the discoverer) himself, ought to disrupt the familiar, but impoverished, dichotomization of "paranoid"/ critical deconstruction on the one hand, versus "straightforward"/descriptive acceptance on the other. Additionally, while "putting to work" echoes certain general features of conventional ideology critique,[75] it is crucial to specify here that whereas immanent critique focuses on exposing the contradictions produced by history upon any positivist or transcendental accounts of "objective" reality, "putting" metapsychology "to work" involves identifying the precise moments in a theoretical formulation when the "exigency" of sexuality is vitiated or obscured. *Homo Psyche* is strategically motivated to perform the initial step of ascertaining precisely where future work needs to be done. Therefore, whereas immanent critique offers a supremely effective analytic for undermining the totalizing claims of ideology, it is as such ill-suited to appraising the transformation of its own critical maneuvers or measuring the invariable distance of an erotophilic aim from an erotophobic outcome.

To wit, my approach in this project is not to hold any one particular thinker or thought responsible for the field's limitations nor to develop an alternative metapsychology that can be subsequently plugged into queer theory,[76] but to treat queer studies as the most creative, vibrant, and practical effort to transform the organization of sociopolitical life and as such, a uniquely fertile site in which to assess the progress of three decades worth of "progressive theory."[77] Of course queer theory is a dynamic field of inquiry, and many of the critics that are the focus of this analysis have modified their interests, views, and ideas about many things over the years. In each chapter, I have tried to respect the breadth of each critic's work while nevertheless focusing on a specific concept (like gender or radicalism) that I believe can only profitably be unpacked by the sustained focus on an exemplary thinker's critical distillation. Furthermore, while each chapter strives to uncover the erotophobic effects of even the most erotophilic intentions, my interest is primarily in tackling, and dismantling accordingly, those concepts which are popular and prevalent in the field so as to create opportunities for theoretical innovation. While it can feel immensely daunting to approach so many beloved formulations with the intention to show where they "go astray," *Homo Psyche* is anchored in the belief that queer studies is impelled by an "exigency" similar to the one Laplanche locates in the "psychoanalytic discovery": that of unconscious sexuality, whereby the "*sexual*" refers to the "enlarged Freudian notion of sexuality" as opposed to the "common sense or traditional notion of a genital sexuality"[78] and to the experience of lived sexuality as it is shaped by *Das Andere*, the "excentric" other. In keeping with the particular aspirations of this project, my focus is on determining how queer theory *uses* Freud/Lacan, rather than on the metapsychological quality of either Freud or Lacan. As such, while my analysis demonstrates the erotophobic results of queer theory's applied Lacanianism, this is *not* the same as saying that *Lacan* is erotophobic. The two distinct registers of analysis here—Ptolemaic/Copernican and Erotophobic/Erotophilic— may overlap but are not ultimately identical; the first metaphor refers to moments in a theory when a thinker "goes astray" from the object of "enlarged" sexuality, whereas the latter formulation refers to the conceptual results of a having "gone astray." In other words, it would make no sense to designate a complex metapsychology like Lacan's "Ptolemaic" because, while there are certainly "Ptolemaic" moments in Lacan, there are also genuinely radical "Copernican" ones as well. While a substantial comparative appraisal of Lacan versus Laplanche would be conceptually interesting on its own,[79] for the purposes of queer theory what matters is how Lacan has been used, in spite of certain "Copernican" promises in his theory, to foreclose erotophilic possibilities.

Unlike traditional ideology critique whose object is variously, empiricism, positivism, and transcendental knowledge, a metapsychological critique proceeds under the assumption that every queer theorist expresses "good" poststructuralist intentions in their endeavor to develop critical formulations that are radical and erotophilic. By focusing on identifying the particular moments where this critical effort is compromised or impaired, *Homo Psyche* testifies to the profound complexity of sustaining a theoretical paradigm that has, at its center, sexuality's "decentering." In this regard, if a certain "deconstructive" practice trains us to hear in Laplanche's differentiation between Freud's "discovery" and his "going-astray" a naïve belief that language could ever go any other way, it's worth considering the foundational role of "antihomophobia" to queer critique, or how "queerness" often nourishes a belief in the sexual drive's particular elaboration. Which is to say that I am unpersuaded by the Derridean-inspired contention that because language is always already mediated, there is no such thing as moments of "discovery." And my project wonders what it would look like to reformulate psychology along the lines of a material "excentric" otherness so that having a psyche no longer licenses pathologizing subjectivization[80] but renders subjectivity as the state of having, and asking, one's *questions*—questions that *I* ask but that also *ask me*. Accordingly, "faithful infidelity" names a critical relation that is organized by a conviction that because every theoretical question is riven by sexuality, it involves fantasy and deviation, too. Of the critical readings I undertake, two of the theorists were teachers of mine whose intellectual provocations I experienced as personal gifts, and all were chosen because I found in them the most sophisticated, creative, and rigorous attempts to challenge erotophobic theoretical conventions. The limitations identified across a range of astonishing critical work confirms Laplanche's fierce contention that ideas must be "put to work" to maintain, as faithfully as possible, the "exigency" that propels them.

1 / What "Theory" Knew: Sedgwick, Queerness, Hermeneutics

The Queer Psyche?

In a recent explanation of why he believes in the importance of writing "explicitly" about sex, the novelist Garth Greenwell describes how the "uniqueness" of sex

> lies in a series of interlocked contradictions. Sex is an experience of intense vulnerability, and it is also where we are at our most performative, and so it's at once as near to and as far from authenticity as we come. Sex throws us profoundly into ourselves, our own sensations, physical and emotional; it is also, at least when it's interesting, the moment when we're most carefully attuned to the experience of another. In no other activity, I think, do the physical and metaphysical draw so near one another—nowhere else do we feel so intensely both our bodies and something that seems to exceed our bodies— and so our writing of sex can be at once acutely descriptive of bodies in space and expansively philosophical. Nothing exposes us more, not just physically, though that's not insignificant, but also morally; nowhere am I more aware of selfishness and generosity, cruelty and tenderness, daring and failure of nerve, in my partners and in myself, than in sex. . . . All of which is to say that sex is a kind of crucible of humanness, and so the question isn't so much why one would write about sex, as why would one write about anything else.[1]

Later in the essay, Greenwell writes that while "our culture is drowning in explicitness" we "suffer from a dearth of representations of *embodiedness*, by which I mean bodies imbued with consciousness." Greenwell's description of the difference "consciousness" makes to bodily experience eloquently captures some of the tensions at the center of queer theory's relationship to psychology. Is sex a legitimate object of psychological inquiry or does it obviate the need for psychological reflection? Is psychology inherently moralizing or does it enable fresh insight into sexual experience? In other words, does psychology sharpen our understanding of what sex *is* and *means*, or does it, by the very questions that it poses, annihilate what makes sex feels dangerous and transcendent?

Among those who ascribe to the association of psychology with intellectual oppression, Lynne Huffer has provided one of the most forceful recent accounts of why psychology should be comprehensively excised from the radical project of queer theory. According to Huffer, "psychoanalysis has proven to be a gilded sexual cage too glittering to be dismantled. If we take away the psyche, what is left us?"[2] For Huffer, it is precisely the inextricability of sexuality and psychology that poses the biggest obstacles to the development of queer studies. Repudiating her own "previously unreflective use of psychoanalysis as a master code for deciphering the mysteries of the world" (187), Huffer insists that, "queer theory's coupling of Freud with Foucault needs to be contested" because "queer theory's pervasive investment in a timeless psyche betrays the ahistoricism of performative conceptions of subjectivity" (129). Through a close reading of Foucault's later work, *History of Madness* specifically, as opposed to the more popular field-wide dependence on *History of Sexuality, Volume One*, Huffer demonstrates that Foucault's "ultimate, unambiguous condemnation of psychoanalysis" (160) has made it incontrovertibly clear that, "as a dominance project of objectification, the 'caged freedom' of psychoanalytic positivism is no freedom at all. Psychoanalysis cannot free us because its rationalist, moralizing structures preclude the possibility of speaking about sexual experience except as it is already captured by a patriarchal scientific gaze" (163). Therefore, insofar as "queer theory reveals itself to be both Foucauldian and psychoanalytic" it "has eaten prodigiously of that juiciest of fruits we call Foucault, but has somehow not taken in, much less digested, the consistent critique of psychoanalysis to be found there" (164). Claiming that "when it stops spinning, queer Oedipus looks much like the old-fashioned model," Huffer mobilizes the Deleuzian critique of psychoanalysis to show that "today's psychoanalytic queer children are not orphans or prodigals; their sexual extravagances have failed to spin them out of the family orbit. . . . For as

Foucault insists, the prodigal queer desire they claim in their 'innermost selves' can only be accessed through a psychoanalytic return to the family they thought they left behind" (128).

Huffer's bewilderment at the relative ease with which contemporary queer theorists "live in Freud like a fish in water" focuses on the incompatibility of the Freudian "master code" with Foucault's historical and "archival approach to rethink the emergence of the modern subject." But in the recent collection of essays, *Clinical Encounters in Sexuality: Psychoanalytic Practice and Queer Theory*, Noreen Giffney and Eve Watson contend that the conceptual tensions between Freud and Foucault are less immediately important than the painful history of psychology's longstanding homophobia. As Tim Dean and Christopher Lane announce in the opening sentence to their collection, *Homosexuality and Psychoanalysis*, "Until recently, the relationship between homosexuality and psychoanalysis was wholly adversarial."[3] Dean and Lane write that, "although in 1973 the American Psychiatric Association decided to remove homosexuality from its list of mental disorders, the legacy of that pathologizing view still lingers. . . . Neither psychoanalysts nor lesbian, gay, and queer people have forgotten that the mental health establishment routinely used to consider same-sex desire pathological" (3). It is precisely an awareness of this history, and the many previous histories just like it, that enables Huffer to claim that, despite its supposedly "liberating" agenda, psychoanalysis is actually responsible for "repeating the despotism of philosophical reason . . . although seemingly a release from the constraints of rationalism, psychoanalysis endlessly performs and augments the Cartesian coup of the seventeenth century" (160). Designating contemporary queer studies' "Freudo-Foucauldianism" as "the most recent episode . . . of a hostile takeover that began when Descartes first exorcized madness from the cogito" (164), Huffer treats psychoanalysis's construction of sexuality as inherently averse to queerness. In her reading—which is grounded in her understanding of Foucault and Nietzsche—psychoanalysis cannot *but* position sexuality as the "bad conscience" of the "internal" subject. As such, there is no version of psychoanalysis that could ever be congenial with the Foucauldian project of emancipating eros from internalized constraint. Even as many scholars have shown that Foucault's relationship to psychology was not actually as purely or simply negative as Huffer makes it seem,[4] or that without psychology "bodies and pleasures" are of limited conceptual use, Huffer contends that we can *either* be "queer" *or* psychological but we cannot be both at the same time.

Tim Dean offers one of the most thorough rebuttals of this line of thinking by persuasively arguing for a revision of current psychological formulations *through* psychoanalysis, and Lacan specifically.[5] For Dean, the answer lies in a *better* psyche, not in *no* psyche at all. Therefore, rather than dismissing and repudiating psychoanalysis, even as "hostility toward psychoanalysis remains a sign of allegiance, a necessary credential for one's political identity as lesbian or gay,"[6] Dean argues that "by emphasizing the unconscious dimension of sexuality, psychoanalysis dramatically enlarges the scope of the sexual" (270) and once "sexuality" is "uncoupled from genitality—all sorts of possibilities emerge for shifting our habits of mind away from both normative heterosexuality and any politics that would require sexuality to be securely wedded to the sovereign self" (272). Articulating a "beyond sexuality," which centers on Lacan's *objet petit a*—"that is not a person and is prior to gender" (274), Dean critiques prominent queer theorists who mistakenly misread psychoanalysis by perpetuating the false alignment of sexuality with identity. Addressing Foucault's impact on queer theory's persistent distrust and entrenched hostility toward psychoanalysis, Dean argues that

> the various sides in this debate miss the point of a psychoanalytic critique of sex, gender, and sexuality, since the purpose of such a critique is not (like deconstruction) to devise ever subtler ways of revealing that what seemed natural is in fact cultural or a positive effect of the symbolic order. . . . By describing sexuality in terms of unconscious desire, I wish to separate sexual orientation from questions of identity and of gender roles, practices, and performances, since it is by conceiving sexuality outside the terms of gender *and* identity that we can most thoroughly deheterosexualize desire.[7]

Dean's deft contextualization of Foucault's critique in the different psychic and performative registers enacted by each social subject complicates the easy reductiveness of consigning (as critics of psychoanalysis do) all of sexuality *with* identity. Later in this same essay, Dean further demonstrates that even though "queer theory's critique of identity as a regulatory norm has also led diametrically away from psychoanalytic epistemologies, encouraged in large part by Foucault's displacement of attention from identities to practices," this historicist solution sustains, in spite of itself, the "problematic distinction between fantasy and verbalization" such that "the concrete reality of sexual practices appears to carry greater political weight than the comparative ephemerality of sexual fantasies" (225). As Dean persuasively shows, "such a hierarchy of political seriousness may itself betoken heterosexist logic: Fantasy remains so phenomenological and conceptually inextricable from perversion that the characteristic relegation of fantasy to zones of secondariness, irrationality, passivity, and immaturity should give us pause" (225). This meticulous parsing of the difference between "unconscious desire" and "sexual identity" enables Dean to show, via Lacan, that if we are attentive to the subtleties of Freud's discovery, "then we can begin to appreciate just how strange, how distant from the normalizing perspective on love and sex, psychoanalytic theory really is. In its most fundamental formulations psychoanalysis is a queer theory" (268).[8]

Sex and Storytelling

Although Huffer mostly explains queer studies' stubborn attachment to psychoanalysis as attributable to the historical, practical effect of how Foucault's *History of Sexuality, Volume One* has dominated the field—as opposed to the more comprehensive critique of psychoanalytic logos found in his (until recently untranslated) *History of Madness*—there are nevertheless several moments where Huffer speculates that there may actually be other, non-logistical, *psychological* reasons for queer studies' continued fidelity to a discourse that has either pathologized them directly, or that Foucault has persuasively shown to be fundamentally complicit with regimes of sexual oppression. Reflecting on the reluctance of queer theorists to disavow the "psyche" as an "ahistorical" container of "inner" depth, Huffer suggests that, "the invitation to speak and to explore the spaces of our previously muted 'inner' life has been simply too strong to resist" (137). This "psychoanalytic couch" offers a "place where perverts are allowed to speak" and once "invited," these same perverts cannot bear to wean themselves from the gratifications of this dialogic exercise. Huffer later suggests that "the thick language of psychoanalysis provides queer theory with precisely what it finds to be lacking in its reading of Foucault. For psychoanalysis is nothing if not a seemingly infinite store of stories about sexual experience; its tantalizing case histories and explanatory structures provide endless material for the project to put flesh on a skeletal sexuality from which eros has been drained" (137). However, while I share Huffer's incredulity at the bewildering alliance of queer studies with certain inherently erotophobic psychological formulations, in my reading, the repeated characterization of an attraction to psychic interiority as the hermeneutic equivalent of an addiction to cocaine completely misunderstands how the interpretation of sexuality is a necessary developmental function of the mind and not only or totally identical with Cartesian rationalism or Nietzschean shame. Drawing on Laplanche's radical revision of psychoanalytic metapsychology, my own project insists on the unexplored critical value of distinguishing a vital developmental mechanism of meaning-making from the "ahistorical" interiority Foucault describes.[9] Furthermore, while I enthusiastically share Huffer's demand for an "ethics of eros" that foregrounds the subject's "coextensivity"—"the coextensive subject is an 'inside' unfolded to bring into view the inseparability of the subject with its 'outside'" (30)—I resist rejecting the psyche as a structure tout court on the grounds that such a reaction (while perhaps understandable) is ultimately philosophically and practically incoherent. Therefore, while I share Huffer's frustration with the persistence of Oedipus and the "bourgeois morality" his deployment represents, I resist the absolute equation of "interiority" with shame, and "depth" with an externally sponsored optical illusion. This total conflation of all *consciousness* with *morality* too easily dismisses an array of astonishingly intricate models of the mind—such as those articulated by Lacan, Hegel, Sartre, and Klein—which, with nuance and immense complexity, distinguish among various registers of experience and symbolization.

Later in this chapter, I will focus on how narrative can be understood as a structural and developmental function and not merely morality's violent intrusion on immediate and self-present erotic life. For now, however, I want to focus on how Huffer's relegation of "stories" to the unique province of psychoanalysis misapprehends how hermeneutics has been, and continues to be, a vital site for the emergence of queer theory. In this vein, it becomes crucial to consider that in many accounts of the field's disciplinary history, it was Eve Sedgwick's determination to "read" literature differently that inaugurated a bracingly new and provocative method for approaching the place of sexuality in social and political life.[10] As Sedgwick observes in the final sentences of her preface to the 1993 edition of *Between Men: English Literature and Male Homosocial Desire*, originally published in 1985 and credited with launching queer studies: "The remarkable creativity of so much subsequent work in the field may say something—I hope it does—for the direct or oblique energizing powers of an unconventional literary intervention like *Between Men*. But it has vastly more to say for the inveterate, gorgeous generativity, the speculative generosity, the daring, the permeability, and the activism that have long been lodged in the multiple histories of queer *reading*" (xx). Therefore, rather than attempting to resolve the abstract debate about whether queerness requires a better psyche or no psyche at all, a return to the centrality of hermeneutics draws attention to how *reading practices* operate as privileged sites for negotiating the relationship of *knowledge* to *sexuality*. It is in the work of attempting to explain *what* people do, and maybe even *why* they do it, that Sedgwick encountered the limits of existing literary paradigms, which prompted her to search for more nuanced explanatory models of desire and affiliation. In their collection of essays, *Regarding Sedgwick*, Stephen Barber and David Clark write, "Sedgwick says that Oscar Wilde was 'hyper-indicative' of his age. Could this not justifiably be said of her with regard to our own time, as heterogeneous as that moment surely is?"[11] Among her contemporaries, Sedgwick's influence on the field is by far the most extensively documented and reflected upon,[12] a feature of her critical persona that may have much to do with the culture of autobiographical life-writing she actively engendered. As Stephen Barber and David Clark write in their introduction to *Regarding Sedgwick*, a unique possibility is "mobilized around the signifier 'Sedgwick.'"[13]

In order to gain purchase on the question of the psyche's role in conceptualizing queerness, this chapter explores the construction of queer hermeneutics—and of queerness *as* hermeneutics—as one place where the dependence of interpretation on psychology is enacted in particularly urgent, sophisticated, and practical ways. If, because of how knowledge is implicated in the regime of sexuality (Foucault)—the distinctiveness of queer hermeneutics is secured by its agonistic relationship to knowledge—then what makes Sedgwick a particularly compelling figure with whom to explore the role of metapsychology in critical close reading is how relentlessly, and in dazzling, Jamesian fashion, her virtuosic and field-defining interventions persistently prioritized an aesthetic appreciation of desire's multiplicity and heterogeneity over concerns with its accessible meaning, maintaining throughout her analyses that desire was *most* charitably explicated the *less* it was assimilated into a preexisting interpretive frame. Indeed, concern with preserving the complexity and nuance of individual desire, by calculating the potentially "ideal" ratio of knowledge to opacity, recurs throughout Sedgwick's career, and this chapter focuses on tracking the impact for queer studies, of her particular attempt to develop "queerness" as a viable, antihomophobic hermeneutic. A deep engagement with Sedgwick's complex and changing relationship to "knowledge" and "sexuality" will demonstrate that Sedgwick worked to defend the particular relationship of "knowledge" to "sexuality" that she qualified as "queer" by admonishing and vehemently rejecting those critical gestures and enterprises that violated the essential *anti*-knowingness of "queer" interpretive practice. A close reading of Sedgwick's oeuvre considers how this fierce policing of the field's critical and sensible boundaries initially treated *all* knowledge about sexuality as a fatal form of *all-knowingness*, and later faulted a default, comfortable *not-knowingness* for inadequately theorizing queer sexuality. By animating Sedgwick's conflicted relationship to "knowledge" as, inevitably, *knowledge about sexuality*, this chapter will show the limitations of a critical practice that depends for its critical rigor on the antinomy between "knowledge" and "sexuality." As such, this chapter puts pressure on the standard polarization of the field into those who either accept or condemn psychoanalysis, and the concomitant conceptualization of all psychology as either presumptively psychoanalytic or objectionable tout court. By introducing *metapsychology* as a method of analyzing the psychological foundations of contemporary queer theoretical formulations, this chapter endeavors to respond to Sedgwick's call for psychological explanations that could radically mitigate the erotophobic tendencies inherent in so many of the most established interpretive practices.

Queerness as Hermeneutics: Or, the Will-Not-to-Know

"Queer theory" specifies a field of poststructuralist theoretical discourse that emerged in the early 1990s at the intersection of women's studies, deconstruction, and gender theory that takes as its antinormative and antihomophobic agenda the problematization of essentialism in its manifold linguistic, performative, social, and philosophical forms. In *Queer Theory: An Introduction*, Annamarie Jagose has written, "While there is no critical consensus on the definitional limits of queer—indeterminacy being one of its widely promoted charms—its general outlines are frequently sketched and debated. Broadly speaking, queer describes those gestures or analytical models which dramatize incoherencies in the allegedly stable relations between chromosomal sex, gender and sexual desire."[14] Originally introduced as a term by Teresa de Lauretis in 1990, "queer theory" has since developed into a heterogeneous discourse that includes, among its foundational features, the determinate resistance to, in David Halperin's words, "the normal, the legitimate, the dominant."[15] "*Queer*," Halperin explains, "does not name some natural kind or refer to some determinate object" but rather "acquires its meaning from its oppositional relation to the norm." As such, "queer" does not "designate a class of already objectified pathologies or perversions; rather, it describes a horizon of possibility whose precise extent and heterogeneous scope cannot in principle be delimited in advance." Specifying the agenda of "queer theory" as a radical critical project, Michael Warner's seminal *Fear of a Queer Planet* argues: "Because the logic of the sexual order is so deeply embedded by now in an indescribably wide range of institutions, and is embedded in the most standard accounts of the world, queer struggles aim not just at toleration or queer status but at challenging those institutions and accounts. The dawning realization that themes of homophobia and heterosexism may be read in almost any document of our culture means that we are only beginning to have an idea of how widespread those institutions and accounts are."[16] The centrality of radical critique to "queer theory's" identity as "queer" is powerfully evident across the discourse, relying, as it does, on the differentiation of "critical" theory from an otherwise un-critical, or, "traditional" theory. The cogency of this juxtaposition depends upon the formulations of "critique" developed by the Frankfurt School of critical social theory that used a Marxist analysis of economic dynamics to challenge prevailing conditions of political action and thought. As Max Horkheimer describes in his essay "Traditional and Critical Theory," "The aim of this [critical] activity is not simply to eliminate one or another abuse, for it regards such abuses as necessarily connected with the ways in which the social structure is organized. Although it itself emerges from the social structure, its purpose is not, either in its conscious intention or in its objective significance, the better functioning of any element in the structure. On the contrary, it is suspicious of the very categories of better, useful, appropriate, productive and valuable, as these are understood in the present order, and refuses to take them as nonscientific presuppositions about which one can do nothing." Further anchoring "critical" theory in a particular intellectual orientation, Horkheimer writes that the "critical attitude of which we are speaking is wholly distrustful of the rules of conduct with which society as presently constituted provides for each of its members. The separation between individual and society in virtue of which the individual accepts as natural the limits prescribed for his activity is relativized in critical theory."[17]

Organized in this way as simultaneously a set of interpretive tools and a radical political enterprise, "queer theory" names an activity of displacing, deconstructing, and rigorously challenging "the ways that the 'natural' had been produced by particular matrices of heteronormativity."[18] The connection here between "rigor" and the activity of "displacement" reflects the privileged status of *not*-knowing in the formation of queer hermeneutics. Therefore, while being "distrustful of the rules of conduct" orients Horkheimer's critical project, queer studies will, drawing on Foucault, extend the range of critique so that "knowledge" signifies more than just a bad version of moralistic dogma that can be systematically dismantled, but the constitutive symptom of sexual repression that must be problematized tout court. Elizabeth Freeman eloquently attests to the *anti*-knowing quality of queer critique when she writes,

At one point in my life as a queer scholar of culture and theory, I thought the point of queer was to be always ahead of actually existing social possibilities. On this model, it seemed that truly queer queers would dissolve forms, disintegrate identities, level taxonomies, scorn the social, and even repudiate politics altogether. . . . Now I think the point may be to trail behind actually existing social possibilities: to be interested in the tail end of things. . . . I find myself emotionally compelled by the not-quite-queer enough longing for form that turns us backward to prior moments, forward to embarrassing utopias, sideways to forms of being and belonging that seem, on the face of it, completely banal.[19]

Freeman then reminds the reader that "because we can't know in advance, but only retrospectively if even then, what is queer and what is not, we gather and combine eclectically, dragging a bunch of cultural debris around us and stacking it in idiosyncratic piles. . . . For queer scholars and activists, this cultural debris includes our incomplete, partial, or otherwise failed transformations of the social field." Freeman's evocative linking of queer studies' potential as a radical social program with its inability to "know in advance . . . what is queer and what is not" is a powerful reference to Eve Sedgwick's definition of queerness as representing a distinctive relationship to "knowledge." Referring explicitly to Eve Sedgwick's resounding call for queer theory to become a "reparative discourse" as against its prevalent "paranoid functioning," Freeman reinforces Sedgwick's model of queer not-knowing when she claims that "this" not knowing "in advance" "what is queer and what is not" is "the essence of what I think Sedgwick means by reparative criticism."

While on the one hand, Freeman's inability to "know" "in advance" "what is queer and what is not" echoes Horkheimer's injunction for critical theory to refrain from non-skeptically assuming, as "nonscientific presuppositions," the "very categories of better, useful, appropriate, productive and valuable," the difference between these two insights hinges upon the distinctive role of "knowledge" in each critical program: In the Frankfurt School, "knowledge" represents the variable, arduous, and elusive goal rather than the presumptive ground of critical analysis, whereas in queer studies, "knowledge" signifies the putative threat to radical, antinormative critique. The relationship between "knowledge" and an antinormative, antihomophobic reading program is extensively thematized by Sedgwick in *Epistemology of the Closet*, wherein the introduction unequivocally states that "a point of this book is *not to know* how far its insights and projects are generalizable, not to be able to say in advance where the semantic specificity of these issues gives over to (or: itself structures?) the syntax of a 'broader or more abstractable critical project.' In particular, the book aims to resist in every way it can the deadening pretended knowingness by which the chisel of modern homo/heterosexual definitional crisis tends, in public discourse, to be hammered most fatally home."[20] The connection between Sedgwick's commitment "*not to know*" and her book's endeavor to generate foundations for an antihomophobic discourse is organized by the links she makes between homophobia and contemporary technologies of "knowledge/truth." Sedgwick writes, "It is a rather amazing fact that, of the very many dimensions along which the genital activity of one person can be differentiated from that of another (dimensions that include preference for certain acts, certain zones or sensations, certain physical types, a certain frequency, certain symbolic investments, certain relations of age or power, a certain species, a certain number of participants, etc. etc. etc.), precisely one, the gender of object choice, emerged from the turn of the century, and has remained, as *the* dimension denoted by the now ubiquitous category of 'sexual orientation'" (8). Arguing that "many of the major nodes of thought and knowledge in twentieth-century Western culture as a whole are structured—indeed, fractured—by a chronic, now endemic crisis of homo-heterosexual definition" (1), Sedgwick contends, in "accord with Foucault's demonstration, whose results I will take to be axiomatic, that modern Western culture has placed what it calls sexuality in a more and more distinctively privileged relation to our most prized constructs of individual identity, truth, and knowledge, it becomes truer and truer that the language of sexuality not only intersects with but transforms the other languages and relations by which we know" (3). The repetition of "knowledge" and "truth" in these sentences points to what is arguably Foucault's most enduring insights: that there is no knowledge of sexuality that is not also and necessarily a discourse of individual Truth.

In *The History of Sexuality: Volume 1*, Foucault asks, "Is it not with the aim of inciting peoples to speak of sex that it is made to mirror, at the outer limit of every actual discourse, something akin to a secret whose discovery is imperative, a thing abusively reduced to silence, and at the same time difficult and necessary, dangerous and precious to divulge?" (34–35). As against the "repressive hypothesis," Foucault contends that "what is particular to modern societies, in fact, is not that they consigned sex to a shadow existence, but that they dedicated themselves to speaking of it *ad infinitum*, while exploiting it as *the* secret" (35). This construction of sex as "*the* secret" transformed sex from a set of bodily practices to a drama of enigma and disclosure, or what Sedgwick would later call, "relations of the closet" (3). According to Foucault, "The essential point is that sex was not only a matter of sensation and pleasure, of law and taboo, but also of truth and falsehood, that the truth of sex became something fundamental, useful, or dangerous, precious or formidable: in short, that sex was constituted as a problem of truth" (56). Having taken "Foucault's demonstration" as "axiomatic," Sedgwick's articulation of the "closet" is defined as a space where "the relations of the known and the unknown, the explicit and the inexplicit around homo/heterosexual definition— have the potential for being peculiarly revealing, in fact, about speech acts more generally" (3). It is therefore precisely in relation to this association between "knowing" sexuality and discourses of "truth" that Sedgwick describes an "antihomophobic inquiry" as "aiming to resist in every way it can the deadening pretended knowingness by which the chisel of modern homo/heterosexual definitional crisis tends, in public discourse, to be hammered most fatally home." As Sedgwick restates even more forcefully later in the essay, "The *special* centrality of homophobic oppression in the twentieth century, I will be arguing, has resulted from its inextricability from the question of knowledge and the process of knowing in modern Western culture at large" (34). This "*special* centrality" of homophobic oppression to "the question of knowledge and the process of knowing" reiterates "Foucault's demonstration":

> the society that emerged in the nineteenth century—bourgeois, capitalist, or industrial society, call it what you will—did not confront sex with a fundamental refusal of recognition. On the contrary, it put into operation an entire machinery for producing true discourses concerning it. Not only did it speak of sex and compel everyone to do so; it also set out to formulate the uniform truth of sex. As if it suspected sex of harboring a fundamental secret. As if it needed this production of truth. As if it was essential that sex be inscribed not only in an economy of pleasure but in an ordered system of knowledge.... And so, in this "question" of sex (in both senses: as interrogation and problematization, and as the need for confession and integration into a field of rationality), two processes emerge, the one always conditioning the other: we demand that sex speak the truth (but, since it is the secret and is oblivious to its own nature, we reserve for ourselves the function of telling the truth of its truth, revealed and deciphered at last), and we demand that it tell us our truth, or rather, the deeply buried truth of that truth about ourselves which we think we possess in our immediate consciousness. (*History of Sexuality*, Vol. 1, 69)

Since this "will to knowledge" that Foucault identifies at the "political economy" of sexuality operates by transforming "sex" into the "secret" essence of each individual's Truth as a modern Western subject, there is no "scientific" inquiry into sexuality—however "rationalist," empirical, or purportedly objective—that is not, by its very discursive operation, participating in "a complex machinery for producing true discourses on sex" and that "enables something called 'sexuality' to embody the truth of sex and its pleasures" (68).

Foucault's problematization of sexuality's discourse persuasively demonstrates why "whenever it is a question of knowing who we are, it is this logic [of concupiscence and desire] that henceforth serves as our master key" (*History of Sexuality*, Vol. 1, 78). There is, as a result, no innocent inquiry into sexuality that does not reproduce and enforce the "*petition to know*. A double petition, in that we are compelled to know how things are with it, while it is suspected of knowing how things are with us" (78). In the context of this categorical indictment of sexuality's epistemology, it becomes possible to trace Sedgwick's elaboration of "antihomophobic" theory as, by definition, a repudiation of "the will to know," "deadened knowingness," and even "homosexuality" as "we know it today" (*Epistemology*, 44). Indeed, when Sedgwick says of her project, "The only imperative that the book means to treat as categorical is the very broad one of pursuing an antihomophobic inquiry" (14), the characterization of the "imperative" as "only" one and "very broad" belies the practical and theoretical implications of this inquiry for the kind of "knowledge" that is available to be pursued. In fact, later in the same introduction, Sedgwick returns to Foucault to demonstrate the dangers of imagining the "development of homosexuality 'as we know it today'" (44). Juxtaposing Foucault with the work of contemporary historians, particularly David Halperin, Sedgwick argues that while "homosexuality as we *conceive of it* today" has provided a "rhetorically necessary fulcrum point for the denaturalizing work on the past," historicizing sexuality nevertheless "has tended inadvertently to *re*familiarize, *re*naturalize, damagingly reify an entity that I could be doing much more to subject to analysis—is in counterposing against the alterity of the past a relatively unified homosexuality that 'we' *do* 'know today.'" It is particularly as *against* these historicizing projects that Sedgwick distinguishes what makes her own particular approach to studying sexuality more rigorously and resolutely "antihomophobic":

> To the degree that power relations involving modern homo/heterosexual definition have structured by the very tacitness of the double-binding force fields of conflicting definition—to the degree that . . . the presumptuous, worldly implication "We Know What That Means" happens to be "the particular lie that animates and perpetuates the

mechanism of [modern] homophobic male self-ignorance and violence and manipulability"—to that degree these historical projects,
for all their immense care, value, and potential, still risk reinforcing a
dangerous consensus of knowingness about the genuinely *un*known,
more than vestigially contradictory structurings of contemporary
existence. (45)

As against the "historians," who, even if and when they incorporate the
"antipositivist findings of the Foucauldian shift" persist in claiming to
"*know*" what constitutes homosexuality, Sedgwick defines her interpretive
method as more fully and more truly "antihomophobic" for repudiating
with more force and more consistency any "consensus of knowingness
about the genuinely *un*known" formations of a dynamic and socially
structured sexual life.

The close reading of these passages intends to point out that a new
relationship between "knowledge" and sexuality was not merely the accidental or arbitrary side effect of elaborating a "queer," as opposed to feminist, critical program, but rather the definitive and constitutive feature of
a distinctly and "categorically" "antihomophobic" interpretive practice.
The centrality of this new relationship between knowledge and sexuality
recurs throughout Sedgwick's multiple attempts to explain the difference
between gay and lesbian studies and what became known as "queer
theory." In "Queer and Now," Sedgwick suggests that "gay" and "lesbian"
still present themselves (however delusively) as objective, empirical categories governed by empirical rules of evidence (however contested).
"'Queer' seems to hinge much more radically and explicitly on a person's
undertaking particular, performative acts of experimental self-perception
and filiation."[21] Later, in "Thinking Through Queer Theory," Sedgwick
sharpens even further the repudiation of "knowledge" about sexuality
that the word and practice of "queerness" is meant to enable. Although
"in many ways, 'queer' and 'gay/lesbian' are overlapping terms ... but
some of their implications are very different. A lot of gay and lesbian politics, for example, accepts the concept of sexual orientation without questioning it in any way."[22] The juxtaposition here between "queerness" and
"gay and lesbian" subjects who "accept the concept of a sexual orientation
without questioning it in any way" and effectively structures the difference around "questioning" rather than any predetermined sexual activities per se. Drawing out the implications of this juxtaposition, Sedgwick
a little later writes, "That's one of the things that 'queer' can refer to: the
open mesh of possibilities, gaps, overlaps, dissonances and resonances,

lapses and excesses of meaning when the constituent elements of anyone's gender, or anyone's sexuality aren't made (or can't be made) to signify monolithically" (200). Then "again," Sedgwick continues, "'queer' can mean something different: a lot of the way people use it to denote, *almost* simply, same-sex sexuality, lesbian or gay, whether or not it is organized around multiple crossings of definitional lines" and yet, "'queer' to me," Sedgwick reiterates, "refers to a politics that values the ways in which meanings and institutions can be at loose ends with each other, crossing all kinds of boundaries rather than reinforcing them" (200). The repeated contrast between "empirical" "gay and lesbian" identities that accept "without questioning" certain discursive appellations and a "queerness" that signifies an "open mesh of possibilities, gaps, overlaps, dissonances, resonances, lapses and excesses of meaning" demonstrates the extent to which "queerness" establishes its identity directly in opposition to the "knowledge" of sexuality as such. If, therefore, homosexuality is the "love that dare not speak its name," there is a way in which, as an imagined antidote to the homophobic "will to knowledge" of sexual discourse, "queerness" is structured to represent the systematic resistance to appropriation by a "name" (such as "gay and lesbian," for example). In this way, it is precisely by virtue of its rigorous detachment from "monolithic" signification—and what signification is not, by definition, "monolithic"?—that "queer" theory secures its radical position as a reliable and militant antagonist of the regime of sexual "truth."

A deep engagement with Sedgwick's complex and changing relationship to "knowledge" and "sexuality" will demonstrate that Sedgwick worked to defend the particular relationship of "knowledge" to "sexuality" that she qualified as "queer" by admonishing and vigorously rejecting those critical gestures and enterprises that violated the essential *anti*-knowingness of "queer" interpretive practice. In the seminal essay, "Paranoid Reading and Reparative Reading, Or, You're So Paranoid, You Probably Think This Essay Is About You" (1997),[23] Sedgwick argues that "the methodological centrality of suspicion to current critical practice has involved a concomitant privileging of the concept of paranoia" (125). In an effort to treat "paranoid forms of knowing" as "one kind of epistemological practice among other, alternative ones" (128), Sedgwick is distinguishing "paranoia" as "characterized by placing, in practice, an extraordinary stress on the efficacy of knowledge per se—knowledge in the form of exposure" (138). Singling out fellow critic D. A. Miller's *The Novel and the Police* as emblematic of theory's uncritical faith in the "paranoid" dynamics of suspicion and exposure, Sedgwick argues that the stakes of this critical tendency extend beyond any given critic's personal hermeneutic "bad" habit to the status of "theory" as an intellectually viable critical endeavor. Sedgwick writes:

> If there is an obvious danger in the triumphalism of a paranoid hermeneutics, it is that the broad consensual sweep of such methodological assumptions, the current near professionwide agreement about what constitutes narrative or explanation or adequate historicization may, if it persists unquestioned, unintentionally impoverish the gene pool of literary-critical perspectives and skills. . . . Another, perhaps more nearly accurate way of describing the present paranoid consensus, however, is that rather than entirely displacing, it may simply have required a certain disarticulation, disavowal, and misrecognition of other ways of knowing, ways less oriented around suspicion, that are actually being practiced, often by the same theorists and as part of the same projects. The monopolistic program of paranoid knowing systematically disallows any explicit recourse to reparative motives, no sooner to be articulated than subject to methodological uprooting. (144)

Sedgwick uses Klein and Tomkins to advance an alternative "reparative" practice that would be "additive and accretive" (149), that would "surrender the knowing, anxious paranoid determination that no horror, however apparently unthinkable, shall ever come to the reader *as new*; to a reparatively positioned reader, it can seem realistic and necessary to experience surprise" (146). In the particular relationship of knowledge that a given interpretive/readerly position entails, who, after all, is the "paranoid" critic but the consummate figure for the most extreme aversion to not-yet-knowing, whose rigid, defensive refusal to "surrender" to not-knowing enforces the very structure of fear-demystification that antihomophobic was, in the first place, mobilized to critique. Therefore, although Sedgwick stops short of linking the "paranoid impulse" of critical work, or what she calls D. A. Miller's "seeming faith in exposure," (139) with the operation of homophobia as a structure of "paranoid" "knowledge," the force of her indictment derives, in no small measure, from the rhetorical connections she establishes between knowledge-paranoia-homophobia, on the one hand, and not-knowing-reparative-queer, on the other.

This admonishment of the "present paranoid consensus" and of the "broad consensual sweep of such methodological assumptions" functions effectively to restrict the "queer" designation to those critical projects that actually "do justice to a wealth of characteristic, culturally central practices, many of which can well be called reparative, that emerge from queer experience but become invisible or illegible under a paranoid optic" (147). Sedgwick further burnishes "queer" theory's "antihomophobic" credentials by demonstrating the complicity of "paranoia" with homophobic thought:

> The dogged, defensive narrative stiffness of a paranoid temporality, after all, in which yesterday can't be allowed to have differed from today and tomorrow must be even more so, takes its shape from a generational narrative that's characterized by a distinctly Oedipal regularity and repetitiveness: it happened to my father's father, it happened to my father, it is happening to me, it will happen to my son, and it will happen to my son's son. But isn't it a feature of queer possibility—only a contingent feature, but a real one, and one that in turn strengthens the force of contingency itself—that our generational relations don't always proceed in this lockstep? (147).

In this constellation of attributes, and as against the specific "present day" "program" of "paranoid" hermeneutic practices, "queer" names a distinctive critical orientation toward "contingency," "surprises," "surrender" that values, as its essential and inviolable commitment, the rigorous, *not-knowing*, in advance, what any given sexual practice or attachment might be doing or *mean*.

Given that Sedgwick has defined the constitutive qualities of "queer" critical practice along the axis of knowing/not-knowing, it can be surprising to encounter Sedgwick's later castigation of her fellow queer critics for too comfortably endorsing a program of "not-knowing" the qualitative "differences" within a rich ecology of affective and sexual phenomena. In "Shame and the Cybernetic Fold: Reading Silvan Tomkins," Sedgwick and Frank mock the commonsense pieties of current academic theory, according to which "theory has become almost simply coextensive with the claim (you can't say it often enough), *it's not natural*," when they ask, "Wouldn't it risk essentialism to understand affects as qualitatively different from each other?"[24] "In fact," Sedgwick continues, "if we are right in hypothesizing that the entire analogically structured thought-real of *finitely many (n>2) values* is available today only in some relation to biological models, and that the concepts of *the essential, the natural, and the biological* have by now become theoretically amalgamated through some historical process, then it makes all the sense in the world that a 'theory' structured in the first place around hypervigilant antiessentialism and antinaturalism will stringently require the sacrifice of qualitative differences among, in this case, different affects" (17). Locating in contemporary theory, a reflexive anti-biologism that "seemingly depends on rigorous adherence to the (erroneously machine-identified) model of digital, on/off representation" (18), Sedgwick contends that, "it would be plausible to see a variety of twentieth-century theoretical languages as attempts, congruent with this one, to detoxify the excesses of body, thought, and feeling by reducing the multiple essentialist risks of analog representation to the single, unavowedly essentialist certainty of one or another on/off switch" (20). Without wanting "to minimize the importance, productiveness, or even what can be the amazing subtlety of thought that takes this form," Sedgwick nevertheless identifies a presumptive attitude of not-knowing with the limitations of contemporary theory, as when she writes that in spite of "its amazing subtlety of thought . . . it's still like a scanner or copier that can reproduce any work of art in 256,000 shades of gray. However infinitesimally subtle its discriminations may be, there are crucial knowledges it simply cannot transmit unless it's equipped to deal with the coarsely reductive possibility that red is different from yellow is different again from blue" (20). Focusing on Ann Cvetkovich's use of "affect" in order to highlight the "common sense" "consensus of current theory" (18), Sedgwick admonishes and berates her fellow theorists for maintaining critical positions that constrain against the productive pursuit of "crucial knowledges," and for extrapolating from the constructivist critique of sexual difference a totalizing refusal to acknowledge *differences* in toto, such that even distinguishing "red" from "yellow" and "blue" seems, to any good graduate of "theory kindergarten" like a "coarsely reductive possibility." Here, Tomkins's affect system functions as an antidote to current "common sense" much the same way Melanie Klein's reparative position promised an alternative to paranoid styles of thought. By deploying Tomkins as an alternative "psychology" that is capable of "displac[ing] the Freudian emphasis on oedipality and repression" (6), Sedgwick repeatedly demonstrates that respecting the "complexity of human motivation and behavior" (7) depends on interpretive gestures that, although conventionally considered "reductive," "coarse," and fatally simplistic, actually uphold the ontological value of material differences—whether among emotions, motivations, colors, or sexualities. Whereas "queer" was earlier equated with the refusal to "know" with "certainty" what any given action or desire might look like or mean, here the integrity or coherence of "queer" critical interpretation is threatened by the knee jerk skittishness around knowledge—the more certain, the more anti-queer, such that "it's the distance of any theory from a biological (or, by mistaken implication, an analog) basis, that alone can make the possibility of doing any justice to difference" (20). How do we understand the meaning of "queer" if it simultaneously represents both, the scrupulous determination to not-know—where "knowledge" is complicit with "paranoid" and homophobic dramas of exposure and absolute Truth—and the possibility of knowing the "differences" among heterogeneous desires, needs, tendencies, and motivations? What relationship to "knowledge" is "queer" theory equipped to enable that can both proclaim the essential and "coarsely reductive" difference between "red," "yellow," and "blue" and yet abstain from "perform[ing] the least possible delegitimation of felt and reported differences and to impose the lightest possible burden of platonic definitional stress" (*Epistemology*, 27).

As evidenced by these famously harsh critiques aimed at fellow critics, Sedgwick's passionate defense of "not knowing" what a given "queer" program would look like did not seem to preclude her from "knowing," fairly certainly, when another critic or a general critical tendency was getting it "wrong." That as a careful reader of Foucault Sedgwick was sensitive to the complex dynamics by which the (critical) drama of exposure structured the (object's) alleged ignorance did not seem to deter her from "outing" a fellow critic's "knowingness" and seeking to vociferously reject that "knowledge" on the basis of its functioning, structurally, as homophobia. Correlatively, Sedgwick's many indictments of her peers did not seem particularly anguished by how the regulation of what constituted actual, rigorous "queer" critique depended, for its cogency, on the serial expulsion of what other critics thought they knew, or wanted to know. Observing the outlines of this pattern, Lee Edelman asks, "Can anyone attentive to Eve's career misrecognize her own distinctive gestures of negation and repudiation, of moving beyond and turning against the formulations, the versions of her own critical self, for which she had come to be known?"[25] Offering an interpretation of these "distinctive gestures of negation and repudiation," Edelman writes, "I'm not interested in globalizing this particular move and making such mastery the secret desire of Eve's writings, both early and late. I want to focus instead on the negativity inseparable from her career-long pursuit of a survivable self—the negativity implicit in her trying and failing to cast out paranoia while also trying and failing to incorporate what affect theory might promise" (59). Edelman's astute attention to the "negativity" that Sedgwick wrestles with in her efforts at repudiation illuminates, in general terms, the psychic stakes of negation and makes it possible to consider how the efforts to locate a paranoid-free "survivable self" potentially enforced a version of "queerness" that maintained a constant deflation of the self as an agent of "knowledge" and "knowingness." In so doing, Sedgwick's writing seemed to suggest that something like transcendence promised the only legitimately antihomophobic relationship between "knowledge" and "sexuality." However, whereas Edelman maps these moves onto the rhythms of an inevitably repetitive cycle, it seems to me this psychic pattern subsumes the substance of her arguments into a more abstract mental habit that misses the structuring effect of these serial negations and repudiations in shaping a particular image of what "queer" hermeneutics could be. I suggest therefore that rather than merely testifying to negativity's persistence in all forms of survival, even reparativity, Sedgwick's "negations and repudiations" indicate a career-long endeavor to elaborate, in delicate, theoretical terms, a radical relationship to *knowledge about sexuality* that she performed, with astonishing and prodigious innovation, in her autobiographical writing.

Autobiographical Erotica

In her account of the motivation for writing *Between Men*, Sedgwick claims as the first audience for her intervention "other feminist scholars" with whom she felt "lifted into the whirlwind of that moment of activist grand theory" at the same time as she admits that, "like many other feminists, I also wanted—needed—feminist scholarship to be different." "In particular," Sedgwick continues, "I found oppressive the hygienic way in which a variety of different institutional, conceptual, political, ethical, and emotional contingencies promised (threatened?) to line up together so neatly in the development of a feminocentric field of women's studies in which the subject, paradigms, and political thrust of research, as well as the researchers themselves, might all be identified with the female. Participating in each of these contingencies, I still needed to keep faith, as best I could, with an obstinate intuition that the loose ends and crossed ends of identity are more fecund than the places where identity, desire, analysis, and need can all be aligned and centered" (xviii). In Sedgwick's writing, there is nothing, so to speak, *innocent* about an "obstinate intuition" insofar as such a phrase routinely performs the heuristic labor of anchoring sharp intellectual insight in the strange persistence of personal, idiosyncratic sensations. A few pages later, Sedgwick concretizes the privileged relationship of "obstinate intuition" to scholarly work, when, in a phrase that continues to be cited as a legitimating credo in so much queer theoretical writing, she proclaims, "Obsessions are the most durable form of intellectual capital" (xiv). Sedgwick describes herself as a young scholar who "needed to keep faith, as best I could, with an obstinate intuition" that in spite of how "neatly" a "variety" of "different" institutional, political and emotional contingencies were supposed to "line up together," it was in fact the "loose ends and crossed ends of identity" that were "more fecund than the places where" everything could be "aligned and centered." Here Sedgwick models to the reader the very relation to desire that she defends as the *queer* intervention in traditional hermeneutics. That is, rather than dismissing her peculiar attractions or reactions on the grounds that they fail to "line up" with her more conscious, or politically correct, or psychologically "hygienic" self-understanding, Sedgwick insists on pursuing the inchoate compulsions that bewilder and besiege her out of some "faith" that actual desire is more "fecund," more *interesting*, for how it confounds our knowledge and our expectations. Wayne Koestenbaum has written on the centrality of "pleasure" to Sedgwick's critical performances, observing that when she "takes a moment to justify her choice of which texts to analyze" she "justifies by not justifying. She confesses that she chose the texts at whim . . . she defends choices made from delight, not from reason, prudence, consensus, or capitulation."[26] While the continued generative of queer studies testifies to the effects of emancipating *reading* from the constraints of "prudence" and "reason," I think it misses a vital dimension of Sedgwick's intervention, in hermeneutics and theory more broadly, to disconnect the "pleasure" she pursued from its connection to dynamic and unconscious sexuality.

In one of Sedgwick's most forceful appraisals of the "I" as a dynamic source of radical contradiction and potential, she writes, "I'd find it mutilating and disingenuous to disallow a grammatical form that marks the site of such dense, accessible effects of knowledge, history, revulsion, authority, and pleasure. Perhaps it would be useful to say that the first person throughout represents neither the sense of a simple, settled congratulatory 'I,' on the one hand, nor on the other a fragmented postmodernist postindividual—never mind an unreliable narrator. No, 'I' is a heuristic; maybe a powerful one."[27] Indeed, it is precisely the tension between, on the one hand, fidelity to desire's non-"Truth" and on the other, an exploration of what desire *might* mean, that organizes Sedgwick's critical project and that she enacts in her autobiographical writing. Regarding the putative relevance of her private sexual life to her scholarly interests, Sedgwick, in the preface to the 2008 edition of *Epistemology of the Closet*, writes: "The dividing up of all sexual acts—indeed all persons—under the 'opposite' categories of 'homo' and 'hetero' is not a natural given but a historical process, still incomplete today and ultimately impossible but characterized by potent contradictions and explosive effects. That's part of the reason why, in a book on gay/lesbian issues that uses the first person freely, emphasizes the importance of perspective effects, and has a special focus on the powerful performativity of coming out, the author herself stubbornly fails to come out in it as either a lesbian or a heterosexual. Not to make a big mystery of it—and because I've written as much in other connections in the ensuing years—I'm willing to say nowadays that when I've had sex with another person, it has been with a man. (Climactic revelation)" (xvi). In this sarcastic announcement of her sexual experience as neither "climactic" nor transgressive, Sedgwick displaces the center of sexuality's gravity away from the acts one does "in bed," or "with another person" in order to suggest that "knowing" the details of a narrow range of genital behavior hardly exhausts the descriptive possibilities of "sexual" life. Sedgwick repeats similar deflationary moves when in referring to her gender identification "as a gay man" she suggests that "I have spent—and wasted—a long time gazing in renewed stupefaction at the stupidity and psychic expense of my failure, during that time, to make the obvious swerve that would have connected my homosexual desire and identification with my need and love, as a woman, of women. The gesture would have been more a tautology even than a connection. Yet it went and has still gone unmade."[28] By sidestepping the tropes of melancholy renunciation or a hidden "secret" sexual wish, Sedgwick treats the coordinates of gender and sexual practice as infinitely mobile and not always or necessarily aligned with the intentions of an intelligible and "successful" subjectivity. This characterization of her non-lesbian identity as a "failure" to "make the obvious swerve" powerfully reconfigures identity as a narrative accomplishment (whether gay or straight) and "sexuality" as an experience that potentially resists or exceeds available representational forms.

Referring to Sedgwick's idiosyncratic conceptualization of "desire" as "algebraic," Wayne Koestenbaum writes: "She mapped human relations with the abstract and paradigm-happy clarity of an anthropological semiologist, in a language of vectors, angles, equations, additions, cancellations, and other chiasmatic patternings" (xi). Indeed, Sedgwick's restless search for new combinatorial possibilities with which to explain, and "map" "human relations" resulted not only in her critical appetite for new thinkers whose new vocabularies could enrich the field's interpretive resources but also in the enactment of "queer" as a practice of explaining her own psychological life outside, or "athwart" the traditional templates of psychic knowability. From this perspective, psychological explanations of human motivation are neither incidental nor supplemental to Sedgwick's investment in a "queer" critical program; instead, "queer" is a method of reading *differently*, of challenging traditional explanatory accounts of sexuality in order to develop a richer, drastically more sophisticated metapsychology that could meet, with far more nuance

and imagination than existing paradigms, the complex, multiply determined movements of experiential sexuality. As Karin Sellberg has
observed in her essay on Sedgwick's use of autobiography:

> Sedgwick herself becomes a queer hub, an "open mesh," through
> which identity becomes reconceptualized in terms of continual
> reformation, and the boundaries between writer and reader are
> made indistinguishable. The act of coming out and the various points
> of exposure function like generators of further making strange, or
> strangening, of identity. It is never solid. Sedgwick moves from spot
> to spot, level to level, and adds more and more voices to her subjec-
> tive cascade, but when it comes down to it, the concept that connects
> them is the compulsion that keeps her moving, the urge to expand
> and expose.[29]

It is in this tradition of autobiographical performance that Huffer participates when, in the text that forcefully calls for queer studies to finally
and decisively forfeit its attachment to the "psyche," a series of first-person
"interludes" interrupt the steady style of "objective" and disembodied
academic argumentation. Grounding her scholarly discovery of Foucault's
neglected archive in the immediacy of her own intensive experience,
Huffer begins her "story about reading Michel Foucault" with a scene of
sensual encounter: "Like many feminists, I admired Foucault's brilliance,
but felt uneasy about his seeming indifference to feminist concerns. Then,
in September 2006, I spent a month in the Foucault archives in Normandy. That experience of what Deleuze calls a 'contact with what's outside the book' not only shifted much of what I thought I knew about
Foucault but also transformed my hot-and-cold feelings. Suddenly I
burned with passion. My archival encounter was nothing less than an
experience of rupture: I was, like Deleuze's book, torn to pieces" (*Mad for
Foucault*, ix). Huffer devotes considerable attention to theorizing the role
of these "interludes" in her work, even defining how they function in relation to her scholarly endeavor: "An interlude appears in the midst of a
story as a moment of rupture, as an interruption in the narrative flow. To
allow for rupture in the flow of a story is to allow for the 'obstinate mur-
mur' of something other to come to the surface to attempt to speak. My
own structure here—where story is fractured by interlude—playfully
reflects Foucault's intervention into a seamless tale that reason tells about
itself" (15). Drawing the link between her own strategic use of "ruptures"
and Foucault's determination to let "those obscure gestures" finally speak,
Huffer frames her engagement with "madness" as the faithful attention to
the "messy tangle of unpublished writing and unedited encounters that

help to form a doubled love story, one that becomes my own story of love. In order to tell that story, I need the suppressed and unpublished marginalia of the Foucault writing machine" because the "'charred root of meaning' I'm calling love makes itself known, somewhat ironically, precisely in those places the Foucault machine has consigned to the silence of the margins" (16). Huffer is acutely aware of how "the doubled structure of flow and interruption I have been describing cannot lead to the neat resolution of a dialectical sublation" for, "indeed, to produce such a resolution would be to repeat the psychologizing gesture through which madness is mastered by a discourse of reason" (17). For Huffer, "not to give in to the psychologizing gesture of mastery means allowing the voice and lump in the throat to enter into dialogue with each other. In that dialogue between the work and its rupture, I can refuse the mastering gesture of the dialectic. And in that refusal, an opening is forged in a language other than science" (17). Much as Sedgwick elaborated how "desire" interrupts the "neat" "alignment" of distinctive identities, we can approach Huffer's use of the "doubled structure of flow and interruption" to create a "dialogue between the work and its rupture" as an attempt to find a language for erotic and sensory experience that exists in a "language other than science." However, whereas Sedgwick wrestled with how to push interpretation beyond its easy reduction to causal determination, Huffer's tactic for preserving the integrity of "obscure gestures" from the "gesture of mastery" involves equating *all* of psychology with mastery, reason, and science. But if this is the case, how can Huffer explain her *own* relationship to the desire that inhabits her, as when, in the description of what led her, in spite of entrenched misgivings about Foucault, to his archives in Normandy, she writes: "In 2006, faced with a long overdue sabbatical, I decided to go to France to get to know Foucault better. Mired as I was, at that moment in my life, in my split self . . . I intuitively felt that Foucault would help me to work through these tangled webs of splittings" (9). Although Huffer's "interludes" tell the story of her embodied, non-cerebral, rapturous encounter with Foucault, the *other* story Huffer does *not* explicitly tell is the one between an intellectual project and her "intuition"— to return to Sedgwick's word for the "obstinate" forces that determine the development of one's particular questions—and these "interludes" function to bring the text back to the specificity of her own unknown erotic trajectory. Therefore, while Huffer insists on distinguishing an ethics of de-subjectivization from the colonizing "mastery" of psychological discourse, her own narrative of the encounter with Foucault *enacts* her belief—which is also at the center of a queer hermeneutics—that pursuing the strange "murmurings" of *otherness within* does *not* necessarily accrue subjective density, but can, perhaps, with a practice of interpretive care, put us in touch with the fundamental *otherness of unconscious sexuality*. Huffer's insistence of an embodied erotic experience *outside* of psychic life ultimately effects a split between sexuality and the psyche that disavows the sexual dimension of all erotic life. But doesn't an erotophilic project require that we preserve the centrality of sexuality and reread the so-called "rational" mind as ineluctably riven by desire, "obsessions," inchoate needs? And so, although in an effort to wrest desire from the language of vulgar psychologization, Huffer urges queer studies to repudiate the psyche, the construction of her own text testifies to how refusing the formal conventions of psychological discourse (out of the fear it becomes automatically identical with morality and Reason) does not in fact prevent her experiential encounter from being *driven* by her particular and "intuitive" cathexis to certain objects and positions. In this way, Huffer's "academic" scholarship is not only "interrupted" by the rapturous erotics of her engagement with the archive, but her surrender to embodiment is everywhere mediated by the compulsions of her own unknown, sexual, and singular psyche.

The Sexual Theories of Children

Laplanche's ingenious differentiation of the "exigency" of the psychoanalytic "discovery" from the particular features of the *metapsychological* paradigm Freud systematically develops provides a necessary intervention in queer studies' contemporary polarization into those who either insist on developing a more queer-friendly psyche (using Klein instead of Lacan or a better Lacan instead of the popular Lacan) versus those who insist on the fundamental antimony between psychology and queerness. Laplanche's meticulous demonstrations of how an erotophobic sexuality haunts psychoanalysis from *within* its most fundamental and avowedly erotophilic conceptualizations, provides an urgent opening in a discourse whose primary relationship to psychoanalysis has been to either uncritically apply it or dismiss it wholesale. Unfortunately, such a rudimentary configuration of the field prevents a more sophisticated appraisal of how and in what ways particular psychological ideas reproduce erotophobic conventions. For example, in Huffer's totalizing denouncement of the psyche as a "symptom" of the field's failure to radicalize subjectivity, the disappointment with queer theory is vague and unarticulated. That is, rather than showing in what specific ways the revolutionary potential of queer theory has been consistently curtailed by its uncritical dependence on psychoanalysis, Huffer's argument repeats the field-wide tendency of equating all psychology with a single version of psychoanalysis, thereby leaving an abstract anti-psychology, or "subjectless" desire,[30] as the only alternative basis for a new queer subjectivity.

Therefore, while for any rigorous explanatory paradigm the value of challenging determinism's grip is urgent and indisputable, one major result of equating *all* knowledge of sexuality with hermeneutic paranoia or intrusive sociality is a veritable prohibition against complex and elaborate psychological speculations—as if all explanatory exercises are inherently exogenous to a functional, sexual subjectivity. Laplanche addresses this fantasy directly when he refers to the "sexual theories of children" as those ideas children invent to manage the anxiety of not-knowing. According to Laplanche, "There exist, in short, certain 'theories,' 'false theories,' that humans create in order to 'bind what was enigmatic.'"[31] Tracing this anxiety back to the child's encounter with the adult world of sexuality, which it can neither use nor comprehend, Laplanche writes that there were "two essentially 'biologizing' childhood theories" that "were able to bind what was enigmatic: the cloacal theory and the theory of castration. Both were absolutely false, the one postulating the birth of babies through the anus, the other ascribing the difference between the sexes to castration" (127). Dismissing Lacan's granting of these "theories" the "illusory and pompous dignity" of the "metaphysical category of 'the Symbolic,'" Laplanche contends that these "sexual theories" are "translation codes," and "tools for interpreting, with varying success, the messages of adults." Significantly, these "theories" are a response "not to the sexual instinct but rather drive-governed sexuality, the sexual dimension that intrudes into the adult-child relationship via the seemingly innocent messages sent by the adult to the child" (127). From this perspective, the drive to explain experiential phenomena in psychological terms is not simply a leftover bad habit from the Enlightenment, paranoia that has been insufficiently worked-through, or a stubborn stupidity that one has failed, with adequate practice and grace, to transcend. Instead, Laplanche demonstrates, a *metapsychological* analytic is required precisely in order to be critical of the psychological explanations we "naturally" invent.

Laplanche's meticulous and unrelenting deconstruction of Freud's "going astray" of a potentially radical psychoanalysis testifies to the urgency of attempting the divestiture of metapsychology from particular psychoanalytic theories. Accordingly, metapsychology refers to "the aggregate of a priori principles that must be in place at the outset for the initiation of analytic interpretation as such."³² Further distinguishing metapsychology from the psychological field, Adrian Johnston explains that whereas the "psychological field" is "defined by the variable particularities of the empirical data divulged through analytic practice," the "very gathering of psychological data" is "made possible by its metapsychological framework." Echoing this distinction and situating the conceptual lineage of the term, Laplanche and Pontalis explain in *The Language of Psycho-Analysis* that "metapsychology" is a term invented by Freud to refer to the study of psychology in its "most theoretical dimension."³³ "It is impossible," Laplanche and Pontalis write, "to overlook the similarity of the terms 'metapsychology' and 'metaphysics,' and indeed Freud very likely intended to draw this analogy, for we know from his own admission how strong his philosophical vocation was." As such, metapsychology is defined by Freud as "a scientific endeavor to redress the constructions of 'metaphysics'; therefore, whereas metaphysics relied upon the classical 'psychologies of consciousness,' metapsychology was original for attempting to construct a psychology 'that leads behind consciousness.'" While Freud invented the term for technical purposes, it is not strictly speaking exclusive to psychoanalysis or clinical research. Indeed, because the ambition of metapsychology was to inaugurate a field of scientific study where metaphysics and mythology otherwise operated as the de facto explanatory modes,³⁴ metapsychology continues to represent a way of thinking about psychic life that locates the coherence of its interpretations in a body of established ideas about the mechanisms, operations, and topologies of non-conscious mental phenomenology. In the Anglophone clinical field, metapsychology has become a locus of intensive controversy with some classical practitioners insisting that it is entirely synonymous with Freud's particular ideas and others treating it as a useless layer of abstract theorizing that should be discounted.³⁵ Without intervening in these debates directly, Laplanche nevertheless observes the immense difficulty in differentiating the object of psychoanalytic study—"enlarged sexuality"—from Freud's particular theorizations. Laplanche repeatedly emphasizes the vitalizing potential of this necessary gap, even going so far as to suggest that one practices psychoanalytically to the extent one maintains a focus on unconscious sexuality, not on the Oedipal complex or death drive, and so on.

As I hope this encounter with Sedgwick's thinking demonstrates, what animates my critical readings is less a preoccupation with whether a given theorist is right or wrong than with the effects for queer theory of a given theoretical idea. In this way, my relationship to queer theory intends to "put to work" existing critical concepts. As Laplanche said of his use of Freudian psychoanalysis, it was imperative for him to refuse the reductive choice between agreeing or disagreeing with Freud, when instead, Laplanche writes, "Putting Freud to work means demonstrating in him what I call an exigency, the exigency of a discovery which impels him without always showing him the way, and which may therefore lead him into dead ends or goings-astray. It means following in his footsteps, accompanying him but also criticizing him, seeking other ways—but impelled by an exigency similar to his."[36]

By treating *sexuality* as an "exigency" that compels both queer studies and a radical metapsychology, this project has as one of its persistent ambitions the aim of developing a theory of subjectivity that is grounded in interpretations of desire as they have been elaborated in some of queer theory's most daring speculations. That is, what would it mean for meta-psychological thinking to conceive of the subject's development differently: to radicalize the presumptive theory of the "subject" that persistently locates deeper meaning in the "substratum" of consciousness, rather than in the "becoming" of a differential, dynamic psychobiological entity? What language of the "self" as an agent and subject of sexuality might be available if, in addition to the vertical axis of depth, we approached desire "genealogically" and as a relationally mediated process of becoming-differential that is driven by a confluence of internal forces and external occasions irreducible to any predictable ontogenetic or transcendental teleology. Working against the tendency, common to queer theory and psychoanalysis alike, to locate an epistemologically secure source of radical and critical thought, Dany Nobus writes that claiming psychoanalysis is inherently queer, "if it is to be truthful to the premises that have supported its clinical and theoretical edifice, thus misses the very point . . . insofar as it fails to acknowledge, as a fundamental and therefore 'normal' principle, the irreducible unpredictability of the human sexual experience."[37] It is this project's wager that engaging with metapsychology enables a process that Nobus describes as necessary for the rigorous encounter between clinical theory and the study of sexuality: a "place whose epistemic parameters and body of knowledge are eternally shifting and changing, and which accommodates fluidity as much as fixity." In this place, "psychoanalysis would not operate from any established source of wisdom, whether conservative or liberal, gay-negative or gay-positive, but act upon what Lacan (2013 [1971]) called a 'knowledge in failure' (*savoir en echec*) (329), which implies that it would approach each and every event in the sexual realm without prejudice and preconception, but with a spirit of discovery, a sense of wonder, and possibly a touch of irony."[38] Perhaps Sedgwick would enjoin us to also bring to "each and every event in the sexual realm" our anxiety, our stubborn needs, confusing intuitions, and appetites, too.

2 / The Genealogy of Sex: Bersani, Laplanche, and Self-Shattering Sexuality

We Have Never Been Sexual

If there is a secret about sexuality, perhaps it is that queer theorists do *not* really like to talk about it. The determination and ingenuity with which queer studies operationalizes an expanded definition of "queerness" that refers to activities and orientations beyond the category of explicitly "sexual" practices, in what Michael Warner describes as "a deliberately capacious way" that recognizes the "many ways people can find themselves at odds with straight culture,"[1] has had, as one of its results, the move away from sex as a serious object of sustained theoretical focus. In their volume *After Sex?*, editors Janet Halley and Andrew Parker refer to this development when, in keeping with their title, they ask of queer theory, "Does sexuality comprise its inside?" and "If so, then does queer theory have an outside?"[2] The considerable irony of "sexuality studies" losing interest in "sex" confirms what Leo Bersani has been saying for decades, that "there is a big secret about sex: most people don't like it."[3] Indeed, Bersani's prescience, combined with his own unwavering commitment to focusing on "sex" as a specific material practice and physical-psychological act have made his work, and especially his formulation of "sex as shattering," the field's most developed meditation on this topic. Therefore, even while the recent collection of essays on Bersani's work begins by asking, "Is Leo Bersani a queer theorist?,"[4] it is precisely his unapologetic detachment from recent trends in the field and lifelong interest in elaborating the specificity and non-metaphoricity of sex that has made his accounts of *what sex is* and *what it means* singularly influential. Spanning a career of writing about literary modernism, art, film and psychoanalysis, Bersani is unwavering in his insistence that sex is something we *do* with our bodies, something that, with varying degrees of agency or surrender, we always *experience*. It is precisely because of this focus on sex as something that affects us that Bersani is able to link sexual practice with ethical concerns, wondering, as he does in everything he writes, how embodied self-relation can proffer a template for radical social modes. Even as recent work has playfully mocked[5] or directly challenged[6] the descriptive pitch of "shattering sex," Bersani's phenomenological account remains the most sophisticated effort to think about the impact of sex on subjectivity. And while the ethical implications of linking sex with negativity occasion passionate debate, the conceptual equation of sex with psychic shattering circulates uncritically in queer discourse where it is rehearsed and presupposed as an established metapsychological fact.

A magisterial account of Bersani's relationship to psychoanalysis has been provided by Mikko Tuhkanen, whose recent essay, "Monadological Psychoanalysis: Bersani, Laplanche, Beckett," carefully reconstructs the constitutive role of Laplanche in supplying certain necessary, elemental terms for Bersani's thought.[7] Tuhkanen's essay zeroes in on Laplanche as the figure whose ideas about sexuality have been most essential to Bersani's work and shows precisely where and when Bersani adheres to Laplanche's formulations and when and how he then decisively diverges. My own chapter is inspired by this scholarship and interested in furthering the conversation enabled by Tuhkanen's work, but whereas Tuhkanen's essay follows Bersani's relationship to Laplanche through a close reading of Bersani's thought, I am interested in assessing the meaning of Bersani's differentiation from Laplanche for what it might elucidate about the particular theory of sex and sexuality Bersani ultimately develops. Specifically, I focus on what it means for Bersani that the moment he decisively diverges from Laplanche is the same moment, in 1970, after the publication of *Life and Death in Psychoanalysis*, when Laplanche turns definitively against his own earlier thought in order to mount a rigorous and systematic reformulation of human sexuality. To the extent Bersani addresses his differentiation from Laplanche, the cause is framed as an abstract theoretical disagreement over the meaning of "primary narcissism."[8] Tuhkanen echoes this narrative when, in his analysis of Bersani's "depart[ure] from Laplanche," he interprets the arc of Bersani's movements as "the becoming-Beckettian of psychoanalysis," a "process that turns on the question of the monad."[9] Using the "monad" to track Bersani's differentiation from Laplanche, Tuhkanen shows that "Laplanche reasonably considers the Leibnizian nonextended monad—the complete substance that contains all its predicates—the apotheosis of the metaphysical prioritization of the individual" (145). Whereas Laplanche "participates in the rethinking, or deconstruction, of classical metaphysics, which prioritizes essence as a self-same, bounded entity that needs to be given before the thought of relation can proceed" (145), Bersani "proceeds to formulate an ethics based on the *singularity of the nonrelated monad*" (147). According to Tuhkanen, "While the monad has a clearly demarcated function for Laplanche—it names, consistently and repeatedly, the reassertion of theoretical egocentrism and, hence, the failure of the psychoanalytic revolution in thinking otherness" (143), Bersani uses Samuel Beckett (and Deleuze) to elaborate an onto-ethical approach with monadic "windowlessness" (142) at its center. Therefore, whereas Laplanche considers the "monad" a "vehicle for the imperial ego's return," Bersani, by contrast, "sees in the theory of object relations, as it develops in Freud, an escape from the implications of death-driven solipsism" (147).

While Tuhkanen's analysis provides an indispensable account of the "idiosyncrasy of Bersani's thought in the contemporary critical field" (143), my own project is interested in how reading Laplanche only through Bersani belies the essential and distinguishing feature of Laplanche's theoretical intervention, which is that it rejects the primacy of the monad by meticulously demonstrating the incoherence of Freud's ideas about the genesis of sexuality. The role of sexuality is missing from Tuhkanen's account of Bersani's relationship to Laplanche, and absent this context it is impossible to evaluate the critical relevance—for Bersani's theory of sex and sexuality—of his differentiation from Laplanche, and from Laplanche's reformulation of sexuality, at the moment he does. By following the story Bersani tells, Tuhkanen's analysis suggests that each thinker basically chooses his preferred story of human origins (monad vs. relational). But whereas Tuhkanen corroborates Bersani's claim that his differing views on "narcissism" are the cause of his divergence from Laplanche, the repercussions of Laplanche's post-1970 thought include a total rewriting of sexuality, such that "monadism" and "sexuality" become structurally incompatible. You cannot, according to Laplanche, be a "sexual monad," and you cannot *not* be sexual. Therefore, while "narcissism" may be one way of describing their different positions, my close analysis demonstrates why the choice between narcissism and monad is actually the expression of a more fundamental difference, rather than its cause. How then does Bersani justify completely ignoring the implications of Laplanche's path-breaking critique—especially since most of Laplanche's writing takes place *after* the 1970 text that Bersani refers to? Indeed, without foregrounding sexuality, it can be impossible to proficiently perceive the incoherence of Bersani's idea that an essential "monadism" is continuous with primal "sexuality."

By engaging Laplanche directly, and not just the Laplanche up until 1970, this chapter restores Bersani's moves to their context in the development of queer critical theory where the stakes of his intellectual choices can be systematically assessed and described. This critical exercise intervenes in the *un*critical adoption of the formula "sex is shattering" for the sake of developing a more rigorous and critical paradigm for sexuality than the sentiment captured and announced in this formulation. Through a sustained engagement with Laplanche's work, this essay explores the precise shape of Bersani's misreading and dismissal of Laplanche's thought and focuses on how the strategic refusal to respond to Laplanche's radical call for "new foundations for psychoanalysis" enables Bersani to maintain precisely the knot—that is, the conflation between sex and sexuality—that Laplanche seeks methodically, by the forensic deconstruction of terms, to untangle. Bersani's determination to advance his own idea of sexuality against the radical critique Laplanche's work opens up results in a defense of a sexuality that is no sexuality at all. Indeed, Bersani's use of Laplanche belies the most radical feature of Laplanche's intervention: his demonstration that, without "new foundations" that grounded the psyche in relation to material others, psychoanalytic theorizations of sexuality were ultimately as erotophobic as the biologistic paradigms they sought to dismantle. This chapter introduces Laplanche as a revolutionary psychological thinker who challenged established psychoanalytic doxa on the grounds it *did not go far enough* in elaborating the "realism of unconscious sexuality."

Bersani: The Reluctant Queer Theorist

Bersani's recurring demand for "new relational modes" is matched only by the constancy with which he claims that sex is shattering, and this chapter begins by wondering about the relation of these two formulations to each other. These ideas are already linked explicitly in Bersani's thought, especially in his more expressly political meditations. The evocation of this phrase, from Foucault, establishes what Bersani considers to be the definitive project of a radical critique that remains steadfastly grounded in sexuality as it *actually* is, not as we would like it to be. Determined to imagine alternative relational configurations, Bersani has been a trenchant critic of the return, in so much queer theoretical activism and writing, to idealizations of dyadic intimacy between two loving, communicating, interior, neoliberal subjects who are compatible with each other, committed, personable, and self-aware. My own work of theorizing the self's transformation in the context of relationality has been immensely inspired by Bersani's vigorous displeasure with the field's limitations. I have been moved and energized by the refreshing force of Bersani's demonstrations that the intransigence of normative intersubjectivity is dangerously contingent upon the repression of sex and sexuality.

In a tone of chronic frustration and stinging disappointment, Bersani often differentiates himself from queer theory "proper" by expressing varying degrees of incredulity and reprimand at his colleagues for failing to let themselves be radicalized by their sexuality. Indeed, in what is arguably his most expressly polemic work, *Homos* (1995), Bersani begins the "Prologue: We" with the statement: "No one wants to be a homosexual."[10] Bersani continues in this vein to impugn "self-identified homosexual activists and theorists" for having "disappeared into their sophisticated awareness of how they have been *constructed as* gay men and lesbians" (5). Singling out as exemplary of this movement Monique Wittig, Judith Butler, and Michael Warner, Bersani argues that "de-gaying gayness can only fortify homophobic oppression" and that one major casualty of "eras[ing] ourselves in the process of denaturalizing the epistemic and political regimes of the normal" (4) is the extent to which "gay critiques of homosexual identity have generally been desexualizing discourses" (5). Bersani follows this condemnation with the provocative taunt that "you would never know, from most of the works I discuss, that gay men, for all their diversity, share a strong sexual interest in other human beings anatomically identifiable as male" (6).[11] Several years earlier in *The Culture of Redemption* (1990) Bersani draws on similar themes when he assails Freud for repressing sexuality's dangerous truth. Bersani writes: "The history of Freud's thought—and, to a large extent, of psychoanalysis itself—is the history of the repression of the psychoanalytic definition of the sexual" (45). While the names of the characters/offenders change, Bersani is unwavering in his application of the formula "sex is shattering" to sexuality's ideological history, a rhetorical construction by which anyone who chooses identity, the ego, culture, and intersubjectivity automatically represses masochism, pleasure, death, and sex.

This essay takes as it's starting point Bersani's conviction that "new relational modes" are contingent on sexual practice. Oriented toward the body as a site of transformational self-experience helps explain the centrality of psychoanalysis to Bersani's thought. Avowedly locating himself in an odd angle to queer theory's dominant tastes and preferences,

Bersani foregrounds his ambivalent relationship to psychoanalysis by acknowledging that "undeniably, psychoanalysis has played a major role in the modern project, analyzed by Foucault, of normativizing the human subject."[12] Bersani nevertheless argues that "Foucault can help us to see—in spite of himself—that psychoanalysis, which he certainly considered, as most queer theorists do today, as operating a massive reinforcement of old relational modes, in fact may have cleared the field—in spite of itself—for 'new relational modes.'"[13] According to Bersani, it is precisely psychoanalysis's theorization of sexuality's self-destructive potential that makes it indispensable to any rigorous speculation on the effect our sexuality might have on others or ourselves. Although Bersani has described his work as "a dialogue (both conciliatory and antagonistic) between" Freud and Foucault and "in the agitated space between Foucault and psychoanalysis,"[14] his thinking depends, for its cogency, on an account of sexualized subjectivity as an experiential event. For this reason, Bersani criticizes Foucault's call for a non-psychoanalytic approach to our "bodies and pleasures" by pointing out the impossibility of isolating a biological/physiological experience from a sensory/psychic one.[15]

Neither wholly for nor against psychoanalysis, neither totally inside nor outside queer theory, Bersani's positioning of himself as essential to, while also apart from, the field has perhaps amplified the meta-critical status of his ideas about the psychic structure of sex and sexuality. Indeed, where ideology critique or Foucauldian analysis might focus on the role of regulation in constructing sexual desire, Bersani locates the connection between questions of subjectivity and aesthetics, sociality and interpretation, at the precise developmental moment when the infant encounters sexuality. It is here, in the organism's "perturbation," when "the body's 'normal' range of sensation is exceeded, and when the organization of the self is momentarily disturbed by sensations or affective processes somehow 'beyond' those compatible with psychic organization" (38), that Bersani deploys Freud to show how sexuality originates at the disjunction between overstimulation and the infant's attempts to master it. This determination to prove the facticity of sex's "shattering" qualities, by threading his genealogy of adult sexuality through psychoanalytic theories of infantile development, renders his thinking unique in the canon of queer political discourse for attempting to provide a metapsychological frame for political and aesthetic speculations. In fact, this use of psychoanalysis to provide human sexuality with an origin story invites us to read his self-described "dialogue between Freud and Foucault" as participating in a genealogical project that aims to rewrite the "history of sexuality" from the perspective of the sensory body.

Sex and Masochism in Bersani and Laplanche

Often referring to his own relationship as a "a faithful infidelity," Laplanche develops a method for using rigorous close readings of Freudian texts to discover which concepts maintain the radical and singular discovery of psychoanalytic science—sexuality and the unconscious—and which ideas or explanations need to be restructured and reformulated. Bersani is drawn to Laplanche's microscopic schematization of sexuality's emergence because in it he is able to locate a signal developmental moment that will serve as the anchor for all of his subsequent thinking about the genealogy of sex and pleasure. In *Baudelaire and Freud*, Bersani articulates the argumentative fixtures of this logic.

> Pleasure and pain continue to be different sensations, but, to a certain extent, they are both experienced as *sexual* pleasure when they are strong enough to shatter a certain stability or equilibrium of the self. The quantitative bias of Freud's argument may bother us; is there really a point on a psychic thermometer beyond which the "heat" of sensation enters into contact with sexual excitement? The crucial point to hold onto is the association of sexuality with the organism's experience of something excessive. Let's push the argument one step further and say that Freud may be moving toward the position that the pleasurable excitement of sexuality occurs when the body's normal range of sensation is exceeded and when the organization of the self is momentarily disturbed (deranged) by sensations somehow "beyond" those compatible with psychic organization. Sexuality would be that which is intolerable to the structured self. (77)

According to Bersani, pain is not incidental to sexuality but in fact essential to it. Quoting Laplanche that "any activity, any modification of the organism, any perturbation [*ebranlement*], can produce a marginal effect which is precisely sexual excitement at the point where this effect [of perturbation, of shattering] is produced,"[16] Bersani adds, "The polymorphously perverse nature of infantile sexuality would be a function of the child's vulnerability to being shattered into sexuality. Sexuality is a particularly human phenomenon in the sense that its very genesis may depend on the *decalage*, or gap, in human life between the quantities of stimuli to which we are exposed and the development of ego structures capable of resisting or, in Freudian terms, of binding those stimuli." From these observations, Bersani introduces the formula that recurs throughout his later work: "Sexuality—at least in the mode in which it is constituted—could be thought of as a tautology for masochism." Masochism, Bersani adds a few paragraphs later, "far from being merely an individual aberration, is an inherited disposition resulting from an *evolutionary conquest*" (39).

The equation that "sex" is a "tautology for masochism" is not merely powerful rhetorically, that is, for the shock value of locating suffering at the center of sex, but it is also conceptually provocative for the continuity it assumes between the infant's encounter with excess stimulation and the adult's experience of sexuality. Laplanche's early-career hypothesis about the infant's "turning around" toward excitation provides Bersani with the basis for this interpretation. In *Life and Death in Psychoanalysis* (1970), the text that Bersani exclusively draws upon, Laplanche writes:

> If, as we believe, the Freudian theory of "propping" should be used as the guiding scheme in understanding the problem of sadomasochism, it is important to recall briefly two major aspects of that theory: the marginal genesis of sexuality and the genesis of sexuality in a moment of turning round upon the self. . . . Propping is thus that leaning of nascent sexuality on nonsexual activities, but the *actual* emergence of sexuality is not yet there. Sexuality appears as a drive that can be isolated and observed only at the moment at which the nonsexual activity, the vital function, becomes detached from its natural object or loses it. For sexuality, it is the reflexive (*selbst* or *auto-*) moment that is constitutive: the moment of a turning back towards self, an "autoeroticism" in which the object has been replaced by a fantasy, by an object *reflected* within the subject.[17]

According to this schema, the infant is overwhelmed by excessive stimuli—verbal messages as well as gestures, sounds, touch, and smells—in the external world. Unable to successfully control or escape this environment, the ego "turn[s] round upon the self" in an effort to manage the excess by surrendering itself to it. As for sexuality, it is in this very *movement* of "turning back towards itself" that the ego experiences the excitation of the *outside* world as, suddenly, its own *internal* excess. Although Laplanche notes that Freud will eventually replace "propping" with "the more abstract and mechanical notion of fusion and defusion," he reiterates that "the crucial point, however, is that its place remains staked out at the same spot in the development of the drive: in the stage in which self-aggression is transformed, in place, into reflexive masochism" (96). For Laplanche, the ego's "turning back towards itself" is an effort to explain the phenomena of sexuality: that when life started you didn't have it but then all of a sudden, you do, and it's coming from the inside. With "propping" as the mechanism and "turning back round itself" as the action,

Laplanche endeavors to account for how the ego generates its own experience of sexuality.

This single moment of the ego "turning back towards itself" forms the theoretical foundation of all Bersani's subsequent thinking about the transgressive power of sexual practice. In *The Culture of Redemption*, Bersani grafts onto the scene of infantile ebranlement a comprehensive hypothesis about the legacy of such a violent process of sexual development. Bersani writes: "Freud's most original speculative move was to deconstruct the sexual as a category of intersubjectivity, and to propose a definition of sexual excitement as both a turning away from others and a dying to the self. The appeal of that dying—the desire to be shattered out of coherence—is perhaps what psychoanalysis has sought most urgently to repress."[18] Elsewhere, in a collection of essays on film with Ulysse Dutoit, Bersani redescribes the transformative potency of "shattering" sex in terms of the self's relation to the outside world. In a close reading of Terence Malick's *Thin Red Line*, Bersani writes, "To be that extraordinarily receptive to the being of the world is perhaps inevitably to be shattered by it (an ontological truth that Witt's death metaphorises)—shattered in order to be recycled as allness. Inaccurate replications—between the subject and the world, among the world's object—shatter individual identities in order to redesign the world as correspondences that can be illuminated by our perception of them."[19] Indeed, although Foucault dismissed psychoanalysis as complicit with the disciplinary regime of regulating desire, Bersani notes, "No one was more alert than Foucault to the connections between how we organize our pleasures with one other person and the larger forms of social organization."[20] It therefore follows for Bersani that in order to discover "new relational modes," it will be necessary to accept that self-shattering is inherent in the constitution of sexuality as such. In an extensive attempt to explain the exemplary status of S/M in theorizations of sexuality, Bersani writes, "The most radical function of S/M is not primarily in its exposing the hypocritically denied centrality of erotically stimulating power plays in 'normal' society; it lies rather in the shocking revelation that, for the sake of that stimulation, human beings may be willing to give up control over their environment."[21] A few pages later, Bersani brings these speculations back to their source in the infant's first experience with sexuality: "So the masochistic thrill of being invaded by a world we have not yet learned to master might be an inherited disposition, the result of an evolutionary conquest. This, in any case, is what Freud appears to be moving toward as a definition of the sexual; an aptitude for the defeat of power by pleasure, the human subject's potential for a jouissance in which the subject is momentarily undone" (100). Tracing his own use of the word "self-shattering" to the "ebranlement" of Laplanche's schema, Bersani concludes that "psychoanalysis has justifiably been considered an enemy of anti-identitarian politics, but it also proposes a concept of the sexual that might be a powerful weapon in the struggle against the disciplinarian constraints of identity" (101).

In a sense then, it is because we have all been masochistic—once upon a time—that Bersani's vision of "new relational modes" involves the wholesale renunciation of "relationships," which, in this schema, are acquired later on, and in their place, a return to that kind of sexual practice that is at the origin of our sexual-psychic life. "If Freud equates sexual pleasure with the shattering of the self's coherence," Bersani writes, "then we could also say that psychoanalysis encourages us to think of the sexual as helping to effect a passage from the physical *individu* to a metaphysical *individuel*" and as a result, "sexuality is perhaps as close as we can come (short of death) to the beneficent destruction of the empirical individual."[22] This "destruction of the empirical individual" is in actuality also a regression to the subject's most originary self-experience because, as Adam Phillips astutely notes in his collaboration with Bersani, "shattering" has "been Bersani's word for the ego's darker design in which the satisfaction more truly sought is a fortifying dissolution not a monumental achievement. And it is a talent for masochism . . . masochism as a developmental achievement that for Bersani through Freud is the way to go."[23] This "talent for masochism," which the ego must acquire in order to survive the excess stimulation of its earliest environment, is available to be re-experienced by the adult who is courageous enough to engage in self-obliterating sex.

Setting aside momentarily the dilemma of how to parse the "shattering" quality of sex if it is to do more than neatly correspond to what is considered, by the social, to be deviant/non-normative, it is important to notice that what underwrites Bersani's political vision is the imagined continuity between the early ego, which "turns around" onto itself and the later adult who experiences sexuality. Even if we do not consciously remember the moment of our own masochistic pleasure, Bersani's interpretation of "shattering" requires that our bodies basically do. What is more, for the genealogy of sex to function as Bersani needs it to, the structure of the early ego—which it might be said, rather heroically "turns around" to face its excitation and submit to it—must be identical to the experience of an older, more developed sexual subject. In his account, every act of "shattering" sex repeats the original experience that set our sexuality in motion. But if sex is the repetition of the original experience of trauma-as-pleasure then the ego is no different than a heroin addict whose first high turned him into a junkie for life. And while it isn't difficult to appreciate the resonance of this account as a phenomenology of sexual pleasure/desire, Bersani's claim that the early ego possesses the characteristics of an "empirical individual" subverts psychic processes into a drama of the ego's agentic and sentimental gestures. This story of the ego that, once upon a time, submitted to its excessive stimulation by "turning around" and *enjoying* it, reinstalls the ego as the master of its own experience. In the name of valorizing fragmentation, Bersani reproduces the ego as an entity that was always present to its experience and, in so doing, reaffirms the status of the self as something that is always yours to scatter, shatter, and enjoy. As we will see, this interpretation of sexuality's development absolutely distorts the potential of ebranlement to inaugurate a radical revision of psycho-sexuality.

Laplanche's Theoretical Turn

Soon after the publication of *Life and Death in Psychoanalysis* (1970), Laplanche realizes that although his account of sexuality's emergence is compatible with existing Freudian accounts of infantile development, his own hypothesis ultimately fails, much as Freud's did, to adequately explain the specificity of sexuality as a "drive" that is structurally and economically distinct from a biological "instinct." In *The Temptation of Biology*, Laplanche offers the following distinction: "*Instinct* denotes behavior that is (1) goal directed; (2) relatively unchanging; (3) inherited, not acquired. *Drive*, by contrast, denotes a force that is (1) not goal-directed to begin with; (2) variable from one individual to the next; (3) determined by the individual's history. The drive par excellence is the sexual one. Even if it's presence is inevitable in a given individual, it is bound to fantasy, which for its part is strictly personal."[24] Laplanche returns to this distinction throughout his work in order to demonstrate that the "instinctualizing" of the "sexual drive" results in Freud's failure to sustain the investigation of "sexuality." Later, in *Freud and the Sexual*, Laplanche explains what he means by drive-"sexuality" as distinct from instinct: "It is not a matter of denying the existence—within the animal, of course, but also within man—of an instinctual sexuality connected to the maturation of the organism and involving neuro-hormonal relays, the complexity of which is now beginning to be recognized. As Freud had already emphasized, this sexuality pushes human beings toward sexual behaviors that are more or less preprogrammed and that are aimed, without this aim being consciously posed, at the self-preservation of the species. But the problem is that this sexuality, which is hormonal in origin, is absent in man from birth to the pre-pubertal period."[25] Furthermore, "It is precisely between birth and puberty that human drive sexuality is situated—the infantile sexuality that Freud discovered and which continues to scandalize today," by which Laplanche specifies that this "sexuality is an *enlarged* sexuality and is not, at first connected to any one erotogenic zone; nor is it connected, in any absolute way, to the difference of the sexes."

It is precisely because this drive is irreducible to innate biological activities and because "this drive sexuality is indissociably connected to *fantasy* as its cause" (44) that Laplanche isolates what he takes to be the urgent question of psychoanalytic science: "What, then, is the relation between drive sexuality and instinctual sexuality within the human being?" Laplanche details several possible resolutions to this question, one of which includes the "leaning-on" hypothesis he popularized in his early work.[26] According to this early hypothesis, "Infantile sexuality first emerges in the exercise of the great functions, in the satisfaction of the great needs of self-preservation. Initially conjoint with the satisfaction of need (feeding, defecation, etc.), sexual pleasure detaches itself secondarily, becoming autonomous with autoerotism and its relation to fantasy" (45). Referring to "leaning-on" (or elsewhere translated as "propping") as a "way to save the Freudian hypothesis," Laplanche writes that the theory "is increasingly invoked, increasingly rediscovered and reinterpreted, and increasingly integrated into the vulgate; but it can have a pernicious effect" because, as he goes on to explain, "if infantile sexuality does not have an innate endogenous mechanism, how can it emerge conjointly with self-preservation? And if it corresponds to a simple representation in fantasy of bodily attachment and self-preservative functions, by what miracle would this fantasmatization alone confer a sexual character upon somatic function?" (21). As Laplanche convincingly demonstrates, this desperate attempt to "save the Freudian hypothesis" relies, for its cogency, on the notion that self-preservation can somehow *morph* into sexual desire. Dominique Scarfone writes, "leaning-on gives the impression that sexuality 'arises' from self-preservative situations a bit as the flower blossoms forth from the bud" as if "an instinctual adaptive function persists long enough, the sexual sphere will kick in."[27] Or as Laplanche reiterates:

> I have frequently, and for a long time, criticized such a "creativist" and "illusionist" conception of human sexuality. In Freud these conceptions find their apogee in the theory of the "hallucinatory satisfaction of desire," which I reject. Indeed, the first real satisfaction can

only be the satisfaction of a *need*; and *its reproduction* . . . can only be the reproduction of an *alimentary* satisfaction. There is in Freud and his successors . . . a veritable sleight of hand: if the sexual is not present within the original, *real experience* it will never be rediscovered in the fantasmatic reproduction or the symbolic elaboration of that experience. (46)

Laplanche locates infantile "creativity" in "the 'drive to translate,' which comes to the child from the adult message 'to be translated.'" Laplanche writes that the child's "creativity . . . does not in fact go so far as to create sexuality: this is in reality introduced from the earliest intersubjective experience, and introduced by the activity of the adult rather than the infant."

Laplanche demonstrates how both Freudian biologism and Lacanian linguistic structuralism fail to account for sexuality's singular characteristics—in Freud's case, by making an unwarranted leap from alimentary satisfaction to desire, and in Lacan's, by reducing individual subjectivity to an effect of language's transindividual "polysemic potentialities." Both models evacuate the source of sexuality's impact—the material other—and with it a rigorous account of sexuality's exigent force. Crucially, "sexuality" in Laplanche's framework retains its radicality by expanding beyond the determined objects and sources of genital sexuality. In order to show how this kind of "sexuality" is primal, that is, "inevitable," Laplanche defines "foundational" as that which is "beyond even the most general contingency." "It is *inevitable* that the mother should arouse pleasurable sensations; that possibility is inscribed in the situation and does not depend upon contingent factors." Elaborating several pages later, Laplanche writes, "*Ultimately*, and whatever distortions may result from the fact, it is possible to become a human being without having a family; it is not possible to do so without encountering the adult world."[28] Laplanche shows why this meticulous differentiation between "instinct" and "drive" is the urgent corrective to Freud's "biologizing going-astray." Dismissing "the sequence of infantile stages described by Freud [as] a barely credible fiction," and prying apart "two respective modes of functioning—'the pursuit of excitation' and 'the pursuit of pleasure in the object,'" Laplanche outlines a profound and original hypothesis about how what propels psychological *becoming* is forceful and enigmatic, internal but nowhere we could really "know." Indeed, this insistence that a "need" cannot set a "drive" in motion (because they have categorically different economies, sources, and aims) offers a powerful alternative model of psychological development because it proposes different motivational lines (self-preservation vs. pleasure) whose relationship to each other is "not one of collaboration or of harmonious blending, but a deeply conflictual relation."[29]

Without challenging the fact of the infant's original susceptibility to excitation, Laplanche nevertheless insists that even if "a somatic reactivity, a general organic excitability must certainly be pre-existent . . . something else is needed in order to make it a *drive*" (48). Determined to account for "that something else" which turns the infant into a "sexual" being, Laplanche introduces the "general theory of seduction." "What matters," Laplanche writes, "is the introduction of the sexual element, not from the side of physiology of the infant but from the side of the messages coming from the adult. To put it concretely, these messages are located on the side of the breast, the *sexual breast of the woman*, the inseparable companion of the milk of *self-preservation*" (69). Therefore, it is precisely because "need" (instinct) requires *communication* between the infant and the adult world that a passageway is opened up for "messages" to be *transmitted* by the adult, who is sexual, to the infant, who is not. "The theory of seduction is the hypothesis best suited to the discovery of the irreducible unconscious" because, as Laplanche explains, "seduction is not a relation that is contingent, pathological (even though it can be) and episodic. It is grounded in a situation from which no human being is exempt: the 'fundamental anthropological situation,' as I call it . . . the *adult-infans* relation. It consists of the *adult*, who has an unconscious such as psychoanalysis has revealed it, i.e., a sexual unconscious that is essentially made up of infantile residues, an unconscious that is perverse . . . and the *infant*, who is not equipped with any genetic sexual organization or any hormonal activators of sexuality" (102). Laplanche fiercely defends what he will later call the "realism of the unconscious" by which he means, that the "unconscious" is neither the source of some mythical, primordial energy, nor the essential center of my true self, but instead the structural effect of the infant's attempts, and failures, to translate the adult's "enigmatic" messages.

What Laplanche calls "enigmatic signifiers," are those "messages" that are "unknown to the adult who is exceeded by her own unconscious." According to Laplanche, the infant is always "translating" messages from his surroundings; often times, referring to the infant as the "original hermeneut"; Laplanche explains how translation is not so much a linguistic or interpretive process, but instead a process for binding affect and energy into symbolization and representation. It is the transformation of diffuse and overwhelming affect into symbolic form that enables the infant's innate regulative capacities to "bind" affect to representation and thereby to survive the assault of overstimulation by the adult environment. However, it is by this same measure that repression occurs because, as Laplanche repeatedly explains, the adult's communications include "enigmatic signifiers," which are unavailable to the adult's own consciousness and therefore untranslatable by the infant alone. The difference, for the infant, between "enigmatic signifiers" and messages that are available for translation hinges on the adult's unconscious. That is, what renders certain messages qualitatively "enigmatic" is not the *content* of the "signifier" per se, but rather the ratio of affect to symbolization.[30] It is precisely those messages that are provocative and unsymbolized for the *adult* that are untranslatable for the *infant*, and repressed as a result. Warning against the misunderstanding of what he means by "enigmatic signifiers," Laplanche writes that "despite the success it has enjoyed—the term 'enigmatic signifier'" could be replaced by "compromised messages" since the "enigmatic" here refers not to some "mysterious" quality of the adult's communications but to the unavailability of these "messages" to the infant's metabolization, translation, and symbolization. It is therefore only through a "realism of the unconscious" and a system of translation-repression, that sexuality is possible as a "drive" that pulses "like a splinter in the skin" within the individual; this "drive" represents a feature of the psyche that is inevitable but not reducible to either biological instinct or genital activity. Indeed, one way to understand Laplanche's "general theory of seduction" is to appreciate it as a structuralist account of sexuality.[31] What Laplanche precisely rejects in Freud's "biologizing" schema is that it incoherently pretends that "sexuality"—as a "drive"—can be produced by an infant's experience of dissatisfaction without acknowledging that no amount of dissatisfaction could ever account for the sudden genesis of "sexuality" as a *drive*. As Laplanche repeatedly insists, this Freudian "metaphysical" speculation relies, for its cogency, on the myth of a primal id that contains, within itself, the sexuality it will possess later on.

Laplanche's Radical Formulations

Exposing the inconsistency of this developmental fable, Laplanche observes that perhaps the most problematic feature of "leaning-on" is that it effectively enables "the abandonment of a theory of human sexuality as exogenous, intersubjective, and intrusive."[32] Returning to the question of masochism—and to the idea of ebranlement from which Bersani derived his notion of "self-shattering"—Laplanche suggests that even if "leaning-on" explains how the "sexual" is capable of arising at the edges of all somatic activity, all kinds of shock, "what remains illogical and unaccounted for is the onset of 'sexuality' with the 'specific-ity of the sexual'"—"precisely its nonvital, marginal character" (199). Therefore, even if we maintain that the infant is impacted by the pain of being overstimulated by the external world, Laplanche concludes, "the theory as a whole remains profoundly biologistic, and above all, endog-enous. It is only ever a theory of the *emergence* of the sexual from another mode of functioning, which is thus substituted for the theory of its implantation" (199). A little later in the essay, Laplanche comments directly on how his understanding of masochism's role in the constitution of sexuality has changed since his earlier speculations. Laplanche explains, "The *Position Originaire* article, a little earlier than *Life and Death in Psy-choanalysis*, had still partially yielded to the inclination to the endoge-nous, insofar as it thought it indispensable to set out from an activity whose origin was the subject—the aggressive subject, transformed by the *drive for mastery*—in order to define a moment of turning-around, which would be the sexual position of masochism. To put it briefly, the 1968 article continued on the track of a leaning-on conceived as a process of endogenous emergence" (209). Whereas Laplanche originally conceived of the ego's "turning-around" as the "moment" where sexuality is *gener-ated*, the new schematization, which is grounded in the distinctiveness of "sexuality" from genital sexuality, the difference between "drive" and "instinct," and the introduction of the "general theory of seduction," makes it immediately clear that the ego can no more generate its own sexuality by practicing its "drive for mastery" than the infant can become sexual by feeling frustrated that nutrition is withheld.

Laplanche's return to masochism and the particular moment of the ego's "turning around" is a place to begin considering the two major and interrelated ways Bersani misinterprets and distorts Laplanche's metapsy-chological schema. That is, in addition to Bersani's neglect of Laplanche's post-1970 work (which constitutes the bulk of Laplanche's writing), this essay's close engagement with Laplanche reveals the distance Bersani's formulations take from Laplanche's original project. First, Bersani con-flates and replaces Laplanche's structural account with his own naturalis-tic, phenomenological one. Therefore, although Laplanche uses "turning around" to explain the conversion of painful stimuli into pleasure, he soon realizes that pleasure and sexuality are neither identical nor neces-sarily co-occurring. That is, even if the ego manages to enjoy the painful assault of unassimilable stimulation, all that ever proves is that the ego has the capacity for surviving its own psychobiological distress. Because Laplanche is insistent on the centrality of an "enlarged" sexuality for any rigorous account of complex psychic structure, it becomes immediately clear that for the infant to go from merely turning pain-into-pleasure to something that is propelled by drive-sexuality requires another intervening event. Laplanche's formulation of the adult other's intrusive, violating impact functions to explain how the ego arrives, by force, at sexuality. But if Bersani persists in treating the ego's "turning around" as an actual encounter with sexuality, it is only because his framework absolutely conflates sexuality and pleasure. That is, if in Bersani's model of sexuality, "masochism is a tautology for sexuality," this is only because "sexuality" is a tautology for pleasure.

Second, Bersani's conflation of sexuality and pleasure leads to sexuality's erasure as a distinctive category of psychic structure. Because pleasure can be gratified and goal-directed, Bersani eradicates any meaningful or functional distinction between "instinct" and "drive" and thereby vitiates the entire foundation of a radical metapsychological project that would take as one of its essential features an account of the human as "driven" by something like "a splinter in the skin," toward objects that increase rather than relieve excitation, by a force that is "nonvital and marginal" rather than goal-directed, repeatable, and satisfiable. If sexuality in Bersani's work adheres to the economy of pleasure/pain, this is because Bersani has elided the distinctive economy of sexuality. Correspondingly, to the extent pleasure/pain is identical to sexuality, it is made possible by Bersani's reassertion of the ego's centrality as the entity who *experiences* feeling (pleasure/pain). By making pleasure identical to sexuality, Bersani ignores the structural and functional specificity of the ego as a psychic agency, and instead treats the ego as a synonym for sovereign individuality. By using ego in the colloquial sense and rewinding to its earliest possible moments of physiological distress, Bersani recenters sexuality to the "truth" of where we find our pleasure. Therefore, whereas Laplanche's account of sexuality hinges on the infant's ultimate passivity, Bersani reinstalls an ego at the origin of infancy who is always already *mastering* its environment, an ego that has all the capabilities and characteristics of an agentic self who is acting psychologically. Indeed, Bersani's romanticization of the heroic ego's epic masochistic initiation into pleasure/pain, who conquers threat by "turning around" and thereby generating the template for its future sexuality, would have been incoherent to Laplanche, for whom sexuality is distinct from the economy of pleasure/pain since sexuality is not merely the repetition of pleasurable experience, and for whom there could be no such thing as an ego who preexists the sexuality that constitutes it.

Bersani's conflation of sexuality with pleasure/pain and phenomenolization of psychic processes is consistent, I would suggest, with the agenda of his genealogical project, which is to use a psychoanalytic developmental schema to find the subject's earliest experience of the sexuality he experiences throughout his adult life. How else are we to appreciate the fixation of Bersani's thought on the single "moment" of the ego's "turning around" toward the stimuli that assault it? Laplanche readily discounts the fascination with locatable "moments" in the development of complex psychic mechanisms. Referring to Lacan's theory of the "mirror stage," Laplanche observes: "Even Lacan does not entirely avoid stageism, and this is not simply in the title of his article, but also in its content: the idea that everything happens one day, in a given month, at a certain moment, all of a sudden. His description of the mirror stage has a highly dramatic character: one fine day, as it were, the mayonnaise takes."[33] If Bersani's allegory of sexual development is likewise characterized by its "highly dramatic character" it is because Bersani is less interested in how psychic processes develop than in the ego's earliest experiences of pleasure. Indeed, since the ego is structurally and functionally indistinguishable from a "person," it becomes clear that to the extent Bersani differentiates himself from Laplanche on the question of the "monad"—even after Laplanche has scrupulously demonstrated the unjustifiability of believing that sexuality can emerge *by itself*, from anything the ego *does*—it is because the "monad" figures for an entity that *experiences* everything, from the beginning.

As Tuhkanen's article notes, "Bersani defines sexuality in terms of monadic solitariness, a nonrelation that, according to him, Freud at once articulates and represses."[34] Therefore, when in *Baudelaire and Freud*, Bersani, in a footnote, writes, "From here on, my discussion differs in important ways from Laplanche's analyses (especially the view I take of the relation between 'nonsexual sadism' [step one] and primary narcissism)" (79), it appears as though Bersani prefers the "monad" to object-relations because, as Tuhkanen observes, for Bersani "it is primarily *the degeneration of the sexual into a relationship that condemns sexuality to becoming a struggle for power* (IRG 25)" (147). For Bersani, the "monad" is pitted against "object-relations" in order to preserve the ethical integrity of sexuality's nonrelatedness. However, it is crucial to observe that his defense of the "monad's" non-relationality is contingent on conflating the "monad" with the autarkic, imperial *ego* who is functionally indistinguishable from the emotional, psychological, and in control *self*. Therefore, although Bersani accuses Freud of having been "fearful of an intrinsic indifference to others in human sexuality," and as a result "managed to reinterpret his theory of primary narcissism,"[35] the presumption that non-relatedness is the scariest possible outcome is belied by Bersani's own thinking, which suggests that it isn't the absence of *relationality* that's terrifying, but that, in fact, what may be nearly impossible to imaginatively sustain is the idea that there is no *self* that we can track back through time, no self-presence that isn't itself the product of violation and intrusion, no ego/monad/person who initiated its own experience of sexuality. Bersani's characterization of Freud and Laplanche as fleeing "radical non-relatedness" in favor of relationality misses the entire thrust of Laplanche's project, which was to expose, as a false binary, the choice between relationality and monadism, by instead demonstrating how the animating tension of even the most radical, speculative theory is between centering and decentering, ipso-centrism and primary alterity.

Shattering as Self-Affirmation

Using the Ptolemaic/Copernican binary heuristically—in order to complicate the easy distinction between radical versus classical theory—Laplanche explains that every revolutionary effort is internally riven by this conflict so that what he calls Freud's "going-astray" emblematizes those moments when "confronted with an obstacle," a thinker "takes the wrong path" away from the "exigency" of the object.[36] Laplanche rigorously identifies these moments in Freud's thought and demonstrates how even a radical discovery like the "unconscious" or "infantile sexuality" is susceptible to being recuperated as a feature of the ego's power and self-presence. Addressing the disappearance of the "unconscious" as representing something in me but which is nevertheless truly foreign and unknowable, Laplanche writes, "From the moment that the unconscious is reduced from its alien-ness to what one could call, along with theologians and those of a certain faith, an *intimior intimo meo* ['something more inward than my inwardness']—we can only observe a return to centering: there is something in me which I've split off from, denied, but which I must re-assimilate. Certainly, the ego is not master of its own house, but it is, after all, at home there nonetheless" (67). Indeed, specifying the ineluctable tendency toward ego-centrism, Laplanche observes, "The Copernican revolution is perhaps still more radical in that it *suggests* that man, even as subject of knowledge, is not the central reference-point for what he knows" (56). This explication of the tension between centering and decentering offers some insight into understanding the movements of Bersani's argument: The choice between a "monad" and relationality is a superficial distinction that Bersani utilizes in order to smuggle into his meta-psychological drama the ego as a familiar and pre-constituted protagonist. This is evident in Bersani's sentimental fable of the ego's "turning around" to generate sexuality, which is endogenous to it, and in his ethical program of insisting that "new relational modes" might take as their template the movements that every person, having been an ego/monad, has already made.

Perhaps nowhere is Bersani's reassertion of the ego's centrality more striking than in his systematic conversion of Laplanche's structural "general theory of seduction" into an interpersonal drama that revolves around the ego's emotional experience. Describing what precisely he means by "enigmatic," Laplanche repeatedly explained, "When I hear talk of enigmas, I prick up my ears. An enigma, despite the German term 'Ratsel' we use it to translate, is not just a simple riddle. An enigma, as I understand it, is to be distinguished just as much from a riddle as from a problem to be resolved, or from a *mystery*."[37] This distinction is crucial for Laplanche because what his schema outlines is not the infant's *feelings* about the "messages" proffered to it by the adult, but rather the structural *effects* on the infant of being assaulted by "messages," some of which it cannot translate. The infant is passive to those "messages" it cannot "translate," and they become repressed instead. But crucially, the infant does not *register* the "enigmatic messages" as "mysterious" and, out of some inability to comprehend them, *reacts* to them instead. Laplanche's theory demonstrates the process whereby the "unconscious" is structured as an effect of those "residues" which the infant could not translate (symbolize/represent). The absence of the infant's conscious decision-making is critical to this schema because what Laplanche is precisely trying to show is that "sexuality" is an expression of those "splinter[s] in the skin" that propel the infant toward objects and aims but are nevertheless untraceable to anything the infant did or felt or wanted.

When Bersani interprets Laplanche's terms, the quintessential passivity of the infant is subsumed into yet another scene of the ego's interior experience. In perhaps his most extended engagement with Laplanche's idea of the "enigmatic signifier," Bersani writes in *Caravaggio's Secrets*, of how "*an ego is erotically solicited into being*."[38] Whereas Laplanche describes a structural process, Bersani announces that:

> it is how we read the summons, the seduction, the soliciting that determines what or who we are. The inability to decipher the enigmatic signifier constitutes us as sexual beings, that is, beings in whom desire or lack is central. However peculiar it may seem to speak of desire as an epistemological category, we propose that desire as lack is constituted, originally, as the exciting pain of a certain ignorance: the failure to penetrate the *sense* of the other's soliciting—through touch,

gesture, voice, or look—of our body. This failure is itself dependent on a more fundamental reading: the reading of the soliciting as a secret. The secrets of the unconscious may be nothing more than the introjection of the secrets the other involuntarily persuades us to believe he or she holds without allowing us to read them. The withheld being with which the other addresses us is the other's desirability. (40)

As the prose and scene-setting of this passage indicate, Bersani subverts passivity into activity, replacing the helplessly implanted infant with a proto-individual who experiences "the exciting pain of a certain igno-rance." Translating "enigmatic signifiers" into a familiar Lacanian topol-ogy, Bersani totally obscures the mechanism (of repression and the constitution of the "drive") that Laplanche uses the concept of "enigmatic signifiers" to outline. Therefore, whereas Laplanche emphasized that the "enigmatic messages" are repressed if they cannot be symbolized, and, unavailable to consciousness, sit lodged, like a "splinter in the skin," as the basis of "drive" sexuality, Bersani again turns the moment of a psychic process into an *interpersonal* drama between the mother who possesses and withholds a "secret" and the infant whose *emotional experience* of "the failure to penetrate the *sense* of the other's soliciting" causes the infant to pursue objects, thenceforth, in a "sexual" way. In his essay on Bersani's use of psychoanalysis to elaborate an ethics of "self-relation," Patrick ffrench addresses what he considers to be the theoretical effects of Bersani's persistent psychologization by clarifying that "the soliciting of the subject is not driven by the intention of an agent. The other who seduces or solicits is not the other *person*, in an intersubjective relation, the other to whom, as Laplanche points out, Freud customarily referred to as *der Andere*, but the other in that other, *das Andere*."[39] Therefore, while "the effect of Laplanche's theory is to decenter the intersubjective relation, render it asymmetrical," ffrench suggests, "What I think Bersani brings to Laplanche, how he inflects the notion of the enigmatic signifier, is to personalize the terms, to insist on the way in which the subject may herself personalize the structure" (135). While ffrench's interpretation offers a compelling account of the work psychologization might accom-plish—in exposing the way "enigma" is psychologized by the subject her-self—such an explanation misses the specificity of "sexuality" as a "drive," which is constituted by affective residues the infant could *not* register, translate, symbolize. Therefore, the contention that "enigmas" are some-what consciously registered, and then personalized, obviates their func-tion in the Laplanchian schema.

Bersani's total refusal to imagine that psychic processes might *not* be merely an effect of how the infant *feels*, is all the more striking in this context since it is on the basis of his mischaracterization of "enigmatic signifiers" that Bersani accuses Laplanche of participating in the grand Western metaphysical tradition of treating all desire as the product of lack. "Lack," Bersani suggests in "The Gay Outlaw," "may not be inherent in desire; desire in homo-ness is desire to repeat, to expand, to intensify the same."[40] Working to develop an alternative theory of desire that is set against a philosophical tradition that asserts the centrality of lack to desire, Bersani insists that "the aim of desire grounded in lack is the filling of the lack through the incorporation of difference," whereas "the desire in others of what we already are is, on the contrary, a self-effacing narcissism, a narcissism constitutive of community in that it tolerates psychological difference" (150).[41] While Bersani's determination to challenge the primacy of desire/lack as the privileged explanatory paradigm of human sexuality is necessary and relevant, it depends, in this instance, on the absolute conflation of "enigmatic signifiers" with "*secrets*" that the ego-as-*person* feels and *experiences* as something he *lacks*. If, as Tuhkanen suggests, Bersani is interested in asking, "Can there be a form of desire that does not aim at the 'annihilating elucidation' of the object, the straightening-out of the other's tortuous puzzles?,"[42] it is worth considering that "desire" is always "personal" insofar as Bersani insists on locating the ego at the center of his schema; it is, therefore, the auto-centric model of endogenous sexuality that creates the conditions for "desire" to be experienced, *as* "desire" by *someone* who knows what he *feels* and wants.

Toward the end of "The Unfinished Copernican Revolution," Laplanche asks, "Can the Copernican revolution be finished?" He means by this that "we cannot reform our language, and with it our perception and our inner sense, to the extent of giving everyday expression in a 'Copernican' language to the movement of the sun, moon and stars. The narcissistic wound inflicted by science is defeated by our narcissistic centeredness as living bodies."[43] According to Laplanche, if Freud repeatedly "goes astray" from his more radical observations, it is an inevitable result of "narcissistic closure" and the psyche's attempt to defend itself against external penetration. With this in mind, we might begin to understand the relationship in Bersani's thought, introduced at this chapter's outset, between "shattering" sex and his call for "new relational modes." What initially seemed curious about the coexistence of these themes becomes representative of the way Bersani locates sexuality as sexual pleasure, and the ego as the agent of its spontaneous emergence. Because the ego originally gave itself over to *enjoying* pain, if only it could do so again, and again, this lesson in surrender would transform the ego from the bad-possessive-relational kind into the good-submissive-singular kind who ushers in a transformative onto-ethics that reconfigures our experience of sexual pleasure. This is a sentimental story though, not only for the regression fantasy it harbors at its base—the good-ego is the original-ego, unmediated by "relationality"—but for its reassertion of the ego's role as the master of its sexual destiny.

In this way, Bersani's call to embrace our fundamental "nonrelatedness," although alleging to be radical, is premised all along on the security of the ego at the center of sexuality and sexuality as the repetition of achievable pleasure. Although there is certainly something compelling about defining sexuality as that which "shatters the structured self," this essay demonstrates the incoherence of this meta-psychic claim on the basis that it preserves the myth of a self that can shatter that which constitutes it *as* a self in the first place. Bersani's consistent personalization of psychic processes reasserts a perceptive and controlling ego into a structure—sexuality—that testifies most acutely to the psyche's mediation by an-other. As such, Bersani's insistent demand for sex to be the way we lose our egos belies the fact that he put the ego there to begin with. There is no self who chooses shattering, even if there are people who feel shattered during sex. Bersani offers a phenomenology of sexual pleasure, and a history of sex as pleasure, from the perspective of the body; his unrelenting defense of the necessity of pleasure is resonant, provocative, and inspiring. But sexuality is not only pleasure and the ego is not merely a less inhibited or truer self. These differences are essential to any rigorous account of sexuality and its development. If there is indeed something sexuality can be said to shatter, let it be the myth that there is a "secret" to sexuality that we, *ourselves*, could ever know or share.

3 /   Boundaries Are for Sissies: Violation
in Jane Gallop and Henry James

Queerness and Vulnerability

In queer theory, "violation" is a touchy subject. Or, more specifically, the exultant celebration of sexuality as ethically radical, psychologically violent, and socially antinormative conduces to a field-wide inability to distinguish "violation" from the routine operation of "queer" sexuality. Queer studies' long-standing self-identification with "antinormativity," broad suspicion of the homophobic ideology subtending the rhetoric of sexual innocence, and reflexive association of sexual emancipation as the decreased preoccupation with logics of constraint have made it uniformly impossible to consider the connection between sexuality and boundaries as a dynamic and complex relation. In his recent study, *Sex and Harm in the Age of Consent*, Joseph Fischel intervenes in this problematic by "pushing back against certain strands of progressive scholarship and activism that equate innocence with vulnerability and/or assume that narratives of innocence and vulnerability are only rhetorical maneuvers to preserve traditional gender and sexual norms."[1] Jane Gallop's *Feminist Accused of Sexual Harassment* (1997),[2] a manifesto against the ideological underpinnings of sexual harassment laws and its threat to progressive feminism and sexual freedom—set against the backdrop of her own real-life defense against accusations of sexual harassment by two graduate students—offers an early and sensational engagement with these questions.[3] Gallop offers an exemplary performance of the contempt and incredulity Fischel attributes to "progressive theory" when in the name of sexuality's transcendental "truth" she insists on the fundamental nonsense of defining "boundaries" between appropriate versus inappropriate sex. Gallop's dramatization of her feminist-minded allergic reaction to sexual "boundaries" as inherently synonymous with anxious idealizations of sexuality anticipates the attitude, shared by many of the field's leading theoreticians, that the very discussion of violation always already signals a fatal concession to heteronormative pieties.

Continuous with Fischel's attempt to differentiate "innocence" from "vulnerability" and to reimagine the asymmetry between different sexual subjectivities, this chapter reads Gallop's text alongside Henry James's short story "The Pupil," in which a precocious young boy develops an intimate connection to his older male teacher, and then suddenly collapses and dies at the precise moment his mother transfers the boy over to his beloved teacher for permanent companionship and care. The short stories and novels of Henry James already enjoy a privileged status in queer theoretical discourse where the proliferation of strange single women, perspicacious children, and overall frustrations of desire's heteronormative trajectory—in addition to speculation over James's personal sexual life—have treated Jamesian characters as oracular proto-queer subjects.[4] Through a close reading of "The Pupil," this chapter focuses on why, at the novel's end, an older man's "hug" kills the young boy who loved him. After working through the possibilities elaborated from within the "anti-boundaries" position of queer critics, this chapter proposes that an absolute scorn for theorizing "boundaries" produces interpretive limitations that fail to understand the violence at the center of James's text and, in so doing, generate a systematic refusal to explore the structural and psychological development of sexuality.

In addition to offering a sustained close reading of an undertheorized Jamesian masterpiece, this chapter looks at how Laplanche's "general theory of seduction" provides a new rubric for distinguishing the fantasy of childhood innocence from the reality of asymmetrical sexual development. Installing a meaningful *difference* in the sexuality of adults and children enables queer theory to approach "violation" as ethically and psychologically complex. Challenging contemporary queer studies to develop a viable model of "sexual harm" that neither capitulates to homophobic tropes nor eschews the language of abuse wholesale, Fischel's critique of current theoretical approaches to sexual harm establishes essential groundwork for this chapter's claim that the current inability to distinguish sexuality from violation, and general conceptual poverty of theorizing violation, betrays a simplistic understanding of boundaries and a defensive orientation toward relationality that perpetuates an ulti-mately erotophobic relationship to sexuality.

"Are Sex Offenders the New Queers?"

In a recent version of how progressive criticism defends sexuality from the rhetoric of "violation," Laura Kipnis summarizes the situation as such:

> Let me attempt to sketch the backdrop of the hysteria, for anyone who hasn't spent time on an American campus lately. There are two conflicting stories about sex at the moment. The first story is all about license: hooking up, binge drinking, porn watching—my students talk knowingly about "anal," and funnily about "dormcest" . . . they're junior libertines, nothing sexual is alien to them. Layered on top of that is the other big story of the moment: sex is dangerous; it can traumatize you for life. It's not a happy combination.[5]

Likening the current campus atmosphere to the Salem witch trials and other outbreaks of social hysteria and paranoia, Kipnis blames the "zeal-ous boundary-drawing" (11) for inaugurating new metaphors that "veer toward the extractive rather than additive—sex takes something *away* from you, at least if you're a woman: your safety, your choices, your future. It's contaminating: You can catch trauma, which, like a virus, never goes away" (7). Although Kipnis does not make any reference to Gallop's 1997 text, her singling out of "zealous boundary-drawing" as a symptom and cause of the contemporary "hysteria" rehearses a set of claims about the relationship of "boundaries" to sexuality that have become axiomatic in contemporary queer criticism.[6]

As Robyn Wiegman and Elizabeth Wilson have argued in their recent field intervention on "queer theory's antinormative conventions," "nearly every queer theoretical itinerary of analysis that now matters is informed by the prevailing supposition that a critique of normativity marks the spot where *queer* and *theory* meet."[7] The shared foundational antinorma-tivity that links an otherwise diverse spectrum of critical orientations leads Wiegman and Wilson to announce, "While its focus and theoretical inheritances vary, antinormativity reflects a broad understanding that the critical force of queer inquiry lies in its capacity to undermine norms, challenge normativity, and interrupt the processes of normalization—including the norms and normativities that have been produced by queer inquiry itself" (4). Pointing out that the "antinormative impera-tive implicit in the designation *heteronormativity* points to a serious methodological quandary for the field," Wiegman and Wilson powerfully express their disappointment and frustration that despite the fact that "queer" has etymological connections to movements that transverse and twist (*Tendencies* xii), "its most frequent deployment has been in the service of defiance and reprimand" (11). Wiegman and Wilson make clear why this "intuitively oppositional and antinormative" stance—although "politically and critically irresistible" (11)—is problematic by returning to Foucault's identification of the "repressive hypothesis." As Foucault observed, and as "every post-Foucauldian queer theorist understands," the "claim that sexuality has been repressed is caught in spirals of power-knowledge-pleasure that make such a claim an enactment of norms (rather than a transgression of them)" (12). Therefore, and with Foucault in mind, Wiegman and Wilson draw attention to the fundamental incoherence of "oppositional" positions, which proceed with "antinormative postures" in spite of how "opposition" itself "underwrites the repressive hypothesis" (12).

Indeed, if "antinormativity" names a defining feature of contemporary queer thought, then "boundaries" perform a vital discursive function insofar as the critical negotiation of them effectively exemplifies and consolidates the field's self-identification as radical, oppositional, and constitutively at odds with norms and normative conventions. Even, and indeed especially, when queer theory's relationship to "boundaries" expresses a proud and totalizing *negation* of their utility, structure, or deployment, contemporary critiques consistently measure the rigor of their antinormativity by advertising their repudiation of the putative "lines" distinguishing the normal from not-normal in social-psychic life. Perhaps nowhere is the operation of this logic more vividly and vigorously defended than in the field's approach to childhood sexuality and, in particular, questions of sexual innocence and abuse. Since childhood innocence is a foundational conceit of normative sexual development, and nonreproductive sexuality is persistently a target for locating threats to the "figurative" and literal "child,"[8] it is not surprising to consider how extensively an antinormative elaboration of queerness hinges on the defiant and unapologetic insistence on the truth of certain counterintuitive claims. Therefore, if the "child" is the "emblem of futurity's unquestioned value"[9] and "normativity" is a "synonym for what is constricting or controlling or tyrannical" (12), then nowhere does sexuality seem more stubbornly oppressed than when it concerns the "commonsense" and "sentimental" legislation of children's sexuality. As many cultural critics have shown, the rhetoric of "saving" and "protecting" the "children" is neither ideologically neutral nor dissociable from compulsory heterosexuality and as such always depends upon the ever-present danger of the aberrant queer. Writing about the ideological association between pederasty, pedophilia, and homosexuality, Ellis Hanson persuasively demonstrates that "scandals over the emergence of gay studies in the academy may be seen as the latest development in a long and anxious tradition of turning pedagogical eros into tragedy or farce, and the scandal always turns on the professional body, which might at any moment dangerously enact the illicit desire it studies."[10] Therefore, if, according to normativity, the adults children always seem to need protection from are "queers" then the "antinormative" opposition to this status quo necessarily requires the vigorous repudiation of "rules" that, in their compassionate safeguarding of children's sexual rights, conceals a corrosive and puritanical attack on sexuality, and queer sex, tout court. This perspective might help explain why queer "oppositional" identity insists on proving its irreverence for social norms or pieties and enables an appreciation of the rhetorical and ideological force of Edelman's ecstatic exhortation to "fuck the social order and the Child in whose name we're collectively terrorized; fuck Annie; fuck the waif from *Les Mis*; fuck the poor, innocent kid on the Net; fuck Laws both with capital *l*s and with small; fuck the whole network of Symbolic relations and the future that serves as its prop" (29).

The field's negotiations of "boundaries" indicates that in queer studies one is never queerer than when taunting and trespassing a boundary, or, in the case of adult-child sexuality, scoffing derisively and refusing to even acknowledge one. Although written nearly a decade before Edelman's *No Future*, Jane Gallop's non-apologia anticipates the call to "fuck the social order and the Child in whose name we're collectively terrorized" when instead of capitulating to the legal/moral accusations of her wrongdoing, she demands an alternative pedagogic model free of sociality's hypocritical, nonsensical, anti-sexual "laws" ("both with capital *l*s and with small"). Gallop offers an exemplary performance of contempt and disbelief when, with incredulity and in the name of sexuality's transcendental "truth," she says, "It is precisely because I believe it is not possible to neatly separate the sexual from other others of relations that I find the movement to bar the sexual from pedagogy not only dangerous but supremely impractical."[11] Grafting these arguments onto a broader claim about the conceptual stakes of "boundaries" for feminism and deconstruction, Gallop defends the freedom of sexuality by asserting that actually, *boundaries are the violation*. As such, "boundaries" that are created to manage the difference between "sexual" and "non-sexual" activity signal, according to Gallop, the total denial of feminism's power as the source of women's sexual liberation. "I credit feminism with teaching me sexual pleasure" (4) Gallop says, and "feminism will always name the force that freed me to desire and to learn" (6). For this reason, impugning a liberated sexuality on the basis that it is "harassment" confounds the unique relationship of feminism to sexuality by criminalizing the transgression of precisely those "boundaries" toward which feminism urges a sustained and empowering imperviousness. Linking feminism with critical theory's psychoanalytic and poststructuralist foundations, Gallop further argues that "boundaries" imperil criticism's radical agenda and ought necessarily to offend any contemporary critic's "deconstructive" sensibilities.

A Small Boy and Others

"The Pupil" is among the least well-known stories in James's remarkable subgenre of short stories where adults accidentally/mysteriously kill the children in their care.[12] Set in turn-of-the-century London, "The Pupil" tells the story of the relationship between Morgan, a gifted and enigmatic student, and Pemberton, his teacher, against the backdrop of Morgan's strange and manipulative family, the Moreens. Pemberton is a recent graduate of Oxford whose failure to secure any writing opportunities requires him to become a teacher. Immediately upon meeting Morgan, Pemberton recognizes that his disciple will be an altogether atypical one: Brilliant and discerning, Morgan is repeatedly described as being hypersensitive to his environment, the affects of others, and his own consciousness, a temperament that is underscored by a weak heart condition. Although Pemberton is initially repelled by the prospect of having to endure the challenges of a talented student, he is quickly charmed by the infectious nature of Morgan's curiosity. Gradually, the two develop an intimate bond that retains the pedagogic schematic even as their conversations revolve around non-academic concerns and their roles reverse. The story ends with the decision of Morgan's parents to give him away to Pemberton while they ostensibly organize their dire financial situation. At the moment when Morgan, now a boy of fifteen, is preparing to go toward Pemberton's embrace, he suddenly collapses of a heart attack instead. His mother and Pemberton rush to help him but it is too late and he dies suspended between the arms of his mother and his teacher.

While James's signature exploration of consciousness is apparent in all his stories about children-adult relations, "The Pupil" is unique for how it entangles differentials such as "age" with the differential of "money" as a means to repeatedly stage the characters' confusion about the *terms* of a relationship between a strange and brilliant child and his older, unmarried teacher. Foucault points out that "age" indexes a unique uncertainty in relationships of "desire and pleasure" when in an interview he says, "Between a man and a younger woman the marriage institution makes it easier: she accepts it and makes it work. But two men of noticeably different ages—what code would allow them to communicate? They face each other without terms or convenient words, with nothing to assure them about the meaning of the movement that carries them towards each other. They have to invent, from A to Z, a relationship that is still formless, which is friendship: that is to say, the sum of everything through which they can give each other pleasure."[13] This question of how to classify the attachment between these boys of different ages is a recurring thematic and representational preoccupation in James's short story, even though to the extent critics have shown interest in this story it has been either to focus on money, sexuality, or childhood, rather than their provocative interconnectedness.[14] In one of the few critical essays that deal with "The Pupil," Millicent Bell argues that "James' great short story, 'The Pupil,' is, among other things, about something considered nearly unmentionable by the genteel—money. By an extinct code of manners and taste that James examines and turns inside out, refined persons were still, in the last decades of the nineteenth century, not supposed to talk much about money, even though their liberty to avoid its mention depended on its sufficient supply."[15] Bell focuses on the class differences that are exposed in the story between Pemberton, "James' gentlemanly young tutor," and Mrs. Moreen. Pemberton "has clearly been bred to the polite concealment of anxiety about dollars or pounds" and who, "not quite typical of the English university men," belongs to "an upper-class membership less long established" and therefore "less secure." "Perhaps," Bell suggests, "the fact that he is an American is meant to suggest a more advanced stage of the economy of wealth than of the hereditary upper class—wealth that is not only more recent in its notions but more liquid and more subject to rapid fluctuation—and necessarily discussable." In contrast, Mrs. Moreen, whose "claims to the aristocratic chic" are undermined by the "suede gloves," which are "soiled" (and thus "a give-away of the insufficiency of Mrs. Moreen's claims to the aristocratic chic"), and "the nervous motion by which with one hand she pulls them back and forth through the other." Bell notes that "Mrs. Moreen has a procuress's instinct for the way love may be made to have an exchange value, may be made equivalent to money" and therefore "seems to guess, accurately enough, that Pemberton will feel young Morgan's appeal."

In Bell's reading, Morgan functions like the prized possession of "a brothel keeper," whom Mrs. Moreen repeatedly advertises "to excite the young man's interest." Mrs. Moreen's eager announcement that "He's a genius . . . you'll love him" is read by Bell to illustrate that Mrs. Moreen "will never cease to remind Pemberton of the reward he gains by knowing her son. She will encourage the tutor's discovery of the precocious young-ster's charm in order to arouse and to strengthen his delighted affection— and so to justify her claim that the teacher's pleasure in his student's rare qualities is itself ample payment. And further—even more shocking, probably—she will convert the boy's own return of devotion to Pember-ton into a substitute for money owed by his parents" (141). Bell's sum-marization of Mrs. Moreen's machinations accurately portrays what transpires in the story, for indeed, Pemberton does find himself immedi-ately taken by the brilliant boy. James writes of Pemberton's response to Morgan: "He rather disliked precocity and was disappointed to find gleams of it in a disciple not yet in his teens. Nevertheless, he divined on the spot that Morgan wouldn't prove a bore. He would prove, on the con-trary, a source of agitation. This idea held the young man, in spite of a certain repulsion" (170). As I think this passage describing Pemberton's experience demonstrates, and as I want to suggest in this section, while money is one of the story's most powerful figurations of the relational dynamics between Pemberton/Morgan, the dynamics of ambiguity between these boys—though representable in monetary terms—are not reducible to an economic problematic. That is, although the story unfolds to the beat of financial concerns—its opening line, "The poor young man hesitated and procrastinated: it cost him such an effort to broach the sub-ject of terms" (168)—the monetary complications are also used to drama-tize the affective instability of this pedagogic relationship, as when upon first seeing Morgan, we learn that "Pemberton was modest, was even timid; and the chance that his small scholar would prove cleverer than himself had quite figured to his anxiety, among the dangers of an untried experiment" (169). What we see from the very first page, then, is that Pemberton's demand to be remunerated, while technically appropriate, clashes with the relational economics whereby his chief anxiety is whether he even *has* anything to offer the young Morgan Moreen for which to be recompensed. From this perspective, James shows us that the unshakable anxiety about "the rate of payment" may have less to do with how "money" reflects the obvious truths of an emotional transaction than with the ways "money" can settle, and make momentarily simple, the terrifying uncer-tainty of what these boys will do together. As such, treating money as the primary narrative force to which all other things must be subverted misses James's assiduous use of money to comprehensively problematize the "relational genre" of their attachment.

The anxiety about the "terms" of their relationship—an anxiety that is expressed primarily financially but that is, as we'll see, profoundly relational as well—is gradually exacerbated by Pemberton's developing awareness that he cannot expect to behave tutorially toward a child that barely resembles a "pupil." As if the story is moving simultaneously on two tracks at opposite directions, we see Pemberton struggle to classify the socioeconomic situation of the Moreen family as well as adapt to his professional/pedagogic function, and although these tracks are expected to complement each other, we learn instead that, if they do, it is not in quite the way Pemberton expects. For example, although Pemberton is initially intimated by Mrs. Moreen's supposed wealth, he observes, "on a nearer view that her elegance was intermittent and her parts didn't always match" (171). Mr. Moreen, whom Pemberton encounters only a few times throughout his time living with the family, was "even more a man of the world than you might first make out" and "further mentioned that [he] aspired to be intimate with his children, to be their best friend, and that he was always looking out for them. That was what he went off for, to London and other places—to look out; and this vigilance was the theory of life, as well as the real occupation of the whole family" (171). The strange glamor of what exactly it might mean for life "experience" to be "the real occupation of the whole family" dissipates as Pemberton increasingly realizes that "their supreme quaintness was their success . . . since he had never seen a family so brilliantly equipped for failure" (172), and a few moments later, "They amused him as much as if they had really been a band of gipsies. He was still young and had not seen much of the world—his English years had been properly arid; therefore the reversed conventions of the Moreens—for they had *their* desperate proprieties—struck him as topsy-turvy" (172). Pemberton observes their "social strangeness," their "chatter of tongues, their gaiety of good humor, their infinite dawdling (they were always getting themselves up, but it took for ever, and Pemberton had once found Mr. Moreen shaving in the drawing-room), their French, their Italian and, cropping up in the foreign fluencies, their cold tough slices of American" (173) and rather amusedly interprets the awkwardness between them around money to reflect something like a clash of their different cultures. Unsurprisingly, Pemberton "had encountered nothing like them at Oxford; still less had any such note been struck to his younger American ear during the four years at Yale in which he had richly supposed himself to be reacting against a Puritan strain." It isn't therefore difficult to imagine his mixed sense of awe and pleasure when he finds that "they could imitate Venetian and sing Neapolitan, and when they wanted to say something very particular communicated with each other in an ingenious dialect of their own, an elastic spoken cipher which Pemberton at first took for some *patois* of one of their countries, but which he 'caught on to' as he would not have grasped provincial development of Spanish or German" (173). When Morgan announces that "'It's the family language—Ultramoreen,'" we are made to understand that Pemberton's estrangement from this "band of gipsies" positions him as more than just a newcomer to an unfamiliar environment, but as an uncomprehending student who is overworking his senses trying to organize his experience. As the one then who is neither caught up in the "topsy-turvy" revelry of his family nor ever completely outside it, Morgan acts like Pemberton's willing teacher, a role reversal that intensifies when Pemberton discovers the scope of Morgan's preternatural brilliance.

"As for Pemberton's own estimate of his pupil, it was a good while before he got the point of view, so little had he been prepared for it by the smug young barbarians to whom the tradition of tutorship, as hitherto revealed to him, had been adjusted." This is an interesting way to launch Pemberton's observations of "his pupil" because it indicates how thoroughly Morgan challenges what Pemberton thought he knew about being a teacher, or having a student. Pemberton observes:

> Morgan was scrappy and surprising, deficient in many properties supposed common to the *genus* and abounding in others that were the portion only of the supernaturally clever. One day his friend made a great stride: it cleared up the question to perceive that Morgan *was* supernaturally clever and that, though the formula was temporarily meager, this would be the only assumption on which one could successfully deal with him. He had the general quality of a child for whom life had not been simplified by school, a kind of home-bred sensibility which might have been bad for himself but was charming for others, and a whole range of refinement and perception—little musical vibrations as taking as picked-up airs—begotten by wandering about Europe at the tail of his migratory tribe. This might not have been an education to recommend in advance, but its results with so special a subject were as appreciable as the marks on a piece of fine porcelain. . . . Pemberton indeed quickly found himself rejoicing that school was out of the question: in any million of boys it was probably good for all but one, and Morgan was that millionth. (174)

Pemberton's recognition "that Morgan *was* supernaturally clever" is crucially situated in relation to "school," which would have "simplified" his intelligence, made "him comparative and superior," so much so that

Pemberton "found himself rejoicing that school was out of the question." Particularly in the context of the Moreens' "topsy-turvy" lifestyle and Pemberton's financial instability, this moment of "rejoicing that school was out of the question" seems to add yet another site of flux and insecurity to a situation that is already strange and unpredictable. For how will he teach this "supernaturally clever" boy who had "a whole range of refinement and perception"?

The evacuation of expectations around what constitutes a "pupil" coincides with an escalation in the tension around Pemberton's salary so that one way of viewing their interrelatedness is to consider that Pemberton realizes the Moreens intend never to pay him at the same time he acknowledges to himself that he intends never to cease being Morgan's companion. Indeed, I would further suggest, that it is precisely through his negotiations over money—and specifically his increased willingness *not* to have it—that Pemberton surrenders any elaborate fantasy he may have one day had to "try to be school himself" (174). We learn that Pemberton and Morgan have spent most of their time together walking and talking, that Pemberton, although still thinking of him as his student, determines "Morgan was a special case, and to know him was to accept him on his own odd terms," that furthermore, "against every interest he had attached himself. They would have to meet things together." This acceptance of Morgan "on his own terms," although framed here in psychological and relational terms, has obvious financial connotations, especially because the haggling over monetary "terms" establishes the backdrop of the story's developmental arc. By the time Pemberton musters the courage to confront Mrs. Moreen with the ultimatum that "unless they immediately put down something on account he would leave them on the spot and for ever," we cannot be surprised to hear Mrs. Moreen express what, as readers, we ourselves have observed: "'You won't, you *know* you won't—you're too interested,' she said. 'You *are* interested, you know you are, you dear kind man!'" Indeed, although Pemberton's "mind was fully made up to take his step the following week," instead "he was irritated to find that Mrs. Moreen was right, that he couldn't at the pinch bear to leave the child" (179). Pemberton responds to his own irritation by blaming the Moreens for having deceived him so effectively for so long: "Wasn't it another proof of the success with which those patrons practiced their arts that they had managed to avert for so long the illuminating flash?" (179). And although it is sufficiently reasonable to link his delayed awareness with the fact they were a "band of adventurers" and "not merely because they didn't pay their debts, because they lived on society, but because their whole view of life, dim and confused and instinctive, like that of clever color-blind animals, was speculative and rapacious and mean" (180), this line of reasoning belies Pemberton's own complicity with the arrangement. In the moments just preceding the account of his confrontation with Mrs. Moreen, we learn that while in Paris "the better part of this baffled sojourn was for the preceptor and his pupil, who, visiting the Invalides and Notre Dame, the Conciergerie and all the museums, took a hundred remunerative rambles" (143). The word "remunerative" is particularly poignant here for the way it draws our attention to where the language of money has migrated; no longer strictly indicative of salaried labor, "remunerative" now refers to the "rambles" the "preceptor and his pupil" enjoy by themselves in Paris. This imagery continues a few paragraphs later when, "During this period and several others Pemberton was quite aware of how he and his comrade might strike people; wandering languidly through the Jardin des Plantes as if they had nowhere to go, sitting on the winter days in the galleries of the Louvre. . . . He used sometimes to wonder what people would think they were—to fancy that they were looked askance at, as if it might be a suspected case of kidnapping. Morgan couldn't be taken for a young patrician with a preceptor—he wasn't smart enough; though he might pass for his companion's sickly brother" (178). The visual imagery in these passages is striking for how poignantly it expresses the transformation of a relationship that was, at least initially, conceived hierarchically, but that becomes a noticeable lateral engagement, so much so that all the walking, strolling, rambling, wandering, and sitting side by side prompts Pemberton to wonder "what people would think they were."

And indeed, *what* are they to each other? Although the language of "preceptor and pupil" still clings to some of the initial descriptions, Pemberton wonders if considering Morgan a "sickly little brother" is more appropriate, or even someone he has "kidnap[ped]." For by the time Pemberton issues his ultimatum to Mrs. Moreen, their relationship has taken shape very *un*-pedagogically. In my reading then, Pemberton's forfeiture of the familiar tropes for relating corresponds to his acquiescence that the Moreens will never pay him because he's never seen himself *less* like a teacher, and therefore less deserving of reimbursement for being one, than in the moment he dares Mrs. Moreen to let him go. As such, whether or not Mrs. Moreen indeed manipulated the situation by using Morgan to entrap Pemberton seems hardly as significant as the fact that "against every interest he had attached himself." As the story progresses, we watch a silent film with two boys "wandering languidly," taking "a hundred remunerative rambles," expeditions punctured only by Morgan's spontaneous questions or "theories" about something. It is Morgan who repeatedly engages Pemberton on the topic of his parents' embarrassing behavior and Pemberton who tenderly reassures him that he'll "hang on to the last" no matter what they have in store for him (176). Not only is it clear that Pemberton relinquishes every aspiration to be instructive, but that what develops instead, or in keeping with his "accept[ing] him on his own odd terms," is a different position in relation to Morgan—not one who "teaches" and gets reimbursed, but one who listens and happily joins him wherever the boy's curiosity leads. This positioning of Pemberton as a beloved companion who listens and enjoys following Morgan's creative and spontaneous concatenations has the effect of establishing distinctive "terms" for the relationship between this young boy and older man. That is, by abandoning "money" as a reliable index of legible value and the transaction of money as a transcendental arbiter of social structure, the young boy and older man formulate their own intersubjective idiom, of what Foucault called "a code that would allow them to communicate."

Reading Henry James

Indeed, the pressure on Jamesian protagonists to conform their particular desires to predetermined economies replicates the practice, in critical interpretations of James's work, to assimilate a story's meaning to existing rubrics of intelligibility. Drawing attention to the special susceptibility of Jamesian short stories to "allegorical" interpretations, Shoshana Felman, in her tour de force essay, "Turning the Screw of Interpretation," writes: "In seeking to 'explain' and *master* literature, in refusing, that is, to become a *dupe* of literature, in killing within literature that which makes it literature—its reserve of silence, that which, within speech, is incapable of speaking, the literary silence of a discourse *ignorant of what it knows*— the psychoanalytic reading, ironically enough, turns out to be a reading that *represses the unconscious*, that represses, paradoxically, the unconscious it purports to be 'explaining.'"[16] Generalizing beyond "psychoanalytic" interpretations, Millicent Bell claims, "The Jamesian narrative does not progress toward an ultimate and irreversible clarification. It also tends to dispense with the linages of normal plot" (17). In *Thinking in Henry James*, Sharon Cameron deepens Bell's description of "consciousness" by showing that, "James is finally less concerned with how consciousness looks (whether it is consistent) than with what it can do, less concerned with any single way it might function than with the fact that it cannot be bound by the singleness of function."[17] According to Cameron, although "one might be misled by a temptation to psychologize," it is crucial that, "James, it might be said, clears the scene so that nothing will occupy it but his own conflicted points of view, which still issue from consciousness" but are not ultimately reducible to a "psychological context" (5). Cameron's emphasis on the link between James's preoccupation with depicting "consciousness" and the inability of consciousness to "be bound by the singleness of function" emphasizes the inherent open-endedness of his texts, something Bell elegantly captures when she writes: "A bemused, detached, central consciousness is the characteristic center of Jamesian fiction. The witness of the press and thrust of outer life who holds himself apart from the visible 'doing' of others is a characteristically Jamesian figure. . . . James' impressionistic emphasis upon transitory perceptions, above all impressions of the eye, the method that suggests that one view of a matter will be replaced by another, is, then, related to this choice of focus, with its renunciation of absolute knowledge of things, its unwillingness to penetrate and ascertain truth" (33).

Linking these characterizations of Jamesian "indeterminacy" and "impressionism" with the particular features of a "stylistic" "queerness," Kevin Ohi writes that the centrality of Jamesian texts to queer literary critique is less about a given protagonist's specifiable homosexual object-choice, than "the disorienting mixings of register and sudden shifts of tone, with unexpected syntactical inversions and equivocal reifications that hover at indeterminate levels of abstraction, with pronouns that divide their allegiance between any number of more or less distant antecedents."[18] Working determinedly against any reductive one-to-one ratio between James's own "personal" sexuality,[19] Ohi argues that "the daunting complexity of James's writing *is* its queerness; the erotic in his work can be most fully understood when it is considered in linguistic rather than representational terms" (2). Ohi's celebration of "queer" style as against a more traditional preoccupation with "content" explains why a figurative vs. material distinction is the organizing dichotomy of the hermeneutic paradigm he outlines in his analysis of childhood "innocence and rapture." That is, in the effort to disrupt the conventional prioritization of "theme" over "style," Ohi treats all objects as stylistic expressions of sexuality. The results of this for queer criticism are intended to rescue the marginalized "figures" of sexuality from ideology's total absorption. The "child" is one such "figure" who—if ideology would allow it—scandalizes sexuality by exemplifying a "sexual pleasure not for reproduction, not for economic productivity or stability, not for identificatory certainty, not for anything but itself."[20] As the embodiment of "sexuality's" fundamental "queerness," Ohi uses what the child symbolizes ideologically—an assault on heteronormativity—to argue, "Childhood is therefore the ground upon which homophobia and other forms of sexual normativity take shape" (8). Equating "the formal and stylistic innovations of aestheticism" with the "theoretical and political critique of ideologies of sexual normativity" (8), Ohi grounds the resistance to "today's ideology" in a refusal of the enforced antinomy between "innocent" childhood and adult sexuality. Ohi takes particular aim at the rhetoric of "violation" that attends, like a shadow, to every articulation of the "innocent" child. "The child," Ohi writes, "allows us to tell ourselves of an origin uncontaminated by the vicissitudes of language and desire, a pure beginning of autonomy uncorrupted by commerce with its outside. Such autonomy, however, presupposes its breach, drafts our self-explanations into a narrative of a Fall that has always already taken place" (6). In this view, it's not clear what the "boundaries" around the relationship of children to sexuality can be other than mere proof of ideology's "current fetishizations of childhood innocence." Furthermore, because "the contemporary insistence on childhood innocence . . . is inseparable from the ideology oppressing all sexual minorities; the articulation of erotic innocence structures contemporary sexual ideology in general" (7).

Although preserving the indeterminacy of meaning is central to Ohi's interpretive endeavor, for example, it is crucial to consider how the reduction of Jamesian characters to their identifiable location on the "aesthetic versus ideological" divide reduces to a simplistic antinomy James's own elaborate engagement with the complex relationship of individual desire to its expression in social forms. To consider "The Pupil" from this perspective, we might wonder how Ohi would understand the fatal "hug" at the story's end? Although Morgan's death at the precise moment he is being handed over to Pemberton's care suggests that for such a sensitive child, the decisive shift in their relational idiom might have been overwhelming, even distressing, within Ohi's framework there is no language with which to imagine how a "boundary" could be crossed that is not, by its very rhetoric of "boundaries," tantamount to retro-projecting "innocence" onto the "sexual" child. Because the beautiful, sexual child is the "truth" of the "innocent" non-sexual one, there is no charge of trespassing "boundaries" that is not, invariably, retraceable to a lurking pastoralizing view. In spite of the, by now, customary disclaimer that there *is* such a thing as *real* sexual abuse,[21] Ohi insists on the *non*-difference between sexual oppression and sexual abuse on the grounds that "contemporary sexual ideology" structures that "difference." Explicitly defining "an anti-homophobic project" as one that "should *not* try to distance itself from pedophilia and child abuse," Ohi, in "Molestation 101: Child Abuse, Homophobia, and *The Boys of St. Vincent*," argues: "Such a collapsing together of pedophilia and child abuse often lurks in popular attempts to clean up homosexual desire for public consumption. ... But queers already have a bad name (precisely, that is, the name queer), and the queer and the child molester—who is treated as synonymous not only with the pedophile but with anyone who dares utter the possibility that children have desires—are demonized in similar ways and, I will argue, for similar reasons. It should then become clear that an antihomophobic project should not try to distance itself from pedophilia and child abuse. The energies mobilized by and against the figures of the child, the child molester, and the queer point to structures underwriting both child abuse panics and homophobia" (196). Ohi persuasively demonstrates that there are common ideological investments underwriting the link between childhood "innocence" and the fantasy of queerness as equal to sexual pathology, pointing to the representational continuities of different terms (molester/queer/pedophile) suggests how these appellations are imaginatively linked, but Ohi's solution to affirmatively embrace these *non-differences* (by defining antihomophobia as a project that "should *not* try to distance itself from pedophilia and child abuse") confirms a model of sexuality that is indeed as fundamentally antithetical to sociality and form as the most homophobic "contemporary sexual ideology" alleges. That is, while the reclamation of "pedophilia" and "molestation" as companionate "queer" designations seems to scandalize conventional critical norms (even "antihomophobic" ones), to what extent does the brazen conflation of all sexuality with deviance actually obscure the incapacity, within an "antihomophobic" agenda, of theorizing a sexuality that thinks with rigor and coherence about what would constitute "boundaries" and their violation?

The Queer = Sexual Outlaw

Perhaps nowhere is this rhetorical maneuver less self-reflectively deployed than in Jane Gallop's extended self-defense, *Feminist Accused*. Rather than meticulously outlining why her own version of sexualization, in a pedagogic context, is not equivalent to the abusive kind of "sexual harassment," Gallop mocks the parochial, anxious, puritanical regime of oppressive sexuality for needing such a facile differentiation in the first place. A distinguished literary theorist at the University of Wisconsin at Milwaukee, Gallop faced charges of sexual harassment by two female graduate students in 1992; one student alleged that Gallop tried to seduce her and when she was rejected, retaliated by criticizing her work, and the other student claimed that a shared kiss in public at an academic conference was an unwanted sexual advance. After an extensive investigation,

Gallop was cleared of the sexual harassment charges but was found, in the case of the first student's allegations, to have violated the university's policy against "consensual amorous relations" wherein a sexualized environment is prohibited even if no sex acts take place. Although Gallop was not sexually involved with either of the students who filed charges against her, the book is filled with anecdotes of her sexual relationships with undergraduate and graduate students, a practice that ceased in 1982 when she met someone (who was neither a teacher nor a student). Instead of being ashamed by the scandal of being accused, Gallop turns the accusations into a scandal in their own right. "While any accusation of sexual harassment seems to promise a juicy scandal," Gallop writes, "this particular accusation is more sensational due to the newsworthy anomaly of a feminist being so accused. While sexual harassment is customarily a feminist issue, feminists usually appear on the accusers' side. For a feminist to be the accused is a dramatic reversal. What kind of feminist would be accused of sexual harassment?"[22]

Gallop grounds her self-righteous incredulity in her own personal experience of intellectual and sexual liberation: "Central to my commitment as a feminist teacher is the wish to transmit the experience that brought me as a young woman out of the romantic paralysis and into the power of desire and knowledge, to bring the women I teach to their own power, to ignite them as feminism ignited me when I was a student" (12). Insisting on the indissociability of sexual and intellectual freedom, Gallop says that, as a student, "I was in an environment extremely conducive to my education, a heady atmosphere where close personal contact intensified my desire to learn and my desire to excel. I learned and excelled; I desired and I fucked my teachers" (42), and then as a teacher, "When I said that graduate students were my sexual preference, when I kissed my advisee in a bar for all to see, I was making a spectacle of myself. And, at the same time, I was being a teacher. The performance turned me on and was meant to turn my audience on, literally and figuratively. The spectacle was meant to shock and entertain, to make people think" (101). Here, Gallop not only legitimizes her particular sexual behavior but furthermore, and in much the same way Ohi describes, redefines "feminist" pedagogy to include as one of its organizing conditions the unconflicted expression of unrestrained sexual pleasure. This ecstatic and flagrant repudiation of "learning" from "fucking," or "shocking" from "teaching" is consistent, in Gallop's topology, not only with being a good "feminist" but, indeed, with being a good "deconstructionist" as well. Introducing her first book on feminism and psychoanalysis, *The Daughter's Seduction*, Gallop frames the goal of her project as "to set up what appears to be an opposition between two thinkers or terms, and then to move beyond the belligerence of opposition to an exchange between the terms. The most stubborn opposition is the continual constitution of 'opposite sexes' which blocks the possibility of a relation between them . . . the goal of the method of this book is to alter the relation from unyielding opposition into a contact between their specific differences—a contact that might yield some real change."[23]

This "method," which is defined as "deconstructive," is committed to showing that the lines we are prohibited from crossing are in fact oppositions that, although "inevitable," are not necessarily "unyielding," that "what appears to be an opposition between two thinkers or terms" is actually something that enough intellectual analysis and grit can help us "move beyond." While this same critical orientation underwrites her defense of "sexualizing" pedagogy on the grounds that this opposition between sexuality and pedagogy is a false one, and that the "lines" dividing these terms are really only rhetorical-psychological hurdles that have been, as yet, insufficiently "deconstructed," Gallop doesn't problematize any of these terms so much as reify them and problematize the accusers. When Gallop begins a paragraph by unapologetically proclaiming, "I think of my students primarily as people," it is as if precisely at the moment when the force of a deconstructive move could be most usefully harnessed to dismantle an opposition, Gallop simply denies any opposition instead. Gallop continues: "As with people in general, I don't like some of them. I'm indifferent to many, and I find some of them especially admirable, congenial or engaging. Although an awareness of our institutional roles definitely gave my affairs with students a certain pleasurable edge of transgression, I slept with students for essentially the same reasons I slept with other people—because they engaged me as human beings, because of a spark of possibility lit between us" (51). To the "boundary" between intellectual and sexual activity, or the line dividing modes of relating, Gallop repeatedly says that she simply *doesn't see it*, that if she crossed it and has gotten into trouble it is because she *did not know a line was there*. Indeed, in an interview with Lauren Berlant several years after the publication of *Feminist Accused*, Gallop says, "There is a shadow version of *Feminist Accused*, which is the 140-page response I wrote to the complaints—literally longer than the book, and very, very, very different. In some way, I had to write *Feminist Accused* to get that other text out of my system. What I hated about writing that other text was drawing lines, saying, no I never did anything ambiguous *in my life*. . . . I wrote the book partly to repossess my experience of the world."[24] Gallop's emphasis on the "hated" "legalistic" demand to be "drawing lines" explains why the therapeutic exercise of "get[ting] that other text out of my system" involves

BOUNDARIES ARE FOR SISSIES / 103

the total purging of "lines" in the name of "ambiguity." As such, the insistently and consistently stunned phrase that runs through her manifesto is indeed something like, *line? what line?*, as if the demand to account for motivation is already an accusation, as if what she is being accused of is "feminism" itself. This is, of course, precisely Gallop's point: that to accuse a feminist of "sexual harassment" is equivalent to accusing a feminist of feminism. But outside of Gallop's own "belligerence" and "shock," it might be worth considering that it's actually her "deconstruction"—as method— that is being impugned by her own demands. For although Gallop comfortably grafts her right to liberated sexual self-expression on feminist foundations, what she cannot sustain, intellectually, is the tension between "sexuality" and "deconstruction." How can Gallop deconstruct false "oppositions" while at the same time defining "feminism" as constitutively oblivious to them? The solution Gallop devises involves evacuating any "oppositions" of any value or meaning so that eventually sexuality names the force that legitimately transcends all the "oppositions" that, by reckoning with, deconstructive analysis labors methodically to identify and work through. It should be clear from the sensational, often sloppy, engagement with this problematic that Gallop's *line? what line?* attitude to sexual "boundaries" is a cheap resolution to the tension between sexuality and form. As an intellectual response, this approach displaces the burden of contending with "difference" onto the disciplinary, hysterical, other side (normativity) and then relies on this disavowal to sustain its identity as the cool sexual outlaw who is *so* "beyond" the silly "oppositions" structuring social-psychic life that it cannot even articulate why differences would ever or in any way matter without violating the integrity of its own enlightened critical pose.

In order to advance their claims for how any good "antihomophobic" or "feminist" project ought to relate to "boundaries," Gallop and Ohi rely on a startlingly simplistic, pre-critical conceptualization of sexuality that entirely misses what sexuality teaches us about the "boundaries" organizing psychic life. In the first instance, the claim to be defending sexuality's "truth" against society's normativizing forces essentializes sexuality in the very effort to defend its ontological complexity. In an effort to describe how extensively he sought to distinguish normative practices of "freedom" from a one-dimensional conceptualization of oppression, Foucault explains:

> I have always been somewhat suspicious of the notion of liberation, because if it is not treated with precautions and within certain limits, one runs the risk of falling back on the idea that there exists a human

nature or base that, as a consequence of certain historical, economic and social processes, has been concealed, alienated or imprisoned in and by mechanisms of repression. According to this hypothesis, all that is required is to break these repressive deadlocks and man will be reconciled with himself, rediscover his nature or regain contact with his origin, and reestablish a full and positive relationship with himself. I think this idea should not be accepted without scrutiny. . . . This is why I emphasize practices of freedom over processes of liberation; again, the latter indeed have their place but they do not seem to me to be capable by themselves of defining all the practical forms of freedom. This is precisely the problem I encountered with regard to sexuality: does it make any sense to say, "Let's liberate sexuality"? Isn't the problem rather that of defining the practices of freedom by which one could define what is sexual pleasure and erotic, amorous and passionate relationships with others? This ethical problem of the definition of practices of freedom, it seems to me, is much more important than the rather repetitive affirmation that sexuality or desire must be liberated.[25]

With this rebuke to "the rather repetitive affirmation that sexuality or desire must be liberated," we can begin to consider just how thoroughly this "notion of liberation" can be seen to be "falling back on the idea that there exists a human nature or base that, as a consequence of certain historical, economic and social processes, has been concealed, alienated or imprisoned." This "repressive hypothesis" underwrites the easy categorization of "antihomophobic = sexuality without social oppression," but what is more, in its claim to speak the actual "truth" of sexuality (that normative pieties are denying), the scorn for "boundaries" validates and enforces an uncritical, and fundamentally conservative, version of sexuality as primitive, "natural," and constitutively *against* the work of structure.

The Violence of Relationality

In Laplanche's framework, sexuality retains its radicality by expanding beyond the determined objects and sources of genital sexuality. Determined to account for "that something else" that turns the infant into a "sexual" being, Laplanche introduces the "general theory of seduction." "What matters," Laplanche writes, "is the introduction of the sexual element, not from the side of physiology of the infant but from the side of the messages coming from the adult. To put it concretely, these messages are located on the side of the breast, the *sexual breast of the woman*, the inseparable companion of the milk of *self-preservation*."[26] Therefore, it is precisely because "need" (instinct) requires *communication* between the infant and the adult world that a passageway is opened up for "messages" to be *transmitted* by the adult, who is sexual, to the infant, who is not. "The theory of seduction is the hypothesis best suited to the discovery of the irreducible unconscious" because, as Laplanche explains, "Seduction is not a relation that is contingent, pathological (even though it can be) and episodic. It is grounded in a situation from which no human being is exempt: the 'fundamental anthropological situation,' as I call it ... the *adult-infans* relation. It consists of the *adult*, who has an unconscious such as psychoanalysis has revealed it, i.e., a sexual unconscious that is essentially made up of infantile residues, an unconscious that is perverse ... and the *infant*, who is not equipped with any genetic sexual organization or any hormonal activators of sexuality" (102).

According to Laplanche, the infant is always "translating" messages from his surroundings and therefore translation is not exactly a strictly linguistic or interpretive process, but instead a process for binding affect and energy into symbolization. It is the transformation of diffuse and overwhelming *affect* into *symbolic* form that enables the infant's innate regulative capacities to "bind" affect to representation and thereby to survive the assault of overstimulation by the adult environment. However, it is by this same measure that repression occurs because, as Laplanche repeatedly explains, the adult's communications include "enigmatic signifiers" that are unavailable to the adult's own consciousness and therefore untranslatable by the infant alone.

Against the simplistic reduction of the "child" to either "innocent" or proto-pedophilic, Laplanche enables us to see why "sexuality" is, by definition, a structure for coping with the unsymbolizable/non-metabolizable sexuality that is everywhere, *in the other person*. In this way, the story Gallop tells of sexuality's omnipresence—and her insistence that a good "feminist" proudly surrenders to it—misunderstands that the sexuality one consciously *feels* is only possible because sexuality—as a "splinter underneath the skin"—is *not* actually available to either consciousness or representation. Sexuality exists as a response to the psyche's overwhelmed encounter with an-other's unassimilable "unconscious" messages; there is no heroic saying "yes!" to it now, as there was no saying "no" to it then. This thinking of sexuality through Laplanche must complicate any reflexive bifurcation of sexuality and structure. Sexuality *is* a structure and, furthermore, its operation also proves how what subtends any assault on the "pastoral" view of sex is a fantasy of sex's ontological "deviance." That is, while certain sexual acts might be considered "socially" deviant, con-flating this symbolic *representation* of sexuality with its structural *mechanism* as a psychic force wages battle with normative ideology by merely developing its own reactionary ideology. Laplanche navigates this impasse by showing that what makes sexuality radical is not the quality of its outward expression but the psychic and relational conditions of its development.

Rereading James

In a return to "The Pupil," we might consider how James's lifelong engagement with depicting gestures that can kill a perspicacious child offer terms for theorizing "boundaries" and their violation that are not simply reducible to gothic tropes of lurid sexual abuse. Indeed, as James will show, sexuality does not necessarily connote the signs of conventional intimacy nor does it presuppose that genitality is the only site vulnerable to trespass. Although we have already noted the extensive critical attention to Jamesian "consciousness," in my reading, it has still somehow gone unnoted that, in Jamesian texts, "consciousness" is not distributed equally, and that, moreover, it is "characteristically" juxtaposed to "desire." While critics tend to focus their interpretive readings on a particular fictional character, theme, or plot, any approach that strips narrative of the *way* it happens in search of *what* it means invariably disregards James's concern—evident throughout his oeuvre—with how "consciousness" negotiates its relation to other ways of being, and to "others" generally. As such, what seems to interest James's narrative imagination is neither a particular plot nor a particular range of what consciousness can do, but rather the encounter between "consciousness" and *everything* else. How else to explain the remarkable complexity of Jamesian plots, their convolutions of betrayal and hypocrisy, and their intricate and multi-layered lies? It is not, that is, as though plot is irrelevant to James or inferior to perception but that a "central consciousness" is never isolated and therefore what matters about plot is how effectively it creates the conditions for our being able to watch "consciousness" negotiate its own impingement by the "desire" of others. Relatedly, James insistently dramatizes how the involutions of "desire" may *feel* to "consciousness" like abrasion, confusion, terror, and enigma. It is by sticking to this *feeling*—the feeling of non-"consciousness" as fundamentally extrinsic—that James defamiliarizes so many of "desire's" dominant tropes. It is, in other words, from within "consciousness" that these formats for self-relating seem remote and agonistic, virtually unbridgeable without (it feeling like) a trespass of some kind.

As we will see, it is indeed this very delicate unhinging of "consciousness" from every other motivational force that enables James to experiment with the un-inevitability of "desire" as an experience of subjectivity and otherness. In his Preface to *What Maisie Knew*, James writes, "Small children have many more perceptions than they have terms to translate them; their vision is at any moment much richer, their apprehension even constantly stronger than their prompt, producible vocabulary."[27] James's precocious children become, in this view, instrumental narrative vehicles for a "detached" "central consciousness" because their kind of perceptive intelligence dramatizes the distance between an "observational" stance and a "desiring" one. Rather than claiming children are inherently innocent, pure, or uncontaminated by desire, James is considering how their distinctive purchase on "consciousness" is made available by their exclusion from other dominant relational economies. James alludes to this dimension of childhood experience when, in the same Preface to *What Maisie Knew*, he includes several pages describing "The Pupil." James explains that the inspiration for the story came "one summer day, in a very hot Italian railway-carriage" when a "a doctor of medicine" told him the story of "a wonderful American family, an odd adventurous, extravagant band, of high but rather unauthenticated pretensions, the most interesting member of which was a small boy, acute and precocious, afflicted with a heart of weak action, but beautifully intelligent, who saw their prowling precarious life exactly as it was, and measured and judged it, and measured and judged *them*, all round, ever so quaintly; presenting himself in short as an extraordinary little person" (151). In James's account, we can see the relationship between precocity and adventurousness in how the "small boy" with "a heart of weak action" is the one who is able to see "life exactly as it was, and measured and judged it, and measured and judged *them*." James then exclaims:

No process and no steps intervened: I *saw*, on the spot, little Morgan Moreen, I saw all the rest of the Moreens; I felt, to the last delicacy, the nature of my young friend's relation with them (he had become at once my young friend). . . . This must serve . . . as my account of the origin of "The Pupil": it will commend itself, I feel, to all imaginative and projective persons who have had—and what imaginative and projective person hasn't?—any like experience of the suddenly-determined *absolute* of perception. The whole cluster of items forming the image is on these occasions born at once; the parts are not pieced together, they conspire and interdepend; but what it really comes to, no doubt, is that at a simple touch an old latent and dormant impression, a buried germ, implanted by experience and then forgotten, flashes to the surface as a fish, with a single "squirm," rises to the baited hook, and there meets instantly the vivifying ray. (151)

In the context of James's own life experience, he would likely have recognized in Morgan the "small boy, acute and precocious" that *he* was in relation to his own "odd adventurous" family, a family that moved around during his entire childhood and youth, whose father, Henry Sr., "turned his household into an impromptu laboratory for experiments in child-rearing and moral philosophy—with results his children found beneficial, confusing, painful, and diverting by turns,"[28] a would-be writer who titled his autobiography *A Small Boy and Others*, as though the only place to begin an account of his own experience is by grounding perception in his apartness from "others."

Because their vulnerability instantiates a gap between "experiencing" and having to *do* anything about it, the separation between "observation" and the obligation to participate that children can be said to so readily dramatize effectively enables James to isolate a particular feature of his phenomenological project—the transformation of "consciousness" into "desire"—in order to ask how an observational stance can ever transmute into an active one. Although the conventional expectation of children is that they eventually grow up, it might be worth wondering why James's "consciousness"-bearing children never seem to, and what, if anything, this has to do with the difference between "consciousness" and "desire" these stories are thematizing. Moral speculation seems everywhere on offer in his stories of children being killed by something adults did; the governess's hysterical curiosity (*The Turn of the Screw*), a parental divorce (*What Maisie Knew*), an embittered marriage ("The Author of Beltraffio"). "The Pupil" may even seem especially susceptible to becoming a parable of either pederasty or pedophilia insofar as its tragic ending appears so obviously to impugn the violence of other people's needs (Mrs. Moreen's greed? Pemberton's sexual desire?) Although Ohi does not write about "The Pupil," his close reading of "The Author of Beltraffio" interprets the death of that story's "exquisitely beautiful boy" as "allegoriz[ing] erotic innocence and the inherent violence of its disavowal and double-speak—and the desperate consequences of its effort to protect children from corrupting representations" (9). If "his mother lets him die of a fever, refusing to admit a doctor or administer medicine," we might extrapolate from this logic that it is the frantic efforts to protect Morgan from the queerness he is already expressing that suddenly kills him, mid-embrace.

One major limitation of these interpretations is that they presume innocence versus awareness to constitute the operating differential structuring adult-children relations. Even Ohi, whose "polemical emphasis" is generated by the sustained refusal to ascribe to normativity's depiction of childhood "innocence," maintains the structural position of innocence by applying it to the queer victim of ideology's projections and denials. Therefore, while it seems plausible to explain Morgan's death as the casualty of some other adult's desire, James's story militates against this interpretation in how assiduously it insists upon Morgan's preternatural brilliance as an intelligence that keenly *understands* the desire and behavior of others. To unpack the links among sexuality, childhood, and consciousness, I want to focus on a moment where Morgan's preoccupation with the idiom of their relationship signals the role of "boundaries" to his experience of Pemberton. During an exuberant volley of affection and desire, Morgan and Pemberton joke about Morgan's frail health and whether Pemberton can continue to stay on with the family without ever getting paid because Morgan will likely die young anyway. The banter is at turns comical and meditative, and orbiting the uncertainty over Morgan's health and Pemberton's salary is the quest to definitively establish, once and for all, what they mean to each other:

> "If I hear of anything—any other chance—I promise to go," Pemberton said.
>
> Morgan consented to consider this. "But you'll be honest," he demanded; "you won't pretend you haven't heard?"
>
> "I'm much more likely to pretend I have."
>
> "But what can you hear of, this way, stuck in a hole with us? You ought to be on the spot, to go to England—you ought to go to America."
>
> "One would think you were *my* tutor!" said Pemberton.
>
> Morgan walked on and after a little had begun again: "Well, now that you know I know and that we look at the facts and keep nothing back—it's much more comfortable, isn't it?"
>
> "My dear boy, it's so amusing, so interesting, that it will surely be quite impossible for me to forego such hours as these."
>
> This made Morgan stop once more. "You *do* keep something back. Oh you're not straight—*I* am!"
>
> "How am I not straight?"

"Oh you've got your idea!"

"My idea?"

"Why that I probably shan't make old—make older—bones, and that you can stick it out till I'm removed."

"You *are* too clever to live!" Pemberton repeated.

"I call it a mean idea," Morgan pursued. "But I shall punish you by the way I hang on."

"Look out or I'll poison you!" Pemberton laughed.

"I'm stronger and better every year. Haven't you noticed that there hasn't been a doctor near me since you came?"

"*I'm* your doctor," said the young man, taking his arm and drawing him tenderly on again.

Morgan proceeded and after a few steps gave a sigh of mingled weariness and relief. "Ah now that we look at the facts it's all right!" (189)

This scene of gentle teasing begins with Pemberton wondering alongside Morgan, whether "you were *my* tutor!" and ends with his exclamation that "*I'm* your doctor," as if finally succeeding to match the object to its appellation. The recognition that pedagogy never was the form of their relating is all the more profound because of their official designation as pedagogically related. Indeed, insofar as their attachment is oriented toward Morgan's emergence through Pemberton's attentive companionship, this bantering assessment confirms that their mode of relating to each other has all along been organized around facilitating the liberty of Morgan's consciousness to range spontaneously, with relative protection from the expectations of conventional reciprocity.

In one of his autobiography's most evocative self-descriptions, James expressly links "consciousness" with perception's freedom from encroachment. Of himself as a "small boy" James writes: "I see myself moreover as somehow always alone in these and like New York *flaneries* and contemplations. . . . Which stirs in me at the same time some wonder at the liberty of range and opportunity of adventure allowed to my tender age. . . . What I look back to as my infant license can only have had for its ground some timely conviction on the part of my elders that the only form of riot or revel ever known to me would be that of the visiting mind . . . there was the very pattern and measure of all he was to demand: just to *be* somewhere—almost anywhere would do—and somehow receive an impression or an accession, feel a relation or a vibration."[29] Here freedom is neither abstract nor merely gestural but is thematized concretely in terms of permission to move unapologetically and unhindered through imaginative experience, a safe spaciousness that, throughout *A Small Boy and Others*, he attributes to the "license" he received. From this perspective, it becomes possible to interpret the hug's fatality as the effect of losing the relational idiom whose "boundaries" promised to hold the relationship of Morgan and Pemberton together. More than just a preference for familiarity over change, what Morgan indicates in his repeated fascination with designating the "terms" of their relationship, and eventual delight at being called a "patient" to his "doctor" Pemberton, is the indissociable link between their style of *relating* and the self-transformation that takes place.

Not for the Faint of Heart

As such, what if what kills Morgan is what, in an extraordinarily emotional letter to his older brother William, Henry James warns could also kill him? In a letter dated August 4, 1899, James responds to having asked William's advice about buying a house. The emotional pitch of this letter is striking in contrast to an epistolary style that is variously flirtatious, pedantic, gossipy, irritable, flattering, and meditative.[30] After James informs William about his intention to buy Lamb House, William responds by consulting an attorney and reports: "Baldwin has just dropt in and I have communicated to him the contents of your letter. He thinks 2000 a very extravagant price for that house in view of the fact that you told him the present proprietors paid not very long ago 1200 for it. It *cannot* have increased in value. You see, the best way is to compute on a basis of *rent*. At a 2000 pound price (=10,000 dollars) you would be paying $500 of mortgage interest. ... I don't know what the place costs you annually now, but it is probably a good deal less than that. Hasn't your lease a good many years yet to run? And is such a place *promptly* saleable, or lettable, in case you should ever wish, or be obliged to give it up? You ought to consult some wary business friend in England before you in any way commit yourself."[31] William's condescension is not unique to this topic; he is constantly dispensing advice on what to eat so as to improve digestion, where to travel, how to organize one's finances, and so on. Although they have quibbled before about William's dislike for some of Henry's fiction, as well as James's dismay at William's children's names, James seems generally amused rather than abused by these interactions. His reaction to William's advice expresses a woundedness we rarely see in James's private writing:

Your two letters make me feel that I have disquieted you more than I meant and drawn upon myself and my project a colder blast than I could apprehend. But I beg you to be reassured. I do, strange as it may appear to you, in this matter, know more or less what I'm about. I didn't mean at all to leave any question about the wisdom of my buying this house, and buying it for every reason of peace of mind, absence of worry as to what may become of it over my head in a place where property is steadily increasing in value, and where *not* to have anything in the air or in the background of a nature possibly compromising to one's *basis*, is for me an absolutely necessary condition of fruitful work. Besides I think I am not unreasonable in letting it count for something that I am intensely, piously *fond* of it—so fond of it that to own it will be a direct operative good, a source of nourishing and fertilizing pleasure to me. At my age it should surely be something that one *wants*, simply, so much to do a thing—for I am not yet wholly senile. Let me earnestly beg of you not to discuss the matter with Baldwin, who was here but one night, and whose judgment of the value of the house I can't for a moment accept as in any way qualified. He knows *nothing* of the place, the conditions, the situation of Rye (as regards houses, demand the *extreme* opposite of everything here), and he scarcely appeared to me to appreciate the place at all. His pronouncement that 2000 is a "very extravagant price" would be grotesque if it were not perfectly ignorant. (For God's sake do not repeat to him *this*; but, PLEASE, drop the subject altogether—with him. I *hate* its being talked of with any one but Alice [James]).[32]

For several pages, the letter continues to point out many facts about the house, to explain impatiently that "the sum in question is in fact, so far from excessive, as to be, as things stand to-day at Rye, extremely reasonable," to provide a detailed purchase history of the property, and to explain his own financial situation and the purchase requirements, which James reassures William are entirely in order. Then, after exhaustively detailing his mortgage arrangements, James writes: "Surely at my age, with full possession of one's facts and one's *data*, and with no burden of precipitate or foolish acquisition (of *any* acquisition), compromising one's past, one may ask to be quietly trusted. I have *accepted* . . . Mrs. B's offer. . . . But my acceptance was in truth only the effect of *all* the extreme desire I had had for three years, ever since I first laid eyes on the house while at Point Hill, to see myself in it as my *home* for the rest of my days. This achieved sense will be inestimably precious to me—will *do* far more for me than anything else *can*." James's defiant insistence that the decision to purchase Lamb House is the culmination of an "extreme desire" is linked in his letter with the need to have something he can designate "my *home* for the rest of my days." Indeed, although James spent his entire life between two countries, often traveling and staying in other people's houses, it is remarkable to read James's poignant conviction that "this achieved sense will be inestimably precious to me—will *do* far more for me than anything else *can*."

Morgan and Pemberton discuss living together at various moments in the story before the fateful final scene. Like companions fantasizing about a distant but beautiful future, Morgan is often heard saying to Pemberton, as he does after Pemberton has left the house and then returned, "'Take me away—take me away.'" When Pemberton asks, "'Where shall I take you, and how—oh *how*, my boy?'" Morgan reassuringly says, "'Oh we'll settle that. You used to talk about it. . . . If we can only go all the rest's a detail'" (197). Morgan's frail health lends their shared fantasy of a future home together an aura of anticipatory sadness but excitement, too, as we learn that "[Morgan] talked of their escape—referring to it often afterwards—as if they were making up a 'boy's book'" (199). For months, these boys walk together "arm-in-arm, good-humored and hungry, agreeing that there was nothing like Paris after all" (201) and we have the impression that Morgan excitedly devises schemes and presents ideas on how they should spend their time, with Pemberton happily accompanying him, listening, glad to "have Morgan on his hands again indefinitely" (198). And yet, when the moment finally comes for Mrs. Moreen to entrust Morgan to Pemberton, saying to Pemberton "'We trust you—we feel we *can*,'" instead of consecrating their shared exuberance, there is only "a moment of boyish joy" before Morgan had "turned quite livid and had raised his hand to his left side" (202). Noticing that already "he was beyond their wildest recall," Pemberton "pulled him half out of his mother's hands, and for a moment, while they held him together, they looked all their dismay into each other's eyes" (202). Mrs. Moreen "wailed," "But I thought he *wanted* to go to you!" (203) and indeed, as readers, we cannot help but wonder the same—wasn't this scene the very "unexpected consecration of his hope"? (202) Interestingly, in the moment's just preceding Morgan's violent heart attack, James writes, "He had a moment of boyish joy, scarcely mitigated by the reflection that with this unexpected consecration of his hope—too sudden and too violent; the turn taken was away from a *good* boy's book—the 'escape' was left on their hands" (202). In this moment of "boyish joy," there is also Morgan's immediate "reflection" that this *way* of going to live with Pemberton was "unexpected," "too sudden and too violent," that, in fact, "the turn taken was away from a *good* boy's book." It is as though the difference between a *"good* boy's book" and a bad one has less to do with the details of an elaborate "escape" plan than the fact that one devises an "escape" for oneself, somehow. It is in this vein worth noting that Morgan's name can be said to prefigure this preoccupation with finding a place to live, for "Morgan" is a name that means "dweller of the sea" and in this way registers his affiliation to infinitude and the freedom to move, but also possibly to solitude and something difficult to contain. It is also therefore hardly incidental that James's own aching articulation of the right to a place that feels like "home" frames the finding of Lamb House as an "achieved sense [that] will be inestimably precious to me—will *do* far more for me than anything else *can*." Although the insistence on finding one's own "home" or "escape" can sound like a child's desperate plea for agency and elaboration, in the context of James's question about how "consciousness" transforms into "desire," freedom is what "consciousness" needs in order to be "true" to what consciousness does.

In his nimble engagement with the question of how to think about harm and "consent" while remaining sensitive to the queer critique of tropes of childhood "innocence," Fischel distinguishes "vulnerability" from "innocence" in order to remain "attuned to asymmetric susceptibility, to the ways young people are disproportionately prone to imposition and interference."[33] Fischel focuses on "sexual harm" as "marked not only by the violation of consent, but also by less spectacular and less individualized threats to or disqualifications of sexual possibility." Fischel develops the concept of "preemption" as *"the uncontrolled disqualification of possibility"* (135), the "way forces—people, education, sex education, cultural and commodity messaging, normative gender and sexual expectations—constrain the young subject and disqualify possibilities for more successful, less damaged modes of intimacy" (14). Specifying the implications of "preemption," Fischel explains, "If political theories of injustice largely target violations or foreclosures of preformed preferences, I shift emphasis to preference formation. If the formation of preferences is always relational, always in some sense requiring the 'interference' or influence of others, what influences are peremptory of young people's flourishing, and what forms are propulsive?" (143). To this formulation, we might add that "preference formation" is not only relationally mediated, but utterly dependent on relationality to structure and enable the particular form "sexuality" takes. In the name of "antihomophobic" projects that are sexually liberating, we might begin by liberating sexuality from its *straight*forward relationship to structure. Instead of the routine standoff between "real" versus "fantasmatic" violation, we might consider the effects, for sexuality's elaboration, of violence that is structural, and inevitable. We might consider how refusing to conceptualize violation is not a badge of queer enlightenment but a reactive attitude that evades contending with the complexity of sexuality's development in an asymmetrical relational context. We might concede that an inability to think with rigor about trespass signals an inability to think critically about pleasure. Queers need boundaries too.

4 / Adults Only: Lee Edelman's No Future and the Limits of Queer Critique

Radical or Extreme

In contemporary critiques of normative sexual life, nothing burnishes queer credibility like telling a child to *fuck off*.[1] Insofar as the "child" represents the sacred symbol of "futurity" and the "future" enforces a logic of reproduction that is structurally aligned with normativity and so always homophobic, then denouncing "children"—even if only *figuratively*—functions persuasively to signify a definitive trespass beyond normative ideology's final frontier. The critical orientation of analysis toward radical conceptual and politico-ethical outcomes is an abiding characteristic of the field, which, as Kadji Amin recently observed, developed as a theoretical discourse by bringing "some of the energy, in-your-face defiance, political urgency, and transgressiveness of on-the-ground queer activism into the academy."[2] Echoing Michael Warner's early claim that "sexual shame is not just a fact of life; it is also political,"[3] queer analysis across a range of heterogeneous projects traces its founding motivations to a refusal of "normal" ("straight") conventions and as such, routinely measures its radical bona fides by how astringently "good" normative objects are transformed into "bad" ones, such that by now "badness" itself becomes a veritable shorthand for *queer* critique. Perhaps no one has bristled as publicly at the bewildering absurdity of this predicament than the poet and writer Maggie Nelson, whose popular memoir, *The Argonauts*, about having a baby while her same-sex partner undertakes a gender transition, begins by expressing frustration with queer theory's

totalizing derision of "normativity" and, specifically, its belligerent antipathy toward normativity's emblem, the "child." Nelson describes the
scene of a friend's reaction to seeing in her home a coffee mug, "one of
those mugs you can purchase online from Snapfish, with the photo of
your choice emblazoned on it" and which features a picture of "my family and me, all dressed up to go to the *Nutcracker* at Christmastime—a
ritual that was important to my mother when I was a little girl, and that
we have revived with her now that there are children in my life. In the
photo I'm seven months pregnant with what will become Iggy, wearing a
high ponytail and leopard print dress; Harry and his son are wearing
matching dark suits, looking dashing. We're standing in front of the
mantel at my mother's house, which has monogrammed stockings hang-
ing from it. We look happy."[4] Although Nelson was initially "horrified
when I received it," when the friend says, "Wow, I've never seen anything
so heteronormative in all my life," Nelson wonders, "But what about it is
the essence of heteronormativity? That my mother made a mug on a
boojie service like Snapfish? That we're clearly participating, or acquiesc-
ing to participate, in a long tradition of families being photographed at
holiday time in their holiday best? That my mother made me the mug, in
part to indicate that she recognizes and accepts my tribe as family? What
about pregnancy—is that inherently heteronormative? Or is the presumed opposition of queerness and procreation (or, to put a finer edge
on it, maternity) more a reactionary embrace of how things have shaken
down for queers than the mark of some ontological truth? As more
queers have kids, will the presumed opposition simply wither away? Will
you miss it?" (13) Here, Nelson demonstrates why dismissing this "boojie" artifact on the basis of its flagrant complicity with norms of capitalist
consumption necessarily ignores the queer components of this scene—
that although "Harry and his son are wearing matching dark suits, looking dashing," Harry is in drag as a man, and his son is the child of another
non-heterosexual union.

Nelson's use of this anecdote to showcase her exasperation with the
impoverished theoretical landscape of contemporary ideology critique
echoes an increasing sense, among practitioners in queer studies, that the
field's foundational antinomy toward normativity betrays a reductive,
short-sighted, and ultimately unsustainable estrangement from the complex realities of queer lives. In the most recent and provocative assessment of this problematic, Robyn Wiegman and Elizabeth Wilson's special
issue of *differences*, entitled "Queer Theory without Antinormativity"
(May 2015), begins by asking: "What might queer theory do if its allegiance to antinormativity was rendered less secure?" (1).[5] According to

Wiegman and Wilson, "Antinormativity not only collectivizes the diverse work of such foundational figures as Leo Bersani, Judith Butler, Michel Foucault, Gayle Rubin, Eve Kosofsky Sedgwick, and Michael Warner, but it also underwrites the critical analyses and political activisms of the field's most important interlocutors, including feminist theory, women of color feminism, and transgender studies. . . . In scholarly venues, antinormativity underwrites methodological investments, serving as the impulse to 'queer' any number of disciplines, objects of study and cultural practices. It also compels a host of theoretical commitments, including those that travel under the contradictory auspices of negativity, utopianism, failure, futurity, and optimism (both cruel and otherwise)" (3). This linking of a range of critical orientations to a shared foundational antinormativity, leads Wiegman and Wilson to announce, "While its focus and theoretical inheritances vary, antinormativity reflects a broad understanding that the critical force of queer inquiry lies in its capacity to undermine norms, challenge normativity, and interrupt the processes of normalization—including the norms and normativities that have been produced by queer inquiry itself" (4). Drawing on Foucault, and the critique of power that Foucault developed, Wiegman and Wilson express frustration that despite "queer's" "etymological connections to movements that transverse and twist (*Tendencies* xii), its most frequent deployment has been in the service of defiance and reprimand" (11). Although "every post-Foucauldian queer theorist understands that the claim that sexuality has been repressed is caught in spirals of power-knowledge-pleasure that make such a claim an enactment of norms (rather than a transgression) . . . queer theory has maintained an attachment to the politics of oppositionality (against, against, against) that form the infrastructure of the repressive hypothesis" (11). Wiegman and Wilson's demand for "scholarship that not only rethinks the meaning of norms, normalization, and the normal but that imagines other ways to approach the politics of queer criticism altogether" (18) invites queer discourse to reevaluate its boundaries and, perhaps, even its critical habits, in order to wonder what queer inquiry would look like "when its critical rigor is constituted by something other than an axiomatic opposition to norms?" (20).

Wiegman and Wilson's powerful critique participates in a rapidly growing body of scholarship that challenges the automatic equation of "queer" with radical politics or thought. As exemplified in the development of concepts such as homonormativity (Duggan), homonationalism (Puar), and queer liberalism (Eng), the last decade of queer writing has increasingly insisted that queer studies reckon with its own complicity in oppressive national and transnational regimes.[6] As gays and lesbians are integrated into the mainstream of social and economic life, the familiar ideological coordinates of first generation queer critique have become destabilized such that, as Nelson's example suggests, even a complex familial arrangement like her own can seem "normative" by the crude standards of contemporary queer doxa. Reflecting on this problematic, recent work in literary studies and philosophy have focused on the "negativity" characterizing contemporary habits of thought in order to argue that, as Elizabeth Anker and Rita Felski show in their recent edited collection, *Critique and Postcritique*, "It is no longer feasible, in short, to assume that critique is synonymous with leftist resistance or that rethinking critique implies a retreat to aestheticism, quietism, belle-lettrism, or other much maligned '-isms' of literary studies. Indeed, the shift away from suspicion may conceivably inspire a more nuanced vision of how political change comes about."[7] According to this view, queer theory's reflexive and entrenched position of "negativity" occludes the very interpretive nuance and ethical expansiveness it claims to defend. Mari Ruti's recent book, *The Ethics of Opting Out: Queer Theory's Defiant Subjects*, similarly expresses "fatigue with the field's by now entirely habitual attempts to slay the sovereign subject of Enlightenment philosophy." Ruti observes that, "It is not an exaggeration to say that 'bad feelings,' broadly speaking, have become the 'good feelings' (or at least the useful feelings) of contemporary queer theory in the sense that they provide—whether through psychoanalysis, affect theory, or Foucauldian genealogies—a way to convey something about the contours of queer negativity" (2). In an effort to draw out the ethical and political implications of this "by now habitual" form of queer critique, Ruti argues that, "it is all too easy to forget that it is a theoretical abstraction that has historically eluded the grasp of most flesh-and-blood subjects. As a result, queer theory's repeated efforts to reiterate its hatred of this subject generate the kinds of ethical dilemmas that the field has not been able to resolve, including the tendency to call for the downfall of subjects who are not already leading overly precarious lives."[8]

While, as Ruti rightly points out, "queer negativity" functions as "a means of countering neoliberalism's insidious hold over the bodily and psychic lives of its subjects" by opposing "capitalist accumulation, normative ethical paradigms, the cultural ethos of good performance and productivity, narcissistic models of self-actualization, the heteronormative family, and related reproductive lifestyles" (7), the growing body of scholarship that tests the limits of queer theory's putative radicalism substantially undoes any easy equation of oppositionality with antinormative critique. As evidenced in Nelson's anti-antinormative backlash against "queer negativity," the question of the child occupies a privileged position in recent arguments about the limited application of an abstract and pure antinormative queer theory to the complex and contradictory subtleties of contemporary lives. The exemplary status of the child in these proliferating debates reflects the rapidly changing political coordinates of gay and lesbian life as well as urgent questions about what constitutes a radical ethics of sexual life.

Lee Edelman's *No Future* provides the theoretical infrastructure for the political-ethical position that defines queer "antinormativity" as the extreme repudiation of social norms. By connecting "queerness" to the Freudian death drive, and queer negativity as structurally antithetical to normative sociality, Edelman argues that queers should say "no!" to the future—of gay and lesbian respectability, the child and the "reproductive futurism" that underlies it—and instead avow and embody the threat they always already signify. "Far from partaking of this narrative movement toward a viable political future," Edelman writes, "far from perpetuating the fantasy of meaning's eventual realization, the queer comes to figures the bar to every realization of futurity, the resistance, internal to the social, to every social structure or form" (4). Referring to *No Future* as "one of the most intriguing places where this dynamic can be found," Wiegman and Wilson refer to a footnote in Edelman's polemic that, they argue, undoes the subtle differentiation, which he otherwise maintains, between negativity which is structural versus oppositional. While Wiegman and Wilson argue that this "footnote seems to imagine that the threat of normativity comes from *outside* Edelman's own text" they deduce from this that "even the most queer theoretical reading can find itself sponsoring a politics of oppositionality" (14). Indeed, having already established Edelman's status as "more committed to queer's negative capability than . . . any other scholar working today in queer studies," the essay quotes Annamarie Jagose's observation that, "It would be a foolhardy critic who twitted Edelman for not going far enough" (5). This recurring suggestion that Edelman's extreme negativity is automatically identical with analytic rigor limits any characterization of disagreement with this position as a sentimental, "optimistic," or anti-theoretical defense. In fact, the near unanimity with which the field locates his thinking *for* the "queer" and *against* normativity reflects the extent to which, whether hailed or rejected, there is a shared consensus within the field that Edelman's critical position is—whatever subjective reaction you have to it—indisputably "radical."

Indeed, the field-wide conflation of emotional militancy with critical rigor recurs even when a theorist such as Ruti observes, "While earlier thinkers, such as Leo Bersani (1995), followed Lacan (1972–1973) in aligning *jouissance* with femininity, Edelman masculinizes the concept, stripping it of its customary feminine intonation" (185). That is, even when critics have drawn attention to the machismo of Edelman's argumentative position, they have abstained from bringing to bear on these interpretations what every analysis of "masculinity" has taught us—namely, that performing muscular power obscures fragility and therefore, by extension, what it might mean for Edelman's ecstatic "radicalism" that it is only articulable through a rhetoric of unconflicted certainty? Therefore, while attention to the quality of "negativity" has prompted critics to urge for alternative approaches and moods, these analyses measure the problem of excessive "negativity" in terms of the range of other affects it forecloses. For example, in *Queer Optimism*, Michael Snediker's persuasive survey of how queer studies "privileges 'suffering' and 'dereliction,'" (4) a "thought-experiment" is introduced in which "optimism" functions as a "space-clearing" that counters the "political claustrophobia" (25) resulting from the narrow and rigid preoccupation with "queerness" as "negativity."[9] While Snediker's close reading of Edelman's "pessimism" astutely draws attention to the "sheer absoluteness of Edelman's dicta" as echoing "something like a superego's militancy" (22), this critique leaves untouched the link between Edelman's rhetorical "negation" and its coherence as a "radical" stance.

As these recent examples demonstrate, across a vast range of critical analyses, Edelman's polemic is singled out as representing the radical ethical position that is technically and theoretically rigorous but otherwise practically, emotionally, and politically unsustainable. However, Wiegman and Wilson's recent demonstration of how "antinormativity" is not automatically or easily independent from the "norm" against which it is defined reveals why any extreme "antinormativity" becomes, by definition, dependent on an equally extreme "norm" and the superficial antagonism between them. Wouldn't it follow from this logic that being "more committed" to queer negativity necessarily involves "not going far enough" when it comes to radical "critique"? Therefore, despite Edelman's enthusiastic identification with political and sexual radicalism, the recent problematization of "antinormativity" enables a critical differentiation between extremism and radicalism and therefore a rigorous evaluation of Edelman's claim to radicalism as attainable through absolute negation.

Although the definition of "critique" is not without its contestations, Felski persuasively suggests that the most basic element of "critique" includes a preoccupation with "self-reflexive thinking. It's domain is that of second-level observation, in which we reflect on the frameworks that form and inform our understanding. The critical observer is a self-observer; the goal is to objectify one's own thought by looking at it from outside, so as to puncture the illusion of any spontaneous or immediate understanding."[10] This identification of "critique" with "second-level observation" unifies a tradition that includes Kant and Marx such that even when the methods, aims, or styles of argumentation differ, all "critique" that goes by this name definitively privileges "second-level observation" over and against "any spontaneous or immediate understanding." With this feature of "critique" in mind, this chapter asks how absolute "oppositionality," as an interpretive and ideological maneuver, ultimately compromises critical self-reflexivity insofar as it locates its "opposition" in a reaction to an object of ideology, rather than the ideological context of its own "spontaneous and immediate" response. From this angle, there may indeed be an *inverse* relation between a theory's "antinormativity" and its available range of critique. That is, at what point do the most extreme articulations of "antinormativity" effectively signal the greatest *distance* from Foucault's critique of "power-knowledge-pleasure" or from Lacan's elaboration of "*méconnaisance*"? If Foucault has taught us that, rather than destabilizing it, an "oppositional posture underwrites the repressive hypothesis" (12), and Lacan has shown how the "unconscious is the discourse of the Other," at what point does a commitment to "antinormativity" as a totalizing conceptual orientation that holds steady the relation between the "ego" and "normativity" enforce, rather than deconstruct, pre-critical theorizations?

That is, does "oppositionality" necessarily function synonymously with the "second-level observation" "critique" demands, and, in what way might "oppositionality" *behave* like "second-level observation" simply by performing its rejection of what is represented, in the first order, by the status quo? By drawing out the norms of "critique," Felski challenges the necessity of "an attitude of vigilance, detachment, wariness" (3), and insists on the possibility that "critique" may become a "less muscular and macho affair than it is often made out to be."[11] This analysis is compelling, not least because it reveals that if "critique" is a "genre," it can be used in heterogeneous ways. That is, whereas Felski's call for "postcritique" follows from her identification of all "critique" with these "muscular and macho" traits, it is also worth considering that precisely *because* "critique" is a "genre" with norms that can be dramatized and mastered, today, brandishing "muscular and macho" traits is enough to qualify criticism as "critique." Therefore, rather than devising an alternative "postcritique" that expands the current range of "our critical moods," this paper explores the ways "moods" function to foreclose rigorous "second-level observation," and specifically, how the performance of "critique" can be deployed defensively to reassert pre-critical methods and beliefs.

By utilizing metapsychology as an analytic that zeroes in on the underlying psychological assumptions inherent in queer conceptualizations of desire, sexuality, sex, and subjectivity, this chapter examines the uninterrogated psychological conventions that subtend the presumptive radicalism of avowedly "negative" or "antinormative" theorizations. Focusing on the contentious and influential insistence that "true" "queerness" demands a rejection of the "child," this chapter explores what kind of normative psychological assumptions this formulation reproduces. I introduce Laplanche's theorization of the adult-infant relationship to problematize the easy, and by now knee-jerk, association of the "child" with normative sexuality. Although the critique of the "child" largely derives its psychological legitimacy from applications of Lacan, a close reading of the metapsychology underpinning these claims will demonstrate that the popular formulation—Child = Social and (therefore) anti-Child = Queer Subject—fundamentally misreads Lacan's complex model of the relationship of the "Other" to "desire." Building on Tim Dean and Mari Ruti's analyses, which focus on how Edelman's particular application of Lacan compromises the radical potential of Lacanian ideas, this chapter focuses on the consequences for "critique" of Edelman's position. Whereas existing Lacanian readings of *No Future* advocate for a more rigorous application of Lacan, my introduction of Laplanche offers an alternative reading of the "child" that addresses the critical and theoretical limitations of an *anti*-child agenda. Laplanche's demonstration of how conceptualizing the "child" in strictly linguistic terms—rather than in the material and relational terms introduced by the "general theory of seduction"—ultimately functions to repress the "realism of unconscious sexuality." This chapter focuses on the *asymmetry* of adult-child relationality and, particularly, the role of this asymmetry in the formation of psycho-sexual life. Among metapsychological thinkers, Laplanche is unique for noticing that psychoanalysis was not immune to erotophobic conceptualizations that went against its own proclaimed commitment to unconscious sexuality. In order to more rigorously articulate and defend the centrality of sexuality to psychic life, Laplanche insisted on "new foundations for psychoanalysis" that departed radically from classical Freudian and Lacanian models of the mind. For queer theory, my use of a Laplanchian critique will demonstrate why, in spite of how bold and allegedly extreme denouncing the "child" may seem, the attack on the figurative or hypothetical "child" actually *defends and perpetuates* an erotophobic relationship to sexuality.

Queer Truth, and the Truth of Queerness

The total conflation of radicalism with "antinormativity" is constitutive of *No Future*'s rhetorical strategy. Using "queerness" as a synonym for "truth," Edelman contends that "truth, like queerness, irreducibly linked to the 'aberrant or typical,' to what chafes against 'normalization,' finds its value not in a good susceptible to generalization, but only in the stubborn particularity that voids every notion of a general good ... its value, instead, resides in its challenge to value as defined by the social, and thus in its radical challenge to the very value of the social itself."[12] Aligning "queerness" "like truth" on the one side, versus the "general good" of "generalization" and "the social itself" on the other, Edelman establishes the groundwork for coding any opposition to *his* "opposition" as necessarily sentimental, lazy, or weak-willed. In their performative theoretical "conversation," *Sex, or the Unbearable*, Berlant resists having her attachment to "repair" characterized by Edelman as a "fantasy of making a big picture of a repaired world of happy lovers, adequate storytellers, and properly recognized beings,"[13] but even as she issues this plea for a different dialogic ethics, her demand to have the rigor of her negativity recognized as such betrays the development of an exchange where her every attempt to theorize reparative possibilities is met with Edelman's insistence that her "hopefulness" or belief in a "scene" is unwarranted, misplaced, fantasmatic, and psychologically and politically naïve. When Berlant diagnoses the problem with Edelman's argumentative tactics, she suggests, "Maybe you believe less in the structural generativity of this worlding work than I do; I don't know. I do know that central to my own approach to this conversation has been not to take on many of your challenges directly in order not endlessly to dig into your positions under the fantasy that in so doing either one of us will persuade the other" (111). Interpreting their impasse to result from Edelman's "bad faith" argumentation, Berlant accuses Edelman of relational unkindness as though his critical responses are *technically* accurate but, in this pedagogic-relational context, ungenerous and unfair.

And yet, what goes unnoticed in this exchange is how the force of Edelman's authority as a "radical" critic derives entirely from his privileged position in relation to subjectivity's structural "truth." Against every other theorist's sentimental aspirations for a "better life," Edelman begins by asserting that, "negativity, in my view, speaks to the fact that life, in some sense, *doesn't* 'work,' is structurally inimical to happiness, stability or regulated functioning" (11). A few pages into *No Future*, a similar repetition of the word "structure" organizes the momentum of Edelman's claims: "Queerness exposes the obliquity of our relation to what we experience in and as social reality, alerting us to the fantasies structurally necessary in order to sustain it and engaging those fantasies through the figural logics, the linguistic structures, that shape them" (7). Here, as throughout Edelman's text, references to "structures" and "logics" of subjectivity and sociality are presented as established, ontological "fact[s]," as if his use of these terms was not, in fact, a particular *application and mediation* of ideas that were developed in other contexts (such as philosophy and psychology) and brought, by him, to authorize a set of singular claims about literary and queer studies. Using Lacan to furnish a literary-political vocabulary for his own argument about the inherent social-psychic negativity of "queerness," Edelman repeatedly insists on the "structural" foundation of his claims, as though his position is the only theoretically rigorous scenario for subjectivity as Lacan has defined it. However, what this angle obscures is the fantasy underlying it: of a pure, unmediated "theory" that he, as a neutral and careful close reader, is faithfully extrapolating from. Once the objects of his inquiry are nothing less than human "drives" themselves, and "drives" behave "structurally" and "negativity" is "structural," then any conclusion that does not resemble his own betrays its own fantasmatic investments. Therefore, in order to project the naturalness of his own interpretation, and to disclaim its interpretive nature, Edelman's rhetorical strategy systematically occludes the manifold leaps and moves he makes in order to link "queerness," "sexuality," "negativity," and "sociality" in the particular way that he has. Therefore, in spite of deconstruction's lessons about the constructedness of every binary, *No Future* positions the "truth" of "queerness" on the "bad" (=good) side of the "drive," which is against the "good" (=bad) side of the "social."

This application of structuralism (as a study of relations) to sexual politics in order to advance what it is calling desire's "structural," transcendental truth enables Edelman to offer a "truly hopeless wager"— by positioning himself as the courageous-sanguine messenger of this unavoidable "truth"—that insists on "taking the Symbolic's negativity to the very letter of the law," a proposition that seems again to suggest that his application of Lacan is, in "fact," really only a dutiful "close reading" of the "very letter of the law." But this insistence that *No Future* is only the natural outcome of accepting the "structural" "truth" of sociality and sex obscures the endless analogies, applications, and category errors that Edelman's argument depends upon for its smooth rhythm *as* a polemic where "truth" is definitive as the "truly hopeless" extrapolation of ontological "facts."[14] For example, in Edelman's argument, the following argumentative structures recur: "truth like queerness" (6), "queer theory as the other side of politics" (7), politics as "like the network of signifying relations that forms the Lacanian Symbolic" (7), politics as that which "names the space in which Imaginary relations . . . compete for Symbolic fulfillment" (8), politics as that which "conforms to the temporality of desire" (9), "death drive names the queer" (9), "death drive marks the excess embedded within the Symbolic" (9), "future" as that which "makes the impossible place of an Imaginary past," and the "Child" as having "come to embody for us the telos of the social order" (11). Furthermore, these abundant analogies and equations are consistently elaborated within a rhetorical structure that is stylistically and conceptually chiastic: by criss-crossing parallel words and ideas, Edelman's prose regularly inverts and resolves at the end of a sentence what it questions and introduces at the beginning.[15] Symmetry is one major effect of chiasmus and indeed throughout Edelman's stunningly beautiful prose, every defense of *jouissance*'s chaotic unbinding is proclaimed in sentences that establish their authority by filling-in *what* every signifier already means and knowing, in advance, *where* in the sentence it belongs.

Commenting on how the fantasy of absolute legibility could be reproduced in even the most avowedly deconstructive critiques, Derrida explains why the metaphysics of presence was not exactly an intellectual flaw that could have been avoided by a more rigorous thinker but rather a feature of thought itself. As Derrida writes in *Of Grammatology*, "The privilege of *phone* does not depend upon a choice that could have been avoided. It responds to a moment of *economy*. . . . The system of 'hearing (understanding)-oneself-speak' through the phonic substance—which presents itself as the non-exterior, non-mundane, therefore non-empirical or non-contingent signifier—has necessarily dominated the history of the world during an entire epoch."[16] If deconstruction is not another doxa but instead a method of reading it is because "self-presence" is not a voluntaristic choice but an effect of how thinking functions in relation to symbolization.[17]

More locally, and returning to the status of critique in "antinormative" thought and *No Future* specifically, this chapter is interested in how the "Child"—as the normative exemplar *par excellence*—functions not only to stabilize a series of incoherent interpretive claims as "structural" "facts" but also to point to a limitation in how the "child," as a psychological position, is conceived in prevailing psychoanalytic thought. Whereas the critical viability of *No Future* hinges on Edelman's distinction of "actual children" from the "Child as figure," this chapter explores how the "child" names a particular relation to time and sexuality that is categorically distinguishable from other/adult developmental moments. In this context, the ostensible extremism of Edelman's call to "fuck the future" reveals itself to be both utopian and misguided to the extent it mistakes an assault on the "figure" of the "Child" with the fantasy of one. Therefore, rather than decrying *No Future*'s self-proclaimed radical message, this essay will show that telling the "child" to "fuck off" (29)—while irresistibly cathartic and emotionally empowering—is actually conservative, traditional, and pre-critical in both its content and its theoretical approach. Although Edelman's argument expects—even depends upon—the reader's offended objections, a deep engagement that reads the "child" back into the psychoanalytic paradigm contests *No Future*'s equivalence of any opposition to *its* opposition with a pious defense of the reproductive future and demonstrates instead that if saying "fuck you" to the "child" seems in any way "radical" it is because of how insufficiently and superficially the dominant model of subjectivity construes the role of childhood in "adult" sexuality. From the perspective of this essay, Edelman's absolute reduction of all identificatory positions to either "with or against" the "Child" misrepresents as the final frontier of antinormative thought a relation to sexuality that is actually uncritical, positivistic, and erotophobic. By distinguishing political ideology from metapsychology, it becomes possible to observe how a "queer" position that is "politically" antinormative could be nevertheless "psychologically" erotophobic.

A Lacanian Critique

Edelman's application of Lacan has been the subject of fierce debate, as other Lacanian theoreticians, specifically, Tim Dean and Mari Ruti, have challenged the accuracy of Edelman's mobilization of Lacanian ideas. These critiques focus on Edelman's gloss on certain key terms, as well as the historical development of Lacan's metapsychological paradigm. In this latter vein, there is significant controversy over the periodization in Lacan's oeuvre,[18] particularly over how to assimilate the changes in terminology and the introduction of new concepts over time. In *The Lacanian Subject*, Bruce Fink observes that Lacan's "attempt to isolate the subject takes many different forms at different points in his teaching" (35) and demarcates the different stages of his teaching/thinking roughly into three stages: phenomenological-Imaginary (1930s–40s), structural-Symbolic (1950s–60s), poststructural-Real (1960s–70s). Within this rudimentary schematization, Fink shows how Lacan's earliest interest in the Imaginary stage expressed a preoccupation with the ways in which the subject was alienated by its specular identification with images outside itself. The "mirror stage" is the principal scene of this phase in his thinking and provides Lacan with a paradigm for constructing the "ego" (*moi*) as an entity that is distinct from the subject. Lacan suggests that, "by identifying with the mirror image, the child assumes a *me* that is radically exterior, strictly inaccessible and unvoraciously complete." Furthermore, "from the idea that the *me* is a mirage, it is easy to infer that the self-consciousness associated with it cannot point the way to a truthful self-understanding . . . the *me* is not the representative of reality, as Freud conceived it, but a showpiece of illusory mastery, a simulacrum of individual control."[19] At this early stage in Lacan's thinking, the goal of analysis is oriented toward the prying apart of the "ego"/*me*, from the subject underneath it.

However, as Lacan's thinking develops throughout the 1950s and desire becomes the major focus of this theorization, another source of alienation is identified, which is language and the network of the Symbolic. Now, in addition to the "other" of the Imaginary, Lacan specifies the role of language-as-Other in alienating the subject from the truth of his desire. During this period, Lacan considers the end of analysis to be signaled by the analysand's "separation" from this Other language (of other people's desire) and this involves a process of accepting one's position in relation to the Symbolic order, instead of incessantly and painfully chasing the object, which will obscure the self's fundamental split. The disappearance of the phrase "separation" after 1964, and Lacan's subsequent elaboration of "traversing the fantasy," points to his new focus on the "real" and the "sinthome." From now on, Lacan no longer treats the subject's "separation" from the Other (as language or as imaginary relations) as the ultimate goal of analysis but formulates instead a complex understanding of how the subject emerges by finally coming "to grips with that random toss—that particular configuration of his or her own parents' desire—and somehow become its subject."[20] This "subjectification" of that "otherness" which is in *me* becomes the goal of analysis, after which point that subject is not recuperated from the historical past so much as created by the analysand through an analytic process, in the present. Whereas Lacan initially imagines that successful analysis is marked by identifying one's "imaginary relations," his eventual recognition of the need for "traversing the fantasy" and, finally, identification with the sinthome, signals his profound reckoning with the complexity of isolating, amongst so many viable "others" (language, imaginary, symbolic relations), a particular *subject* that could, in some small way, avail itself of its pleasures.

With this context in mind, it becomes crucial to observe that whereas Lacan struggles to differentiate the subject from its statements of desire (always attentive to how *desire is the language of the Other*), Edelman seems, unproblematically, to take the desires of "queerness" at face value. Consider the positivizing effects of Edelman's analogical moves: the queer = sinthome, sinthome = death drive, Child = future, social = Child, politics = Imaginary (+ Symbolic), truth = queer. Therefore, although *No Future* does not focus on queerness as a sexual practice, it uses the "queer" designation to name the "death drive, this intransigent jouissance, by figuring sexuality's implication in the senseless pulsions of that drive" (27).[21] The use of "figuring" in this sentence is significant and it recurs throughout Edelman's text. Indeed, as a measure of the conceptual labor this word performs, we might observe how insistently it substitutes every signifier with a definitive, *a priori* "meaning" in order to develop the effect of smooth, rhetorical links between conflicting, heterogeneous terms. To focus on a few examples (italicization added): The "queer" *figures* the "death drive," "queerness ... *figures*, outside and beyond its political symptoms" (3), the "queer comes to *figure* the bar to every realization of futurity" (4), the "*figural* Child alone embodies the citizen as an ideal" (11), the Child "*figures* our identification with an always about-to-be-realized identity" (13), "true oppositional politics implicit in the practice of queer sexualities lies ... in the capacity of queer sexualities to *figure* the radical dissolution of the contract" (16), politics "centers ... on the *figurality* that is always essential to identity, and thus on the *figural* relations in which social identities are always inscribed" (17), "to *figure* the undoing of civil society ... is neither to be nor to become that drive ... rather according to that *figural* position means recognizing and refusing the consequences of grounding reality in denial of that drive" (17), "politics (as the social elaboration of reality) and the self (as mere prosthesis maintaining the future for the *figural* Child), are what queerness, again as *figure*, necessarily destroys" (30), "homosexuality, understood as a cultural *figure*" (39), "All sexuality, I've argued is *sinthom*osexuality, but the burden of *figuring* that condition ... falls only to certain subjects" (73).

With its etymological roots in the Latin "figura," meaning "shape, figure, form," *figure* refers to the symbolic potential of language, to the representational capacity of all signifiers to be attached to any variety of objects. "Figure" *makes* the "child" equivalent to the "future," just as, in an attempt to embrace the implications of this logic, the "queer" is *made* synonymous with negativity by "figuring" for what's beyond the "child." Edelman repeatedly notes that these "figural" equations derive from conservative ideology ("Without ceasing to refute the lies that pervade these familiar right-wing diatribes, do we have the courage to acknowledge, and even to embrace, their corrective truths?" [22]), and seems unbothered by aligning these "right-wing diatribes" with the subject's ontological truth. However, whereas other readers have already noted the problematic implications of this logic,[22] I am less interested in the efficacy of Edelman's political strategy or in his deformations of metapsychological concepts than in the effects, for queer critique, of *plugging in* to every signifier an equivalent "figure" that can only ever—when added up— arrive at one, True result. What kind of impasses result from Edelman's systematic conflation of "symbolic" identity with the transparency of subjectivity's sexual "truth?"

Although Edelman insists that "queerness" can "never define an identity" (17), he nevertheless outlines the queer as precisely *that* subject which the social *abjects*. Indeed, it is by claiming as a "structural position" precisely the negation that the social prefers to disregard that "queerness" develops its position *as* "queer." Edelman's unconflicted reliance on the social/Symbolic for determining the essential features of "queerness" conflates a political strategy with a metapsychological one: Is "queerness" here referring to the subject's "symbolic" position or to his "desire"? Although at the level of the Symbolic the "queer" might "figure" for the anti-future, how can the symbolic register *speak* for the subject at the level of his unconscious desire? Put another way, how can acceding to what is "radical" within "symbolic" relations coincide, even *equate*, with the radical truth of one's particular "drive"-based sexuality? If Edelman's polemic is rejected on the basis of its political inefficacy ("what some will read as an 'apolitical' formalism" [157n19]) then *No Future* is mistakenly faulted for its abstract/idealist approach to praxis; but what this rejection occludes is the theoretical incoherence of *No Future*'s claims. Specifically, while Lacan's formulation of the "Other" compelled him to generate a multiplicity of clinical techniques for differentiating the "subject" and his "desire" from the many languages of "others"—scansion, separation, traversing the fantasy, variable length sessions, subjectification[23]—Edelman defines, a priori, what every signifier "symbolically" *means* and then equates "accepting the burden" of this "symbol" with an act of ethical "desire." But what happened to the radical indeterminacy of signifiers, or the process of "traversing" one's originary "imaginary" relationship to sexuality? How did the Lacanian rigor of an analytic *process* whereby you locate your *sinthome* amongst the false perceptions of what you *think* is *your* desire, transform, in Edelman's version, to a clear, unmediated and unconflicted choice about the "truth" of what you really, always already want? Here, the difference between the "mirror stage" and "subjectification" is crucial, for while both involve a mechanism of identification, Lacan is vehemently opposed to any therapeutic process that equates cure with the analysand's identification with yet another/different, "better" image.[24] Indeed, his lifelong battle against American ego-psychology[25] demonstrates why, for Lacan, any promise of a cure that routes itself through "imaginary" or "symbolic" relations reinforces the primacy of the "Other" over and against the subject's encounter with the singular aspect of his unconscious desire. As Lacan repeatedly points out, what makes imaginary identification so pernicious is that identification with a new and better "image"—of the analyst, as the subject who knows more, or in this case, the "queer" theorist who knows the "negative" better—alleviates the subject's suffering by adhering to a new master without making a dent in the analysand's capacities to find out what is un-transparent, not-self-present, unsymbolizable about what *it* wants. As such, when Edelman argues that the "ethical burden to which queerness must accede in a social order intent on misrecognizing its own morbidity . . . [is] to inhabit the place of meaninglessness associated with the sinth-ome" (47), he liquidates the radical process by which the "sinthome" is recognized as such. For Edelman, the "sinthome" is *immediate* to the sub-ject, *felt* as something that he *truly* always *knows* he *wants*.

This *positivization* of the "sinthome" has devastating effects for Edel-man's conceptualization of sexuality because, with the conflation of sexu-ality with the structure of the "sinthome," Edelman transforms sexuality into, merely, the opposite of conventional morality. Although anchoring the "sinthome" to a negation of the child seems, at least superficially, to embolden *No Future*'s radical credentials, a deeper consideration of how the "child" functions in the formation of sexuality reveals that rather than securing sexual radicalism, Edelman's "fuck you" to the "child" perpetu-ates an erotophobic relationship to sexuality that hinges on a fantasy of purifying sexuality of its chaos, mutability, perversion and, particularly, of its origins in an irresolutely *asymmetrical* relationship to otherness and time. In Edelman's formulation, the queer's recognition of the neg-ativity that normativity denies is equivalent to the analysand's "travers-ing the fundamental fantasy" to identify with his "sinthome"—but whereas Lacan locates "meaninglessness" *in* the patient's particular "sin-thome," Edelman turns the "sinthome" into the transcendental "figure" of "meaninglessness" in general. This is why Edelman can propose that deconstructing normativity's investment in the "child" automatically produces the conditions for "queer" enlightenment. And yet, without a rigorous process (whether clinical or critical) for differentiating one's "sinthome" from the desire that is mediated by "others," Edelman's impas-sioned call to "identification" betrays a wishful, uncritical belief in the power of the Imaginary to persuade the Real. In so doing, Edelman rewrites psychic liberation as achievable by a merely more extreme iteration of ideology critique, thereby vitiating any potential for experiencing "queerness" to radicalize knowledge and epistemology. As such, in addition to perpetuating an incoherent psychic strategy, Edelman's model of radicalism depends upon a version of ideology critique that de-contextualizes, and therefore de-dialecticizes, the complex conditions by which "radicalism" is ascertained. Theodor Adorno wrote of this tendency in ideology critique when, in his letter to Walter Benjamin in *The Work of Art in the Age of Mechanical Reproduction*, he criticizes Benjamin's "romantic" and "casual" determination of cinema as "inherently" revolutionary. After challenging Benjamin's assertions that the "laughter of the audience" is necessarily "good and revolutionary" (calling it instead "full of the worst bourgeois sadism") and rejecting Benjamin's defense of "distraction" and the "aura," Adorno concludes his critique by adding "only one more small item: the idea that a reactionary is turned into a member of the avantgarde by expert knowledge of Chaplin's films strikes me as out-and-out romanticization."[26] Vehemently resisting this "romanticization" of cinema, Adorno writes, "What I would postulate is *more* dialectics" as the only possible strategy for avoiding the "casual" assignment of historical objects to a "revolutionary function." Adorno's "negative dialectics" shares with Lacan's ethics of the "act" a vigorous refusal to presume the immediacy or transparent knowability of what constitutes a radical, sinthom-atic expression of any given subject's particular truth.

Theorizing Radicalism

Adrian Johnston interrogates the relationship of metapsychology to transcendental philosophy in order to demonstrate why a schematic understanding of the "drive's" *internal* contradictions is fundamental to any logically sustainable philosophical paradigm. Using the tragedy of Oedipus as an example, Johnston explains, "The truly tragic dimension of Sophocles' play, from a properly formulated psychoanalytic perspective, is the lesson that the removal of the repressions and inhibitions holding *trieb* in check doesn't open out into an ecstatic, Dionysian release of *jouissance*. What makes Oedipus emblematic of all subjects isn't just that he manifests the hidden wishes of the individual as conditioned by the general structure of the socio-symbolic unit of the family, but that he depicts how transgressively *overcoming* the impediments to the drives doesn't enable one to simply enjoy enjoyment."[27] Johnston integrates Freud and Lacan in order to correct the pre-psychoanalytic misconception that "Oedipus represents the position of the libidinal individual, an individual burdened with desires that run counter to both the conscious sense of self as well as the interdictions of social reality" (xix). As against this popular Freudian doxa, Johnston designates the "drive" as internally split between, what he calls, "the axis of iteration" and "the axis of alteration." This means that a *discontent prior to civilization exists* because the "axis of iteration insists on an unaltered repetition of an initial satisfaction" while "the representational components of the axis of alternation are subject to modification by temporal factors" such that a "pure, undiluted repetition of the initial satisfaction sought by the axis of iteration is, strictly speaking, impossible" (151). Johnston further develops this insight by explaining that, to the extent the subject "imagines" "pure" enjoyment lies on the other side of social construction, it is because the "unconscious forges an alliance with reality as an ostensible enemy" (286) in order to justify its necessary distance from "trieb's" absolute realization. With this in mind, being *cured of the cure* means being led to that final point where one is capable of accepting that what was fantasmatically expected/anticipated prior to the end of analysis—'when the analyst cures me, then I'll be happy, content, and free of pain'—is itself a chimera produced by a neurotic manner of coping with the self-defeating dynamic of the libidinal economy. After passing through this difficult moment, the analysand at least might be able to secure a bit more satisfaction from the little pleasures of quotidian existence, once these pleasures are not completely overshadowed by unattainable standards of nonexistent enjoyment" (338). Although securing "a bit more satisfaction from the little pleasures of quotidian existence" cannot compete with "fuck the future" as a bumper sticker for the liberated life, Johnston's reformulation of the problem with *jouissance* (a problem that is *internal* to the "drive") enables us to consider how Edelman's relentless positivization of mobile, multivalent signifiers and unconflicted endorsement of the "imaginary" as the "structural" "truth" of the "real" functions recuperatively to reassert a pre-critical belief in the subject who *knows* what it wants and *has* the power, deep down, to get it.

In his searing critique of *No Future*, Tim Dean observes, "Edelman renders the symbolic order as exclusively heteronormative" and "reduces the heteronomous relations among imaginary, symbolic, and real orders— which Lacan mapped topologically through figures such as the Borromean knot, in order to characterize relationality's incredible complexity—to a series of binary oppositions."[28] Noting that, divorced from its clinical context, "psychoanalysis degenerates into a dogma whose principal function lies in producing the rhetorical effect of authority" (129) and demonstrating the extent to which Edelman's version of psychoanalytic concepts consistently relies upon a common sense and literal interpretation of metapsychological terminology (like the "death drive," "symbolic," the "future"), Dean hypothesizes that this "polemical quality, producing an impression of barely restrained fury, helps account for the book's appeal" and suggests that "the appeal of *No Future* lies less in its thesis or conceptualization than in its rhetorical style and the irrational passion that style conveys" (126).[29] Dean later links this "irrational passion" with the general polemical pitch of Edelman's argument, suggesting that "uncritically naming the 'drive' 'the death drive' essentializes the drive's negativity" and that the "death drive" is not only an "instance of hyperbole in Freud's thinking—a point Lacan makes in *Seminar XVII*," but also a rhetorical move that "lends itself to conceptual redundancy, rhetorical exaggeration, and emotional responses typical of the genre of melodrama" (130). While Dean is not alone in drawing attention to *No Future*'s militant and hyperbolic tone, I resist Dean's dismissive categorization of "passion" as either "irrational" or "melodrama[tic]" for how it categorically equates traditionally "feminine" characteristics with compromised rationality and furthermore reduces to a single dimension the astonishing stylistic virtuosity of Edelman's voice.

Indeed, the sonic pleasure of Edelman's prose testifies to the sensuality of *No Future*'s critical position. Which begs the question: Why not perform the *jouissance* of playing "Darth Vader" as necessary, *not* because it represents objectively the queer's structural truth, but merely *because* it is a style of reading that offers inexorable pleasure? In spite of Edelman's repeated proclamations that sexuality wants and offers "nothing," the sensual beauty of his prose enacts a relentless endeavoring to use language for making "something"—*something* beautiful, exhilarating, clear, resolute, and true. When Edelman locates queerness in that "place, to be sure, of abjection expressed in the stigma, sometimes fatal" (3) and describes "queerness as a burden" the "queer" should once and for all "accede to" rather than attempt, in vain, to overcome, when he says that the "queer must respond to the violent force of such constant provocations not only by insisting on our equal right to the social order's prerogatives, not only by avowing our capacity to promote that order's coherence and integrity, but also by saying explicitly what Law and the Pope and the whole of the Symbolic order for which they stand hear anyway in each and every expression or manifestation of queer sexuality: Fuck the social order and the Child in whose name we're collectively terrorized; fuck Annie; fuck the waif from *Les Mis*; fuck the poor, innocent kid on the Net; fuck Laws both with capital *l*s and with small; fuck the whole network of Symbolic relations and the future that serves as its prop" (29), he isn't just, as Dean suggests, generating a "*jouissance* comparable to that of Edelman's antagonists"; rather, he is modeling a rhetorical form that sounds inexorably *driven* by the force of a relationship to language that resembles what we know of the sinthome's relationship to sexuality. In which case, although we might register the tension between Edelman's erotophilic political agenda and the erotophobic consequences of his argumentative moves, we cannot repudiate the "passion" of his prose without losing what this passion has, as passion, to teach.

Furthermore, to separate the fury of this "fuck you" from the sexuality it is defending seems to underestimate the vital function "no!" provides in the construction of identity. Therefore, while Dean trenchantly highlights the manifold ways Edelman's application of Lacan distorts some of Lacan's most fundamental insights, Dean's focus on Edelman's *mis*-application of Lacan fails[30] to consider how the systematic disregard of Lacanian (and Foucauldian)[31] critical models might, in fact, be instrumental, rather than merely accidental, to the consolidation of the field's "queer" identity. I am thinking here not only of how "no" precedes "yes" in the child's development of a separate and autonomous "self,"[32] but also how negation generally consolidates identity by stabilizing iteration and variation into a moment of determinate coordinates and opposition. Indeed, approaching the "no" of *No Future* with an interest in how "no" functions critically enables us to wonder what the "child" has to do with the defense of "queerness" and what imaginative and psychological possibilities remain for a sexuality that continues to be conceived as possessed by the "queer" "adult" who supersedes the "child." While as an abstract emblem of "reproductive futurism," getting rid of the symbolic "child" may have liberating effects on the imagination and organization of social life, a close reading of Laplanche's paradigm of sexuality's development in the context of adult-infant relationality demonstrates why we must worry about the ways rejecting a "child's" *asymmetrical* relation to adult sexuality ultimately reproduces a reassuring psycho-sexual symmetry.

A Laplanchian Critique

After an early defense of traditional Freudian ideas about the origins of "unconscious" sexuality, Laplanche's extensive career is marked by attempts to critique the limitations of a strictly linguistic (Lacan) or biologistic (Freud) developmental paradigm. In order to retain the exigency of the psychoanalytic discovery, Laplanche reinstalls the "child"—as a unique position in relation to temporality and the adult Other—in order to isolate the specific psychic mechanism that explains how adult sexuality is created by the child's encounter with specific others in the outside world. Having distinguished "instinct" from "drive" and demonstrated that whereas "instinct" "pushes human beings towards sexual behaviors that are more or less pre-programmed and that are aimed, without this aim being consciously posed, at the self-preservation of the species," "drive-sexuality" is "not, at first, connected to any one erotogenic zone; nor is it connected in any absolute way, to the difference of the sexes."[33] It is precisely because this drive is irreducible to innate biological activities, and because "this drive sexuality is indissociably connected to *fantasy* as its cause" (44) that Laplanche isolates what he takes to be the urgent question of psychoanalytic science: "What, then, is the relation between drive sexuality and instinctual sexuality within the human being?" Laplanche details several possible resolutions to this question, one of which includes the "leaning-on" hypothesis he popularized in his early work.[34] According to this early hypothesis, "Infantile sexuality first emerges in the exercise of the great functions, in the satisfaction of the great needs of self-preservation. Initially conjoined with the satisfaction of need (feeding, defecation, etc.), sexual pleasure detaches itself secondarily, becoming autonomous with autoerotism and its relation to fantasy" (45). Referring to "leaning-on" (or elsewhere translated as "propping") as a "way to save the Freudian hypothesis," Laplanche writes that although the theory "is increasingly invoked, increasingly rediscovered and reinterpreted, and increasingly integrated into the vulgate [. . .] it can have a pernicious effect" because, as he goes on to explain, "If infantile sexuality does not have an innate endogenous mechanism, how can it emerge conjointly with self-preservation? And if it corresponds to a simple representation in fantasy of bodily attachment and self-preservative functions, by what miracle would this fantasmatization alone confer a sexual character upon somatic function?" (21).

Laplanche demonstrates how both Freudian biologism and Lacanian linguistic structuralism fail to account for "sexuality's" singular characteristics; in Freud's case, by making an unwarranted leap from alimentary satisfaction to desire, and in Lacan's, by reducing individual subjectivity to an effect of language's transindividual "polysemic potentialities." Both models evacuate the source of sexuality's impact—the other—and with it a rigorous account of sexuality's exigent force. Laplanche vigorously rejects the self-begetting fiction proposed by Freud and Lacan, insisting instead that the origin of "drive"-sexuality can only be explained as the result of a child's encounter with the adult's *existing* unconscious sexuality. As such, while "instinct" sexuality has biological origins, "drive"-sexuality originates in the necessary intersubjective exchange between adult and child. For Laplanche, the child's "creativity . . . does not in fact go so far as to create sexuality: this is in reality introduced from the earliest intersubjective experience, and introduced by the activity of the adult rather than the infant" (47). As Laplanche explains, "It is *inevitable* that the mother should arouse pleasurable sensations; that possibility is inscribed in the situation and does not depend upon contingent factors." As such, Laplanche writes, "*Ultimately*, and whatever distortions may result from the fact, it is possible to become a human being without having a family; it is not possible to do so without encountering the adult world."

According to Laplanche, only the "general theory of seduction" accurately reflects the truth of this inevitable and universal predicament. "What matters," Laplanche writes, "is the introduction of the sexual element, not from the side of physiology of the infant but from the side of the messages coming from the adult. To put it concretely, these messages are located on the side of the breast, the *sexual breast of the woman*, the inseparable companion of the milk of *self-preservation*" (69). Therefore, it is precisely because "need" (instinct) requires *communication* between the infant and the adult world that a passageway is opened up for "messages" to be *transmitted* by the adult, who is sexual, to the infant, who is not. "The theory of seduction is the hypothesis best suited to the discovery of the irreducible unconscious" because, as Laplanche explains, "seduction is not a relation that is contingent, pathological (even though it can be) and episodic. It is grounded in a situation from which no human being is exempt: the 'fundamental anthropological situation,' as I call it . . . the *adult-infans* relation. It consists of the *adult*, who has an unconscious such as psychoanalysis has revealed it, i.e., a sexual unconscious that is essentially made up of infantile residues, an unconscious that is perverse . . . and the *infant*, who is not equipped with any genetic sexual organization or any hormonal activators of sexuality" (102). Laplanche fiercely defends what he will later call the "realism of the unconscious," by which he means that the "unconscious" is neither the source of some mythical, primordial energy, nor the essential center of my true self, but instead the structural effect of the infant's attempts, and failures, to translate the adult's "enigmatic" messages. What Laplanche calls "enigmatic signifiers" are those "messages" that are "unknown to the adult who is exceeded by her own unconscious." According to Laplanche, the infant is always "translating" messages from his surroundings; oftentimes, referring to the infant as the "original hermeneut," Laplanche explains how translation is not merely a linguistic or interpretive mechanism, but a process for binding affect and energy into symbolization and representation. For the infant, the difference between "enigmatic signifiers" and messages that are available for translation hinges on the adult's unconscious. That is, what renders certain messages qualitatively "enigmatic" is not the *content* of the "signifier" per se but rather the ratio of affect to symbolization.[35]

According to this model, the "child" temporalizes desire by situating sexuality in the *asymmetrical* relationship to adult sexuality. The "child" is not just a figure for the "future" but the condition for adult sexuality in the *present*. Therefore, equating the "child" with the social "good" and the "queer" with structural "truth" perpetuates the fantasy—upheld by normativity and antinormativity alike—that desire is ahistorical rather the consequence of a "child's" unavoidable relationship to time. As such, we can no more say "no" to the "figural" "child" than we can say *no* to the "unconscious" sexuality that is determined by all of us having been children, once upon a time. Not only does the binaristic opposition between the "queer" and the "child" collapse under the weight of metapsychological interrogation, but the position from which queer theory might function as a critique of sexuality's construction is vitiated by the absolute identification of the "child" with the "symbolic" *out there*, dissociable from what "queerness" is, "under the splinter of the skin," for every adult. Although Edelman's application of Lacan represents an attempt to rally queers toward "not giving ground on their desire," this slogan reinforces the fantasy of desire's *immediacy*; whereas in Lacan, the clinical process painstakingly facilitates an internal psychic encounter, Edelman mobilizes ideology critique as a convenient shortcut to a priori designate one's misalignment with the social as desire's radical "truth."

But by insisting on sexuality's *in*difference to the proper behavior of liberal subjectivity, Edelman interprets the "drive" as, at its purest, misanthropic. And yet: how can a "drive" that does not have the properties of a good citizen possess the traits of a villain? While, as a polemical gesture, interpreting the "drive" in the least personable light provides an exhilarating antidote to the insistence that desire and the Law neatly align, the conversion of sexuality into a misanthropic *character* belies the development of sexuality *outside* the register of fully formed emotional traits, *outside* the nomenclature of stable features, and in the uncoordinated, ever-shifting process of involuntary intimate relationality.

As such, by locating Ideology as the primary source of the command to "love" the "Child" and the "anti-Child" "queer" as the only legitimate defense against the steady march of a future-oriented Symbolic Order, Edelman perpetuates the sentimental view that we *don't* "hate" the child already. By conflating psychology with ideology, Edelman's polemic misrecognizes how the psychological force of a compulsory demand to "protect" a "helpless" "child" in itself already reflects awareness of the threat a "child" poses to the adult's repression of unconscious sexuality.[36] Edelman's projection of a structural and constitutive psychological tension into the pure antinomy of a (passive) Subject versus (big bad) Ideology sustains the romantic hope that rejecting the "figural" "Child" will, once and for all, radicalize our relationship to sexuality. But while "no future" efficiently stabilizes the rhetorical coordinates of queer critique, the total refusal to differentiate the fantasmatic child of ideology from the sexual child of adult-infant relationality recuperates the hope that erotophobia can be vanquished by heroic acts of emotional negation. Therefore, to the extent Edelman's analysis provides a template for the conscious defiance of normativity, its "no!" is like an anthem and its antagonism indispensable. But to the extent this construction of an alternative identity hinges on the uncritical reassertion of a "real" that is indistinguishable from the "symbolic," a "queer" that can get what it wants because it *always* wants *nothing*, a structural "desire" that is immediate and transparent to the psyche it inhabits, or a formula for radical change that denies the need for a rigorous, critical/clinical process that can apprehend the bewildering specificity of the subject's "sinthome," then contempt for the "child" betrays the wish for a *less* conflicted sexuality, a more *positive* relation to the indeterminacy of sexuality, an extreme attempt to make "adult" sexuality structurally *misanthropic* as against its material formation within the *asymmetrical* relationship to overwhelming, necessary others, and then—no wonder negation feels so damn free—*No Future* is a lullaby.

Laplanche's "general theory of seduction" helps us understand why naturalizing the "symbolic" / "figural" characteristics of the "child" effectively entrenches the dissociation of sexuality from childhood by taking sexuality out of time, history, difference, and relation. After all, how might normative ideology's command to love the innocent "children" operate to conceal the very violence that *having* children *does* to them? From this perspective, the difficulty absorbing the structural effects of infantile "seduction" is not reducible to any one side of the normative-antinormative divide. The operational fantasy of an "adult" who knows exactly what it wants requires that we cannot ever feel just how "desire" comes from having been a kid. What would a queer inquiry that took this challenge to its critical confidence look like? Perhaps it is as Lacan said of the time-structure of desire, what he called the "futur antérieur," where "what is realized in my history is not the past definite of what was, because it is no more, or even the present perfect of what has been in what I am, but the *futur antérieur* of what I shall have been for what I am in the process of becoming,"[37] which is to say, perhaps, that only time will tell.

5 / Psychology as Ideology-Lite:
   Butler, and the Trouble with Gender Theory

The "Subject" Makes a Comeback

In recent work of feminist critical theory, there is a growing call to
think about the "self" as an essential component of radical political thought.
While superficially the inclusion of subjectivity in social theory may
seem obvious or unremarkable—after all, social change aspires to
improve people's lives and its utopian aspect hinges on a deep understanding of human behavior—in the context of late twentieth-century
critical thought, the increased interest in theorizing subjectivity marks
a new turn in a long-standing debate about whether the "self" hinders
or enables a project of political transformation. For the past several
decades, major arguments in feminist criticism have revolved around
whether the "self" is indeed a vital guarantor of emancipatory potential
or a pernicious obstacle to truly radical political ideals. The "feminism/
postmodernism" debate has been one primary locus for this question.

In what is often considered a forceful exposition of the anti-
postmodernist position, Seyla Benhabib, in *Situating the Self* (1992),
argued that, "a certain version of postmodernism is not only incompatible with but would undermine the very possibility of feminism as the
theoretical articulation of the emancipatory aspirations of women."[1]
Intended to expose the stakes of what seemed then to be a casual appropriation by feminists of sexy new postmodernist tropes, Benhabib systematically demonstrated that "this undermining occurs because in its
strong version, postmodernism is committed to three theses: the death of

man, understood as the death of the autonomous, self-reflective subject, capable of acting on principle; the death of history, understood as the severance of the epistemic interest in history of struggling groups in constructing their past narratives; the death of metaphysics, understood as the impossibility of criticizing or legitimizing institutions, practices, and traditions other than through the immanent appeal to the self-legitimation of 'small narratives.' Interpreted thus, postmodernism undermines the feminist commitment to women's agency and sense of selfhood, to the reappropriation of women's own history in the name of an emancipated future, and to the exercise of radical social criticism, which uncovers gender 'in all its endless variety and monotonous similarity.'"

If Benhabib outlined a feminism that eschewed postmodernist ideas, one could see Wendy Brown's *States of Injury* (1995) as a powerful pro-postmodernism rebuttal. Through an engagement with Nietzsche and Foucault, Brown argues that

> feminist wariness about postmodernism may ultimately be coterminous with a wariness about politics, when politics is grasped as a terrain of struggle without fixed or metaphysical referents and a terrain of power's irreducible and pervasive presence in human affairs. Contrary to its insistence that it speaks in the name of the political, much feminist anti-postmodernism betrays a preference for extrapolitical terms and practices: for Truth (unchanging, incontestable) over politics (flux, contest, instability); for certainty and security (safety, immutability, privacy) over freedom (vulnerability, publicity); for discoveries (science) over decisions (judgments); for separable subjects armed with established rights and identities over unwieldy and shifting pluralities adjudicating for themselves and their future on the basis of nothing more than their own habits and arguments.[2]

Refusing Benhabib's claim that postmodernism "undermines" feminist interests and aims because it deprives women of their "agency and self of selfhood," Brown instead asserts, "Dispensing with the unified subject does not mean we ceased to be able to speak about our experiences as women, only that our words cannot be legitimately deployed or construed as larger or longer than the moments of the lives they speak from; they cannot be anointed as 'authentic' or 'true' since the experience they announce is linguistically contained, socially constructed, discursively mediated, and never just individually 'had'" (41).

From one angle, the rise and instant popularity of queer theory can be viewed in the context of this feminism/postmodernism debate. While there was certainly a diverse array of factors that precipitated the emergence of a new disciplinary formation focusing on "sexuality studies,"[3] one foundational starting point for the types of intellectual inquiry that qualified as "queer" was the radical departure from identitarian conventions. As Annamarie Jagose describes it, "Identity has been reconceptualized as a sustaining and persistent cultural fantasy or myth. To think of identity as a 'mythological' construction is not to say that categories of identity have no material effect. Rather it is to realize . . . that our understanding of ourselves as coherent, unified, and self-determining subjects is an effect of those representational codes commonly used to describe the self and through which, consequently, identity comes to be understood. [This] understanding of subjectivity questions that seemingly natural or self-evident 'truth' of identity which derives historically from Rene Descartes' notion of the self as something that is self-determining, rational and coherent" (78). This constitutive suspicion toward *all* identities has enabled queer theory to instrumentalize an astonishing range of conceptual and performative possibilities. By *de-linking* sex from gender from sexuality, queer theory enabled a radical rethinking of accepted categories for action and thought. Less accidentally, queer theory has also affected a total shift in the anti- vs. pro-postmodernism debate by demonstrating the superior conceptual flexibility of doing critical theory *without* the autonomous subject at the center.

In an essay that addresses the fate of feminism in the wake of the queer intervention, Brown posits several causes for the weakening of feminist momentum, only to conclude, "The forces disintegrating revolutionary feminism did not only come from without. Within Western feminist theory, poststructuralist insights were the final blow to the project of transforming, emancipating, or eliminating gender in a *revolutionary* mode. . . . The point is not that poststructuralism undermines the project of transforming gender but that it illuminates the impossibility of seizing the conditions making gender as well as the impossibility of escaping gender."[4] The role of "gender" in Brown's account is extremely significant here insofar as it testifies to the outsized role that "gender" played in the transformation of the postmodernism/feminism debate into the new landscape of queer theory. Specifically, whereas previous generations of feminist thinkers focused on trying to overthrow patriarchy, masculinity, and sexist oppression, a new model of "gender" as "performative" radically reoriented the coordinates of social criticism and change. "Indeed," Brown continues, "In its very challenge to the line drawn in the revolutionary paradigm between 'conditions' and 'effects,' it undermined the possibility of objectifying those conditions and of conceiving agents who could stand outside them to transform them. Moreover, poststructuralist feminism's appreciation of the psychic coordinates and repetitions constitutive of gender locates much of its production in social norms and deep processes of identifications and repudiations only intermittently knowable to its subjects, even less often graspable, and thus unsuited to a paradigm of transformation premised upon seizing and eliminating the conditions producing and reproducing gender ... thus, gender is regarded (and lived) by contemporary young scholars and activists raised on poststructuralism as something that can be bent, proliferated, troubled, resignified, morphed, theatricalized, parodied, deployed, resisted, imitated, regulated ... but not emancipated" (111). As Brown's description eloquently demonstrates, it is not a new model of poststructuralist political analysis that, on its own, has radicalized feminist concerns, but the feminist rethinking of "gender"—as separable from sex and sexuality—that has invalidated so many existing theoretical tools.

Judith Butler's work on gender has long been exemplary here. Whereas previous generations of gay and lesbian thought had insisted on *naturalizing* same-sex desire between people of the same gender, Butler, via Derrida and Foucault, argued instead that there was no such thing as an essential "gender" that belonged to each person. Instead, gender was a performance that was repeated according to existing cultural scripts and tropes. So, while decades of feminist and cultural thought had been aiming to liberate people by condoning the continuity between their gender and their sexuality, Butler called the entire *category* of "gender" a cultural fiction. By appropriating the arguments of deconstruction and poststructuralism, Butler was able to argue that all along our thinking about sex, gender, and sexuality has been entirely backwards: We imagine that heterosexuality is the norm and determine the identity of everything else in relation to this standard when, in reality, heterosexuality is neither the norm nor necessarily natural, so much as it is the product of discursive production. Narrating her own relation to the feminism that came before, Butler explains:

> My own history within feminism has always been an uneasy one, and I found myself increasingly enraged as a graduate student and young faculty member as countless feminist frameworks seemed either to elide or pathologize the challenge to gender normativity posed by queer practices. The writing of *Gender Trouble* was perhaps the acerbic culmination of that history of unease and anger within feminism. The binary between "men" and "women" seemed not only to be a constant presupposition within feminist work, but was elevated to the theological status of the "irrefutable" within some French Feminism.

The implicit and compulsory presumption of heterosexuality supported the normativity and irreversibility of that binary and posited relations of complementarity or asymmetry between its terms in ways that only shored up, without marking, the heterosexist assumptions of the paradigm. As I wrote against such moves, I meant to open up another possibility for feminist thought, one that would overcome its complicity in heterosexist presuppositions, and mark an alliance with lesbian and gay struggles. That the work was taken as a queer departure from feminism signaled to me how deeply identified feminism is with those very heterosexist assumptions.[5]

The unique status of Butler's work in the development of gender theory (both insofar as *Gender Trouble* is often considered to have inaugurated queer studies and in the ways poststructuralist feminism displaced earlier forms of feminist thought) has long made her writing a vital source for theoretical engagement. In the two decades since *Gender Trouble* was published, serious efforts to challenge or critique her work often focused on her readings—of Nietzsche, Foucault, Freud, Althusser—and proposed alternative interpretations of these major thinkers that would resolve many of the problems in Butler's gender paradigm. This essay participates in the tradition of reading Butler closely while at the same responding to a broader shift currently taking place in feminist-oriented critical theory—namely, the resurgence of the "subject" as a dynamic resource for social critique. If earlier versions of poststructuralist feminism accepted Butler's ideas on gender, welcoming, what Brown has called "a women's studies 'beyond sex and gender,'"[6] then recent criticism might perhaps best be understood as an assessment of the limitations of the "performative" subject. As such, while there is ample criticism of the postmodern position from those who summarily reject it (as the previous passage from Benhabib indicates), there is a growing body of work that accepts many foundational claims of poststructuralist critique yet nevertheless calls attention to major deficits in the "gendered" post-identity subject as it is currently conceived. Amy Allen captures this particular position exquisitely when, in *The Politics of Our Selves* (2005), she writes, "Even if a rational critique of subjection can be disentangled from power relations enough to give it the necessary critical bite, it will not be enough to envision what it takes for subjected subjects to overcome the power relations that constitute them. Thus, to the extent that a feminist critical theory is interested not only in diagnosing power relations in all their complexity but also in charting possible directions for social transformation, our analysis of power will have to tell us something about how subjection shapes not only our critical capacities but also our will and our desires. Not only that, but our account of autonomy will have to illuminate not just the possibilities for rational, critical reflexivity but also the prospects for reworking will and desire in a direction that motivates emancipatory self-transformation."[7] In a slightly different but related dimension, Lois McNay's *Gender and Agency* puts pressure on the kinds of autonomy that are possible for the newly "gendered" subject by demonstrating that the predominant model of agency is "negative" and as such, "tends to highlight the retentive dimension of the sedimented effects of power upon the body. This underplays the protensive or future-oriented dimension of praxis as the living through of embodied potentialities, and as the anticipatory aspects inherent within subject formation."[8] Both Allen and McNay apprehend debilitating deficiencies in popular models of power that do not have a robust account of the "subject" at their center. As Allen's reading of Butler suggests, "Conceiving of resistance in terms of a refusal to be a subject, or of an embrace of unrecognizability, does not seem particularly promising, both because it is unclear what this would mean and because such a refusal denies the subordinated the recognition that . . . we all crave" (94). Therefore, not only do Allen and McNay persuasively demonstrate the theoretical and practical limits of the "performative" subject, but they also draw the connection between Butler's conceptualization of "gender" and the incoherence of contemporary critique.

Particularizing the effects of progressive theory's assault on the "subject," Mari Ruti develops a sustained interrogation of "queer negativity," according to which queer pseudo-radicalism seems directly proportionate to ever-more drastic attempts at killing the "Subject" because "allowing the subject to survive in any shape or form would amount to an ethical failure."[9] Ruti traces this totalizing "moral preoccupation with the demise of the subject" to the field-wide conflation of all "subjects" with the "sovereign subject of Enlightenment philosophy" (9). Acknowledging the ways "queer negativity" functioned initially to counter the neoliberal culture of positivity, Ruti nevertheless observes that "antinormativity has become a default politico-ethical stance to such an extent that what matters is not the practical viability but rather the sheer extremity (or rhetorical allure) of the arguments made," such that, "the strand of queer theory that advocates various versions of the ethics of opting out often promotes the ideal of antinormativity so indiscriminately that one act of defiance seems just as good as any other, irrespective of the 'content,' let alone the outcome, of the act in question. . . . In its eagerness to reach the next radical edge, the most hyperbolic positions conceivable to stand on, this theory sometimes misses its aim" leading to what "Lacan calls 'empty' speech, speech devoid of any meaning" (38).[10]

Ruti proposes an alternative paradigm for queer subjectivity that distinguishes Lacan's theorization of the Real from the version of Lacan that queer theorists routinely equate with anti-relationality. For Ruti, "What is unique about Lacan is precisely that he theorizes autonomy (defiance) in the context of a conception of subjectivity that is *otherwise* completely antithetical to the ideals underpinning the sovereign humanist subject" (56). Lacan's crucial differentiation of "autonomy" from the sovereign "humanist subject" presupposes a fundamental relationality that, according to Ruti, many interpreters of Lacan repeatedly fail to seriously consider. Contrasting the Lacanian "act" with Butlerian "performativity," Ruti urges a new Lacanian model of queer subjectivity that allows, "in Zizek's assessment," for a "much stronger subjectivity autonomy" (50). Rather than Butler's insistence "that because every part of the subject has been infiltrated by power in the Foucauldian sense, the real cannot be anything but a symbolic construct" (48), Lacanian theory "asserts that we are *not* eternally beholden to the Other that rendered us socially intelligible—that there is a way out of our servitude to the Other (as well as to the multiple avatars who function as avatars of the Other)" (52).

Ruti's efforts to develop a more rigorous Lacanianism to counter Butler's use of Foucault are consonant with related efforts by Shannon Winnubst to develop a more "robust Lacanian lexicon" together with the "psychoanalytic concept of cathexis"[11] as a necessary corrective to Butler's total dependence on Althusserian "interpellation" for theorizing subject formation. Focusing on the distinctiveness of neoliberalism from classical liberalism, Winnubst persuasively argues that "a concept that has dominated post-Hegelian, leftist theory, interpellation has been the primary heuristic for analyzing sociopsychic formation across the last four decades, whether explicitly in Marxist and neo-Marxist analyses or implicitly in feminist and queer analyses. While it has offered many insights about subject formation, the limits and possibilities of social resistance, and (of course) the basic functioning of ideology, interpellation has also failed to grasp many of the messy and irrational aspects of sociopsychic formation" (66). By showing that "the neoliberal subject of interests is no longer the sedimented effect of assuming a social scripted position" but instead "purely the effect of his or her practices" (68), Winnubst diagnoses *Gender Trouble* as neoliberalism's "playbook" rather than a critical paradigm for complex subject formation under a neoliberal regime.

Psychology as Micro-Ideology

My own understanding of queer theory's theoretical limitations is deeply engaged with these arguments but differs sharply in its diagnosis of the problem. Specifically, whereas the tendency among critical theorists has been to modify certain aspects of Butlerian subjectivity, my own metapsychological analysis demonstrates that, in fact, Butler's "subject" isn't psychological at all. As such, efforts by contemporary critics to rectify how Butler conceptualizes particular features of the "subject"—such as autonomy, agency, freedom, and so on—misses the underlying deficit of Butler's model, which is that what she calls the "subject" fails to correspond to a complex psycho-sexual being. Although Butler repeatedly situates her project as "a certain cultural engagement with psychoanalytic theory that belongs neither to the fields of psychology nor to psychoanalysis"[12] this differentiation of her "cultural engagement" from psychology proper actually functions throughout her oeuvre to redefine the "psyche" along "cultural" lines. Perhaps nowhere is this discursive strategy more evident than in *The Psychic Life of Power* (1997), where Butler's determination to answer the question, "What is the psychic form that power takes?" leads her to announce that such a task "has been eschewed by writers in both Foucauldian and psychoanalytic orthodoxies" (3). Disclaiming any promise "of a grand synthesis," Butler nevertheless proceeds to offer what, in her diagnosis, Foucault's theory of power is lacking: a comprehensive "psychological" account of how the subject is formed in submission to power. Butler writes: "I am in part moving toward a psychoanalytic criticism of Foucault, for I think that one cannot account for subjectivization and, in particular, becoming the principle of one's own subjection without recourse to a psychoanalytic account of the formative or generative effects of restriction or prohibition" (87). Since, by her own estimation, a coherent theory of subjection requires a psychoanalytic theory of the subject, Butler's ambition to provide a better theory of power's "psychic life" stands or falls with her successful development of a "psychological" account of power. And yet, as my analysis of gender melancholia will show, Butler's use of psychology works to systematically deny any meaningful and practical distinction between "psychology" and "ideology." As such, whereas Ruti expresses shock and incredulity at the blithe ease with which critics annihilate the subject, suggesting that perhaps they do so because "it seems to have virtually nothing to do with the personal realities of those who advocate it, most of whom live semicoherent, semicontinuous lives in semiconsistent (usually tenured) lifeworlds" (39), my own analysis suggests that the delight critics express in their assault on the subject reflects that there isn't, in fact, a functional or meaningful subject there to begin with. That is, if the stakes of "queer negativity" do not seem, to its most prominent practitioners, relevant or high it isn't only because the most zealous combatants inhabit "tenured lifeworlds," but because the "subject" has already been vacated of any practical psychology—that is, it doesn't hurt to die. A close reading of Butler's "psychic" narrative of gender development will demonstrate that despite acknowledging critical theory's dependence on the articulation of cogent psychological foundations, "psychology" has been systematically evacuated of its conceptual and practical utility as a distinctive and dynamic critical process. Taking Butler's relationship to psychoanalysis as exemplary, this chapter will show how in contemporary queer studies, "psychology" is treated as *ideology writ small*.

Because Butler's most thorough attempt at formulating a detailed account of "psychic" activity occurs in her theorization of gender development, this chapter focuses on a critique of gender as it is elaborated and applied across Butler's oeuvre. To further particularize the consequences of Butler's gender performativity for queer theory, this chapter will ground its analysis in a close reading of Radclyffe Hall's *The Well of Loneliness* (1928). The novel, which was banned upon publication in Britain and includes a commentary by sexologist Havelock Ellis, depicts the protagonist's sexual "inversion" and specifically the struggle to feel comfortable as a female within a family that consistently views her femininity with suspicion and hostility. The protagonist, who dresses mostly in male clothing and lives with her former teacher, Puddle, eventually falls in love with Mary, a beautiful woman, only to later violently renounce a future life with Mary and proclaim a life of loneliness and exclusion instead. Heather Love writes:

> ... with its inverted heroine and its tragic view of same-sex relations, *The Well* has repeatedly come into conflict with contemporary understandings of the meaning and shape of gay identity. During the 1970s, the novel was attacked primarily for its equation of lesbianism with masculine identification; in the years of the "woman-loving-woman," it was anathema with its mannish heroine, its derogation of femininity, and its glorification of normative heterosexuality. Although the recent recuperation of butch-femme practices and the growth of transgender studies have sparked renewed interest in the book, Hall's embrace of the discourse of congenital inversion is still at odds with the antiessentialism of contemporary theories of sexuality. The dissemination of the Foucauldian notion of reverse discourse has also

caused some critics to reconsider Hall's embrace of the language of inversion, but for many, such a revision has been insufficient to exonerate the novel.[13]

This summarization of the novel's singular status in the field enables Love to conclude that, "*The Well*, still known as the most famous and most widely read of lesbian novels, is also the novel most hated by lesbians themselves." Indeed, so indissociable is the critical reception of Hall's novel from any particular content of the novel itself that over the past several decades, many of the most sophisticated critical engagements with *The Well* have endeavored to interpret the strange relationship between the classic novel's immense popularity and the persistent aversion it generates in its readers.[14] Love draws on Butler's model of gender melancholia when, toward the end of her essay on *The Well*, she writes: "Butler's project has allowed us to understand gender melancholia as a condition associated not only with nonnormative gender embodiments but also with gender as such. The antihomophobic charge of this project is undeniable. And yet such a project is incomplete without an account of what it feels like to live out the melancholia structuring all sexual and gender identity" (124). According to Love, the novel's ending—in which "Stephen seals her own lonely fate, accepting her role as martyr and tragic lover as she affirms the priority of this heterosexual union" (125)—is so persistently unpalatable to lesbian and queer critics because of how it confronts the pain of a gender melancholia that had been previously disavowed. Mapping the reader's rejection of Stephen's grief onto the broader historical agenda of gay liberation, Love suggests, "Celebration will only get us so far, for pride itself can be toxic when it is sealed off from the shame that nurtures it" (127). For Love, *The Well* can show why "we need a genealogy of queer affect that does not overlook the negative, shameful and difficult feelings that have been so central to queer existence in the last century" (127).

Continuous with Love's determination to take seriously the novel's affective landscape of despair and desolation, my reading of *The Well*, and of how *The Well* is read, will show that rather than a slow-motion depiction of gender melancholia, it is Butler's model of gender as melancholia that totalizingly obliterates the complex psychic economy of the novel. Reading *The Well* from within Butler's (Freudian) frame leads to the simplistic, and false, alignment of romance as the emblem of a happy lesbian ending. That is, although critics feel betrayed by Stephen's choice to "sacrifice" Mary because it ostensibly confirms the Law's demand that lesbians die all alone and miserable, such an interpretation consistently fails to consider the context of this violent, apocalyptic moment and how "lone-liness" might actually signal a more radical sexual and ethical choice than existing theorizations imagine. Drawing on Jean Laplanche's ideas of gender as "assignment," this essay will show that while Butler offers a compelling account of how the social expectation of heterosexuality gets reproduced with particular implications for the assumption of a "mascu-line" or "feminine" "identity," her paradigm cannot ultimately account for the development of "gender" as a psychic experience because it cannot consider the psyche as a distinctive register that is produced by particular relationships to differentiated and psychological others. This analysis will demonstrate that Butler's systematic negation of psychology reflects an abiding problem for thinking about sexuality and, specifically, what Laplanche calls, the "realism of the unconscious." For Laplanche, in order for theories of sexuality to avoid the reductiveness of Freudian biologism or Lacanian linguistic structuralism, a radical revision is required that situates the adult-infant seduction at the origin of sexual development. Therefore, while, as abstract categories, "masculine" and "feminine" can be produced by an abstract "Law," "gender" as it is lived and felt can only be produced by the encounter with specific, conflicted, and sexual adults.

"The Well of Fucking Loneliness"

In *Palatable Poison*, their recent collection of critical essays on *The Well*, Laura Doan and Jay Prosser explain the logic of their title as a refer-ence to the ways in which critics continue to "express aversion to its sub-ject and/or aesthetic mode of representation. Yet they find in its poison a pabulum sufficiently palatable that *The Well* is responsible for generating a wealth of criticism, indeed gives rise to some of the richest feminist thought to appear during this period."[15] As Doan and Prosser note, the novel's morbid representation of lesbian romance constituted a "damning plot" that was impossible for most critics to justify. For many critics, "Stephen's masculinity did not accord with the lesbian feminist ideal that, as Wiesen Cook, quoting Virginia Woolf, put it, "Women alone stir my imagination" (15). A "narrative of damnation" rather than of "enabling escape," for most critics Radclyffe Hall's text emblematized the very "homophobic and misogynist stigmatization of lesbianism from which the lesbian feminist sought to emerge" (16). Esther Newton's historical contextualization of the novel explained why, given the time period in which "sexuality was wholly apportioned to the masculine," Hall actually "had no other choice but to appropriate masculinity as an instrument to symbolize lesbian sexuality."[16] In spite of Newton's reappraisal, Love observes, "With her avowed desire to be a man, her powerful gender dysphoria, and her romantic failure, Stephen represents the melancholic image of the butch lesbian that critics and activists have tried to overcome in recent years" (115). While these readings are considered by Love, and Doan and Prosser to be redemptive analyses that attempt to reconcile the novel's agonizing tone with the liberationist agenda of 1990s gay, lesbian, and emergent "queer" activism, Teresa de Lauretis's famously "perverse" reading of the novel uses the psychoanalytic paradigm of the "fetish" to reinterpret Stephen's self-hatred as a longing for her mother's body.[17] Judith Halberstam critiques de Lauretis for not taking sufficiently seriously Stephen's desire to be a man and argues instead that Stephen's "female masculinity" is a successful way of managing the pressures of biologism and social disapproval.[18] Whereas Halberstam considers Stephen's self-hatred as a product of her conflict with social mores, Jay Prosser claims the novel as "the first in a transsexual canon" in which Stephen's persistent grief testifies to her longing for a differently gendered body.[19] Love astutely observes that common to all these interpretations is a determination by critics to either recuperate Stephen's "loneliness" or locate its causes in some historical elsewhere. Resisting the temptation to "wish away" the "melancholic trace" of Stephen's "loneliness," Love argues that "any attempt to resolve her sense of loneliness into a longing for either masculinity or femininity misses a crucial aspect of her experience. Of course these feelings are ideological, but they are also real. Stephen is doomed to experience her own body as essentially unlovable; the reasons for this failure are crushingly specific—her sense of failure and longing has everything to do with being a mannish woman before the war in rural, quasi-aristocratic England. And yet this does not mean that a change in circumstances would render Stephen perfectly happy, perfectly satisfied" (119).

Love's suggestion that readers embrace Stephen's suffering rather than disavow it treats the affective landscape of the novel as constitutive, rather than incidental, to the formation of queer identity. And yet, while this call to respect the value of shame and other "backward feelings" provides a crucial corrective to the field's valorization of "pride" and heroic self-acceptance, the causal link between Stephen's "gender" and her suffering is so unanimously accepted in the critical imagination that as yet no reading expresses incredulity that, as theorists of radical sexuality, our despair at Stephen's willful "loneliness" actually aligns us with the normative romance plot. While it is not difficult to understand the threat that Stephen's "lonely" and martyr-like submission to "destiny" poses for an emancipatory political agenda, my own reading shows how this preoccupation with the "tragic" dimension of Stephen's self-experience consistently misses the particular context in which this dramatization of suffering takes place. Although Stephen's harrowing, tormented tone leaves little room for ambiguity on what she feels about her "lonely" fate and wretched "unwanted being," it is nevertheless the case that the long-standing uncritical acceptance of the *transparency* of Stephen's psychological experience reproduces a superficial interpretive schema of romance = happy ending and loneliness = tragic homophobia. Particularly, this narrative framework routinely refuses to consider the psychological "quality" of Stephen's relationship to Mary, and correlatively, what it means that instead of domestic normalcy with Mary, Stephen commits to "write" instead.

The critical tradition of reflexively interpreting Stephen's renunciation of Mary as a tragic act of internalized homophobia follows directly from how the novel, and particularly Stephen's own narrative descriptions, frame the text's climactic event. When Stephen is confronted with Martin Hallam, a rival male suitor who expresses interest in Mary, she is initially shocked but also immediately confident and reassured. When Martin confronts Stephen with the allegation that "life with you is spiritually murdering Mary. Can't you see it? Can't you realize that she needs all the things that it's not in your power to give her? Children, protection, friends who she can respect and who'll respect her" (425), Stephen responds that she has "great faith in my writing, great faith" and that this will "compel the world to accept me for what I am." When this reasoning fails to persuade Martin, the rivals agree to a "curious warfare" over Mary, and Stephen "fell back upon her every available weapon in the struggle to assert her right to possession. Every link that the years had forged between her and Mary, every tender and passionate memory that bound their past to their ardent present, every moment of joy—aye, and even of sorrow, she used in sheer self-defense against Martin. And not the least powerful of all her weapons, was the perfect companionship and understanding that constitutes the great strength of such unions. Well armed she was, thanks to both present and past—but Martin's sole weapon lay in the future" (428). After several chapters of their "curious warfare," "secretly waged," Stephen suddenly realizes that "the woman she loved was deeply unhappy" and resolves to surrender, determined to dismiss Mary and send her to a "future" with Martin instead. We learn that after holidays spent with friends but in exile from her childhood home, Stephen's "perceptions were even more accurate and far-reaching, for to her there had come the despairing knowledge" of Mary's unhappiness (429). Although "at first she had blinded herself to this truth, sustained by the passionate stress of the battle, by her power to hold in despite of the man . . . yet the day came when she was no longer blind, when nothing counted in all the world except this grievous unhappiness that was being silently borne by Mary" (429). This description of Stephen as having been "blind" in her previous devaluation of heterosexual privilege and suddenly becoming "no longer blind" to the, supposedly, "hard truth" of Mary's unhappiness / social exclusion frames Stephen's final rejection of Mary as an excruciating defeat, a painful acquiescence to society's moral conventions and a betrayal of her own "courage" to prove that there was never anything wrong with her love or relationship to Mary. When in the novel's final pages, Stephen resolves to coordinate a plan with Martin whereby she will reject Mary and he will "wait under this arch . . . until Mary needs you, as I think she will . . . it may not be long" (434), and then watches from her window as Mary runs for comfort into Martin's arms, it is not difficult to appreciate why generations of readers have responded much as Valerie Seymour, Stephen's close friend who moments before this dramatic sequence says, "Good heavens, you're worth twenty Mary Llewellyns! Stephen, think it over before you decide—it seems mad to me" and, then noticing Stephen's "dull" resolve, "got up" and exclaims, "Being what you are, I supposed you can't—you were made for a martyr!" (434). Valerie's frustration with Stephen's martyrdom anticipates a staple of the novel's critical reception. Indeed, so continuous is the link between how the *novel* describes Stephen's "martyrdom" and how *critics* interpret these acts, it becomes worth considering to what extent the "courageous," self-hating, invert-as-martyr functions less as an objective feature of Stephen's terrible "fate" than as a trope the novel effectively exploits to obscure its more radical defense of Stephen's sexuality and gender.

Stephen's relationship with her teacher, Miss Puddleton, the "queer little woman" (68) and "little grey figure" who is shaped like "a miniature box" (67)—and accompanies Stephen in her successive homes, initially being her tutor and eventually taking care of various administrative and domestic tasks—offers an underutilized resource for mapping the psychic landscape of the novel. Nicknamed "Puddle" by Stephen when she is still a younger child and then described as "an insignificant creature, this Puddle, yet at moments unmistakably self-assertive" (69), Puddle is single-handedly responsible for introducing discipline into Stephen's life and education; upon Puddle's entry into Stephen's life, "now Stephen found herself put into harness for the first time in her life" (68) and though Stephen bristles at the sensation, she would also "gaze at Miss Puddleton in a kind of amazement; that tiny, square box to hold all this grim knowledge!" (68). Growing gradually to appreciate Puddle's severity and wisdom, Stephen announces that "'I can always be comfortable with you, Puddle . . . you're like a nice chair; though you are so tiny yet one's got room to stretch, I don't know how you do it'" (70). It is against this backdrop of teacher-student companionship that Stephen comes to depend increasingly on Puddle's camaraderie and experience. When, after her father dies and Stephen's infatuation with another woman is revealed to her mother, forcing her into exile from her childhood home, Puddle offers to join Stephen abroad in London and later in Paris. As Stephen "graduates" from her position as a student, Puddle assumes a more mentoring, "guardian" role, often implying that her own history being a "queer little woman" informs her implicit understanding of Stephen's experience. When, having grabbed at random a book from her father's library, Stephen discovers in a text by sexologist Ullrich Kraft-Ebing the "truth" of her sexual "inversion," and, devastated, "she sank down completely hopeless and beaten," Puddle confesses to her former pupil, "All that you're suffering at this moment I've suffered. It was when I was very young like you—but I still remember" (205). This powerful, often tacit, alliance between them situates Puddle as a source of wisdom, and in many instances throughout the novel where Stephen is lost or confused, it is Puddle whose spectacular clarity and decisiveness prevails to guide Stephen and protect her.

As a result of Puddle's unique status in the text, it is important to observe that her opinion about Mary, and the novel's romantic love plot more generally, is drastically at odds with Stephen's characterizations. As Stephen begins to develop into a serious writer, for whom "work" had "become a narcotic," Puddle takes on all the responsibilities of arranging a writing life for Stephen—"Puddle it was who found the flat . . . and Puddle it was who now kept the accounts, paid the rent, settled bills and managed the servants" (211). Puddle's unconditional support of Stephen's writing does not stop her from worrying about Stephen's loneliness, and we learn that even though Puddle encourages Stephen to push herself to become a great writer, "but one thing there was that Puddle still feared, and this was the girl's desire for isolation. To her it appeared as a weakness in Stephen . . . and she did her best to frustrate it" (214). However, in spite of Puddle's determination to foster Stephen's social comfort, we find out that when Stephen describes Mary, who is "not quite twenty-two," instead of rejoicing at Stephen's newfound happiness, Puddle "glanced at Stephen and fell silent" (302). Mary's "youthfulness" gradually comes to represent a kind of immaturity, as Stephen herself repeatedly observes, with amusement, that Mary is thoroughly unfamiliar with even small tasks like "where to buy Stephen replacement stockings" and what to do during those "long hours of idleness" while Stephen was working. Mary's "youth" is repeatedly emphasized as the source of her inability to be efficient in household duties, or confident in social excursions, or even imaginative about pleasurable activities (340). Indeed, Stephen recurringly observes that Mary's "youth" symbolizes her distance from the exigencies of either the material world or the economy of creative production, as when Stephen considers that "she looked much less than her twenty-two years in her simple dress with its leather belt—she looked indeed little more than a schoolgirl" (323). Indeed, as Stephen grows increasingly preoccupied with writing her novel, she keeps noticing that Mary "did not look very well" and "at times she seemed a little downhearted, so that Stephen would snatch a few hours from her work in order that they might go out together" (345). Stephen describes Mary as "feeling happy, would revive for these few hours as though by magic" only to retreat again, "find[ing] herself lonely, with nowhere to go and no one to talk to, because Stephen was back again at her desk, why then she would wilt, which was not unnatural considering her youth and her situation" (345).

Stephen's awareness of Mary's chronic suffering ought to complicate the justification Stephen articulates, when, in renouncing Mary, she claims to "suddenly" arrive at the "despairing knowledge" that Mary was unhappy. In fact, Mary's unhappiness is a constant feature of their relationship and for its entire duration Mary would "wilt" without Stephen's full attention, and it is the burden of this dynamic that Puddle refers to when she confronts Stephen with the observation, "'You're not working, and yet work's your only weapon'" (340). Although Stephen is initially "sore" from "Puddle's words," they "kept hammering in her brain" as she struggles to negotiate if she "could finish her book—she who had Paris in springtime with Mary?" when there was "so much to see, so much to show Mary" (325). In fact, the centrality of the tension between "writing" versus "Mary" is particularly crucial for how it replicates the dynamic between Stephen's mother and father. Although throughout the novel, Stephen characterizes her parents' matrimonial union as perfect, almost mythically so—"seldom had two people loved more than they did; they loved with an ardor undiminished by time; as they ripened, so their love ripened with them" (12)—this language of extreme idealization is nevertheless repeatedly undermined by references to her father's irremediable grief and loneliness and her mother's persistent unhappiness. From the young Stephen's perspective, it is her birth—as a girl instead of the son they expected—that introduces hardship into her parents' bucolic lives (14), but as the novel develops, it becomes increasingly evident that it is not only Stephen's awkward negotiation of her femininity that compels her father, out of pity, to be kind to her, but that Sir Philip found in his daughter a "deep sense of friendship, with a deep sense of mutual understanding" that was otherwise absent from his "perfect" marriage to the "gracious beauty of Anna, so perfect a thing" (27). Indeed, this repeated reference to Anna's "perfection" functions in much the same way as the adjective "youth" worked to designate Mary in abstract, mythological terms. In contrast to the nuance and rich descriptions Sir Philip uses when observing Stephen's "curious suggestion of strength in her movements" (26), lively mind, capacious sensitivity, talent in hunting (44), the language of the text gives the reader no sense of Anna's personality, apart from her "gracious" "perfect beauty" and visceral aversion to Stephen's appearance and touch.

A major effect of these linguistic choices is to communicate a categorical difference between the complex and layered individuality of Stephen and Sir Philip, on the one hand, and on the other hand, the abstract, disembodied features of Mary and Anna. A further implication of this juxtaposition is that Stephen's attraction to the "youthful," "innocent" Mary reproduces Sir Philip's experience of being married to a "gracious" and "beautiful" woman who was "perfect" and yet with whom he could not freely share the contents of his own mind. Throughout the novel, we see Sir Philip reading in his study, reading in their bedroom, trying to figure something out while Anna, helpless and estranged from this aspect of her husband, tells him it is time to go to bed, or go to sleep, and so on. Sir Philip's closeness to his daughter offers a sharp contrast to his "perfect" marital union because whereas Philip strives to constantly protect Anna from difficult subjects and feelings, he regularly speaks freely with his daughter about deep existential concerns and, crucially, decides to educate his daughter even though Anna asks, "Did you love me any less because I couldn't do mathematics? Do you love me less now because I count on my fingers?" to which Sir Philip replies by "kiss[ing] her and saying, 'that's different, you're you.'" Although Philip was smiling, Anna registers "a look that she knew well had come into his eyes, a cold resolute expression, which meant that all persuasion was likely to be unavailing" (54). If the relationship between Sir Philip and Anna resembles Stephen's relationship to Mary, it is because in both cases there is one individual who worries, protects, thinks, organizes and another party who accepts, endures, appreciates, and responds. While this distribution of emotional labor breaks down along normative lines that are traditionally associated with "masculine" versus "feminine" differences, calling these traits "masculine" or "feminine" does little to elucidate why Stephen would initially inhabit this "masculine"/paternal role, only to reject it at the novel's end.

Furthermore, although conceding that Martin represents the better "moral" choice for Mary seems to represent Stephen's final defeat and tragic capitulation to the heterosexual matrix, such an interpretation evacuates any relational system of its psychological quality and particular dynamic and relies instead on the absolute equivalence between anatomy (individuals have a similar body part) and sexuality (the type of desire they experience). That is, what if the putative "sameness" of "gender" actually works in this text to obscure their profound sexual "differences"?

Gender as "Assignment": A Laplanchian Paradigm

I am thinking here of "sexuality" in the enlarged sense defined by Laplanche. Within Laplanche's definition, "sexuality" can only maintain its radicality by expanding beyond the determined objects and sources of *genital* sexuality. To represent this "enlarged sexuality," Laplanche invents a neologism in French by transforming the German adjective "sexual" into a free-standing noun.[20] It is with this understanding of "sexuality," as irreducible to genitality or "gender," that it becomes possible for the first time to consider what it means that immediately upon conceding Mary to her rival Martin, Stephen is overcome by the "demand" to "write," to inhabit her own body as a vehicle for articulating sexuality: "They were calling her by name, saying: 'Stephen Stephen!' The quick, the dead, and the yet unborn—all calling her, softly at first and then louder" until, in a moment of ecstatic climax, Stephen's "barren womb became fruitful" and "now there was only one voice, one demand; her own voice into which those millions had entered. A voice like the awful, deep rolling of thunder; a demand like the gathering together of great waters. A terrifying voice that made her ears throb, that made her brain throb, that shook her very entrails, until she must stagger and all but fall beneath this appalling burden of sound that strangled her in its will to be uttered" (437). This final scene of Stephen giving "birth" to "her own voice" signals that what is unleashed upon the break-up with Mary is precisely the "sexuality" that Stephen was, via her role as paternal protector of Mary, trying to repress. This is what Puddle refers to when, throughout the novel, she warns Stephen that tending to Mary means "you are not working," and why ultimately Stephen does *not* surrender to heterosexuality so much as deploy it as an alibi for the surrender to her own erotic longing for impregnation and becoming.

How can we understand the total absence of criticism that addresses this story's triumphant ending? Why do generations of readers continue to accept the transparency of Stephen's psychological experience, take her feelings as objective representations of the event and disregard the text's sophisticated mobilization of certain narrative tropes to challenge sexuality's normative regime? A closer examination of the novel's psychic economy will demonstrate that, contrary to the popular belief that Stephen's sacrifice of Mary constitutes a romantic tragedy—an interpretation that Stephen herself forcefully insists upon—the novel's dramatization of Mary's violent rejection actually works to exemplify the psychological violence through which "gender" is produced in *relation* to others, and therefore to enact Stephen's determined differentiation from the "gender" she had been "assigned," which revolves around the painful struggle with who her father was, and who he expected her to be.

Gender and Laplanche

In his essay, "Gender, Sex and the Sexual," Laplanche defines gender as an "assignment" because "assignment underlines the primacy of the other in the process—whether the first assignment is the declaration at the town hall, at the church or in some other official place, a declaration involving the assignment of a first name, the assignment to a place in a kinship network, etc.";[21] however, in order to differentiate this use of "assignment" from the "Lacanian inflation of the notion of the signifier," Laplanche explains that "a word of warning" is required:

> It is said that "gender is social," "sex is biological." Caution must be taken with the term "social," because here it covers up at least two realities that intersect. On the one hand there is the social, or the socio-cultural, in general. Of course it is in "the social" that the assignment is inscribed, if only in that famous declaration at the beginning of life that is made at the level of the institutional structures of a given society. But the inscriber is not the social in general; it is the little group of close *socii*, of friends and blood relations. This is, effectively, the father, the mother, a friend, a brother, a cousin, etc. Thus it is the little group of *socii* who inscribe *in* the social, but it is not Society that does the assigning. (174)

The intervention Laplanche makes in the discourse of gender and sexuality rests on this meticulous differentiation between the specific "little group of *socii* who inscribe *in* the social," and an abstract "society in general." Drawing out the radical implications of this distinction, Laplanche observes that, "This idea of assignment or of 'identification by' *completely changes the vector of identification*" (174) for it is no longer possible to claim, as Freud and Lacan do, that identification originates in the *child* when, as a consequence of the child's dependence on adult caretaking, the communication of attachment between parents and children is compromised by the "noise" of *adult* sexuality. For example, Laplanche writes, "A father may consciously assign the masculine gender to his offspring but have expected a daughter, even have unconsciously desired to penetrate a daughter. Actually, this field of the unconscious relation of parents to their children has been very poorly explored" and therefore, Laplanche contends, "It's what is 'sexed' and also above all the '*sexual*' of the parents that *makes a noise* in the assignment" (176).

Disputing the supposed transparency of anatomy, Laplanche argues instead that, "There are several levels (not to mention other registers) within anatomy itself: there is scientific anatomy which may be purely descriptive or may be structural . . . and then there is 'popular' anatomy" which is "perceptual, even purely illusory" because it reinscribes the "phallic logic" whereby, owing to the human's upright posture, "the perception of genital organs is no longer the perception of *two* genital organs but only of one. The difference between the sexes become a 'difference of sex'" (177). By dismissing the stability of "gender" as identical to "biology," Laplanche establishes the metapsychological foundations for his claim that, "The perceptible difference of sex as sign or as signifier has practically nothing to do with biological and physiological male/female difference" and as a result, "gender"—via the adult-child relation—"comes before sex, a point that upends habits of thought, the ruts of routine thought that put the 'biological' before the 'social'" (180).

At the center of Laplanche's lifelong attempt to establish "new foundations for psychoanalysis" that challenged Freudian biologism and Lacanian linguistic structuralism, Laplanche introduces the "general theory of seduction." According to Laplanche, "The theory of seduction is the hypothesis best suited to the discovery of the irreducible unconscious" because, as Laplanche explains, "seduction is not a relation that is contingent, pathological (even though it can be) and episodic. It is grounded in a situation from which no human being is exempt: the 'fundamental anthropological situation,' as I call it . . . the *adult-infans* relation. It consists of the *adult*, who has an unconscious such as psychoanalysis has revealed it, i.e., a sexual unconscious that is essentially made up of infantile residues, an unconscious that is perverse . . . and the *infant*, who is not equipped with any genetic sexual organization or any hormonal activators of sexuality" (102). Laplanche fiercely defends what he will later call the "realism of the unconscious" by which he means that the "unconscious" is neither the source of some mythical, primordial energy, nor the essential center of my true self, but instead the structural effect of the infant's attempts, and failures, to translate the adult's "enigmatic" messages. According to this model, the infant is always "translating" messages from his surroundings and therefore translation is not exactly a strictly linguistic or interpretive process, but instead a process for binding affect and energy into symbolization. It is the transformation of diffuse and overwhelming *affect* into *symbolic* form that enables the infant's innate regulative capacities to "bind" affect to representation and thereby to survive the assault of overstimulation by the adult environment. However, it is by this same measure, that repression occurs because, as Laplanche repeatedly explains, the adult's communications include "enigmatic signifiers" that are unavailable to the adult's own consciousness and therefore untranslatable by the infant alone. The difference, for the infant, between "enigmatic signifiers" and messages that are available for translation hinges on the adult's unconscious. That is, what renders certain messages qualitatively "enigmatic" is not the *content* of the "signifier" per se, but rather the ratio of affect to symbolization. It is precisely those messages that are provocative and unsymbolized for the *adult* that are untranslatable for the *infant*, and repressed as a result.

Putting together the "attachment" relation with the development of "gender," Laplanche suggests that "communication does not only occur with the language of bodily care; there is also the social code, the social language" and "these messages are chiefly '*messages of gender assignment*'" (176). For this reason, Laplanche argues that the popular focus on "gender" in opposition to "sex" risks restoring the supposed facticity of biology and completely annihilating the category of the "*sexual*." Laplanche observes how even in "radical" feminist positions, the requirement for "gender" to be "constructed" depends upon a "biological" precondition. "In all of this," Laplanche points out, "the Freudian *sexual* risks becoming a major absence" (167). With this warning Laplanche means to demonstrate that by centering "gender" in the *child's* identificatory actions, the vector of identification is wrongly reversed so as to obscure the primacy of the *adult* in the production of *my* "gender."

Refusing *Gender Melancholia*

Following Heather Love's interpretation of *The Well* as offering "a painfully slow-paced and explicit account" of the "melancholy of gender" (121), this chapter aims to show that instead of an accurate depiction of how gender is psychologically produced, Hall's "slow-paced" depiction of Stephen's painful struggle dramatizes the violent relational process by

which "gender" is "assigned," and the narrative reconstruction that ultimately reverses and eschews the sequence of "gender" development by
claiming the *self* as its origin. As critics of *The Well* have routinely observed,
Stephen's sense of herself as a "wretched" and "unwanted being" can be
traced to her earliest experiences of being a "girl," where her parents antic-
ipated having a "son" instead. What has been systematically neglected,
however, is the causal links between how Stephen perceives the "problem"
of her "gender" and the role of her parents in defining, as a "problem," the
"gender" they "assign" her. Throughout the novel, Sir Philip's preferential
attachment to Stephen is normalized as the natural effect of his pity for
her "sexual inversion." We are repeatedly reading that, when staring at his
daughter, Sir Philip would "frown and become lost in thought" (26), that
he would stay awake in his study reading Kraft-Ebbing to learn about the
"truth" of her strange "gender-sexological" condition. While Sir Philip's
treatment of Stephen stands in sharp contrast to Anna Gordon's visceral
revulsion at the look and touch of her daughter (15), a closer examination of the language surrounding Stephen's birth problematizes the narrative of Stephen's "gender" as *preceding* her parents' relationship to it.
Rather, close attention to the relational context of Stephen's "gender"
development reveals that Sir Philip's absolute determination to have a son
who would emulate and "resemble" him "*completely changes the vector of
identification.*"[22]

In the first few pages of the novel, we learn of Sir Philip that, "It never
seemed to cross his mind for a moment that Anna might very well give
him a daughter . . . he christened the unborn infant Stephen, because he
admired the pluck of that Saint. He was not a religious man by instinct,
being perhaps too much of a student, but he read the Bible for its fine
literature, and Stephen had gripped his imagination. Thus he often dis-
cussed the future of their child: 'I think I shall put Stephen down for Har-
row,' or: 'I'd rather like Stephen to finish off abroad, it widens one's outlook
on life'" (12). In fact, so entrenched is Sir Philip's expectation of a son, and
so elaborate his fantasies of what kind of son the child will be, that when
a girl is born he "hid his chagrin" and "insisted on calling the infant Stephen, nay more, he would have it baptized by that name. 'We've called her
Stephen so long,' he told Anna, 'that I really can't see why we shouldn't go
on—.' Anna felt doubtful, but Sir Philip was stubborn, as he could be at
times over whims. The Vicar said that is was rather unusual, so to mollify
him they must add female names. The child was baptized in the village
church as Stephen Mary Olivia Gertrude—and she throve, seeming
strong, and when her hair grew it was seen to be auburn like Sir Philip's"
(13). Although the novel repeatedly portrays Sir Philip as somehow

conceding to Stephen's sexual "inversion" by allowing her to participate in activities traditionally reserved for "boys," it is Sir Philip's adamant, "stubborn" refusal to acknowledge Stephen as anything other than his rightful "son" that determines the particular shape of Stephen's "gender." Therefore, while Stephen considers her sexual flaw to originate in her faulty "gender," it is the *adult*—in this case Sir Philip—whose vehement insistence on having a "son" forces Stephen to be identified as a girl-who-should-have-been-a-boy. "You're all the son that I've got," he tells her, as if to suggest that his determination to have a son supersedes any expression on her part. Stephen hints at some awareness of this arrangement when, after her father announces, "I want you to have the same education, the same advantages as I'd give to my son," Stephen gently exposes the fantasy that is trying to pass off as magnanimous equality by saying, "But I'm not your son, Father," a rejoinder that immediately makes "her heart fe[el] heavy—heavy and sad" and "her own eyes clouded and she stared at her boots, ashamed of the tears that she felt might flow over" (61). This momentary disconnect in the smooth flow of "gender's" "assignment" is resolved at the scene's end by returning full circle to Sir Philip's desire and reinstating the determinative power of the parent's unconscious relation to the child, as when Sir Philip, having secured Stephen's agreement to be "educated" like a "son," says to her: "'Stephen, come here—look me straight in the eyes—what is honor, my daughter?' She looked into his anxious, questioning eyes: 'You are honor,' she said quite simply" (62). What the acknowledgement of Stephen as a "daughter" seems to offer with one hand, it therefore retrieves with the other, for by recuperating his own image as the embodiment of "honor," Sir Philip recuperates his primacy in the kind of "gender" she develops—"girl" or "boy" becomes irrelevant, as long as Stephen agrees to *become like him.*

It is precisely the psychological process of how "gender" is "assigned" within particular relationships to intimate others that gets uniformly obscured by critical readings of the novel that naturalize as the source of Stephen's "gender" problem some innate, private, ontological "truth." Treating Stephen's "gender" as something that expresses either social nonsense or psychic "truth" fundamentally obscures the sequence of "gender" as developing *in relation* to psychological and *sexual* others. The role of particular *sexual* others is completely negated in Butler's account of subject formation where her attempt to undermine the categories of "masculine" and "feminine" leads her to equate "gender" with "false" signifiers that can be "performed" or renegotiated. According to Butler's account of subject formation, "feminine and masculine dispositions are the result of the effective internalization of that [the homosexual incest] taboo."[23]

Arguing for the *"precedence"* of the "homosexual incest taboo" (that is, before the Oedipal dilemma), Butler uses the "cultural" prohibition on homosexuality to prove the inevitability of an individual's gendered "psyche." As Jay Prosser has shown, Butler's elevation of the prohibition against homosexuality to the status of the earliest and most definitive ideological taboo relies on Monique Wittig's analysis of "heterosexuality as a social system which is based on the oppression of women by men and which produces the doctrine of the difference between the sexes to justify this oppression."[24] Following Wittig's claim that "what founds society, any society, is heterosexuality" (24), Butler asserts the priority of "homosexuality" in her revision to the Freudian psychoanalytic schema and thereby uses a "politico-cultural" account of heterosexuality to explain the development of "psychic" structures.[25] For Butler, the alleged radicalism of her position derives from dissociating "sex" from "gender" so that, while some kind of biological "sex" is primary, "gender" as an identity is not; but a paradigm wherein "gender" might *not* match "sex" begets the question—how *could* "gender" as a complex psychic constellation ever match "sex" as an anatomical apparatus? The radical performativity of this model reinforces the gender/sex binary whereby "gender" is only a performance in relation to a "part" that is determinative and fixed (you can resignify what penis / no penis means but this presumes it ever means "one" transcendental thing). But what happens when, drawing on Laplanche, we consider that the "sex" of the child never means *just* one thing because the context of its symbolization takes place in *relation* to the fantasies of particular *sexual* adults. Butler's account of the primacy of the taboo against homosexuality places at the origin of "gender" development an abstract Social Law. Here the parent is operated as a psychically and sexually neutral carrier of dominant normative ideology. But how do we explain the categorical differences between what ideology wants, and what particular adults do? That is, even if the prohibition against homosexuality is a component of every child's encounter with sociality, surely not every parent "abides" by or "prohibits" the Law in the same way? Furthermore, by what *mechanism* does a cultural law produce an individual's psychological "gender"? Between "culture" and "psychology" Butler situates the "parent" but such a figure has been emptied of any psychic content and transformed into merely the channel through which Society reaches its youngest subject. To consider this a "psychological" account risks using "psychological" as merely a synonym for "personal" and the "psychic life of power" as really meaning "the personal version of ideology."

Butler's account presumes that a *parent* acts upon desire the same way ideology does—in "Melancholy Gender—Refused Identification," Butler writes: "for if we accept the notion that the prohibition on homosexuality operates throughout a largely heterosexual culture as one of its defining operations, then it appears that the loss of homosexual objects and aims ... will be foreclosed from the start" (171).[26] In this "psychological" account, there is no meaningful or structural differentiation between a "culture" that is "largely heterosexual" and the particular "objects" who relate, sexually, within it. By equating a social and legal taboo with a psychological one, Butler proposes that kinship arrangements are actually lived by adults in some psychologically homogenous way so that the "parent" is really only a smaller scale source of the "cultural" law. But if so, who are these adults who behave like an abstract Ideological directive, who unconflictually and absolutely "prohibit" homosexual attachment— were they not themselves children once? Are they not themselves *sexual* and therefore subjects of the same prohibition? Are they not themselves bearers of a sexuality that is dynamic and ongoing and even, according to Laplanche, "reactivated" by the encounter with an infant's sexuality? Turning the Parent into a sexually neutral agent of the Law treats adult-child relations as merely the passive instantiation of a vulgar ideology, and thereby refuses to distinguish the operations of ideology from the complex mechanisms of psychological development. Perhaps most problematically, Butler's reduction of psychology to merely ideology-on-a-smaller scale confirms the individual as the irreducible center of his own formation—while it is the "adult/Society" who produces abstract, reductive interdictions, the "child" is an agent of complex identifications whose "gender" represents a promise of autonomy and emancipation.

Psychology = Ideology Writ Small

Drawing from this, we can begin to appreciate how Butler's conceptualization of "gender" as at the nexus of cultural-psychological experience in fact belies its behavior as a thoroughly ideological mechanism. Put another way, despite Butler's repeated insistence that "gender" performativity describes an individual's complex internal negotiation of social norms, in actuality, "gender" functions in Butler's model identically to ideology. Seeing it this way further confirms the limited emancipatory options available to the Butlerian subject; that is, if "gender" is the inevitable effect of being "hailed" by the social/normative regime, the only possible means of rebellion are restricted to the performative domain—resignification, disidentification, "drag." Shannon Winnubst has recently observed that "in Butler, the role of Althusser . . . is apparently so profound that she does not even recognize the need to cite him: his name is not listed in the index. Her arguments are, however, thoroughly Althusserian, arguing over and over that 'gender is performatively produced and compelled by regulative practices of gender coherence,' which sounds remarkably similar to the processes Althusser calls interpellation. To make the matter even worse, her example (arguably the exemplar) of birth as the site of gendering is precisely the same example Althusser describes in 'Ideology and Ideological State Apparatuses,' published in 1970."[27] Winnubst's critique of contemporary critical norms astutely traces the link between Butler's poststructuralist account of gender and the broader economic context of neoliberalism. Focusing on the distinctiveness of neoliberalism from classical liberalism, Winnubst persuasively argues that "a concept that has dominated post-Hegelian, leftist theory, interpellation has been the primary heuristic for analyzing sociopsychic formation across the last four decades, whether explicitly in Marxist and neo-Marxist analyses or implicitly in feminist and queer analyses. While it has offered many insights about subject formation, the limits and possibilities of social resistance, and (of course) the basic functioning of ideology, interpellation has also failed to grasp many of the messy and irrational aspects of sociopsychic formation" (66). By showing that "the neoliberal subject of interests is no longer the sedimented effect of assuming a social scripted position" but instead "purely the effect of his or her practices" (68), Winnubst diagnoses *Gender Trouble* as neoliberalism's "playbook" rather than a critical paradigm for complex subject formation under a neoliberal regime. Although *Gender Trouble* is "not framed as an analysis of gender in the neoliberal episteme," it nevertheless "maps out many of the philosophical moves involved in this kind of unmooring of gender from deep political and historical structures . . . the category of gender begins to exemplify the cultural embrace of social difference as fungible, as evacuated of any political heft of historical weight—as oh so cool" (127).

Although Winnubst focuses primarily on *Gender Trouble*, Butler's later efforts to correct the psychic limitations of her earlier model, specifically in *Psychic Life*, mentions the role of Althusser in her theory. She claims that "the scene of 'interpellation' offered by Althusser is one instance of this quasi-fictive effort to give an account of how the social subject is produced through linguistic means. Althusser's doctrine of interpellation clearly sets the stage for Foucault's later views on the 'discursive production of the subject.' . . . In Althusser's essay, 'Ideology and Ideological State Apparatuses,' the subordination of the subject takes place through language, as the effect of the authoritative voice that hails the individual" (5). From here, Butler proceeds to claim that, "Significantly, Althusser does not offer a clue as to why that individual turns around, accepting the voice as being addressed to him or her, and accepting the subordination and normalization effected by that voice. Why does this subject turn toward the voice of the law, and what is the effect of such a turn in inaugurating a social subject? Is this a guilty subject and, if so, how did it become guilty? Might the theory of interpellation require a theory of conscience?" (5). Indeed, it is precisely to this end—providing "a theory of interpellation" *with* its requisite "theory of conscience"—that Butler focuses her efforts throughout the book. What is more, it is presumably the very effort to answer "why" the subject turns around that Butler calls "psychic." "That conscience," she writes, "understood as the psychic operation of a regulatory norm, constitutes a specifically psychic and social working of power on which interpellation depends but for which it can give no account" (5).

In this way, we might understand that what Butler is calling "psychic" is the effort to explain the "why" of interpellation. And yet the problem she sets out to solve remains entirely within the scene and structure of interpellation. Using Hegel to explain the subject's dependence on recognition, Butler attempts to resolve the question of "why the subject turns around" in order to demonstrate that (unlike Althusser and Foucault) her own paradigm is capable of accounting for human motivation. But while the account of a subject "turning around" *because* it depends upon recognition by another offers a causal narrative for the subject's actions (a *reason* he agrees to be "hailed" by authority) this story of the hailed Hegelian subject still fails to resemble how an actual mind develops in relation to others. That is, even as Butler's later attempts to include Others in the scene of interpellation mime the coordinates of a psychological event, the mechanisms she describes are no less schematic, rigid, and limited, and her subject no less autarkic and enclosed, than it was before. How does a subjectivity form via "turning around?" Earlier Butler referred to her project as a "theory of conscience" to complement a "theory of interpellation" and indeed, her account of turning around is consistent with the possible development of particular function—such as a conscience, or superego, for example. But is the individual *only* his conscience? Is one's conscience the center of subjectivity? Although Butler insists that accounting for the motivation beneath interpellation is tantamount to offering a psychological account of subject formation, the speculative Hegelian-Althusserian allegory she develops does *not* in fact correspond to any process in mental terms. The account of "why" the subject turns around refines her original account considerably so that now she is able to explain the general conditions of the subject's dependence on those same structures it later struggles to eschew. However, this refinement of interpellation notwithstanding, Butler's paradigm continues to reduce the subject to its ideological operations. While perhaps from within the austere materialism of first-generation Marxism describing the underlying "reason" for interpellation may *seem* like a description of "psychic" life, and referring to an internal sequence rather than an external one may sound as though it is automatically focused on the mind, the continued utility of critical theory depends upon an appreciation of the subject as a complex and multi-dimensional construction.

To insist, with Laplanche, on the fundamental incommensurability between Society and "the little group of socii" within it requires a reformulation of "gender" that rigorously differentiates between abstract gender categorizations, such as "masculine" and "feminine," and the psychological development of "gender" as an "assignment" that takes place within a series of singular, actual relational arrangements. As against the abstractions of linguistic structuralism, Laplanche reminds us that, while it is "in 'the social' that the assignment is inscribed," it is nevertheless the case that, the "inscriber is not the social in general" (173). The "inscriber" is specific; it is Sir Philip not "the Law." The distinction between "the social in general," and the particular "inscriber" enables another differentiation that has been absent from critical interpretations of *The Well*—that is, between "gender" as a *psychic* development versus Stephen's *narrative* account of it. Restoring the novel's psychic context makes it possible to see Stephen's final rejection of Mary as a willful repudiation rather than a sacrifice—not only does Stephen immediately get overtaken by the voices of "these strangers with their miserable eyes" (436) but she discovers "only one voice, one demand; her own voice into which those millions had entered" (437). The ecstatic impregnation by these "strangers" contradicts Stephen's portrayal of herself as a suffering "martyr" who renounces Mary out of shame and internalized self-hatred. Instead, breaking-up with Mary functions to permit her access to her own body as a resource for enjoyment and becoming so that her "barren womb became fruitful" and instead of merely being the lover who could not provide Mary with a child, she experiences the "rockets of pain" as she ecstatically gives birth to "her own voice" (437).

By focusing on the psychic quality of the text's final scene, we are confronted with a bewildering antinomy between Stephen's bold and self-preservative actions and the affective landscape of tragedy and failure in which she relates it. If Stephen dodged a bullet in rejecting Mary, why doesn't she seem to celebrate it? In fact, it is precisely this final refusal to *feel* liberated that prompts Terry Castle to declare the novel, "Hall's often monstrously overwrought parable of homosexual *Bildung*" (398). Confessing her own lifelong aversion/protectiveness toward the novel, Castle concludes, "No one tries to hide it: the book has its mortifications and one must wrestle with them as best one can" (398). It might seem interesting that Castle's eventual acceptance of the book is verbalized in a style that could have come directly from the novel itself—the third person pronouns, the tone of omniscient authority, the use of a religious word like "mortifications" and the connotations of a powerless reader who "must wrestle as best one can." What would it mean to consider that it's actually Stephen's helpless acceptance of the power of relationships that provokes generations of readers to feel as Castle does in her opening sentence: "Oh god not again: *The Well of Fucking Loneliness*" (394). For the duration of her childhood, we readers watch as Stephen endures the scorn and revulsion of her mother, the anxious seductiveness of her father. We watch as Stephen is told that her sexual "inversion" is a problem, even while we follow, in slow-motion, as her "gender" is "assigned" within the context of her adult parents' enigmatic, fantasmatic, sexual lives. We watch as Stephen blames and hates herself for how her body looks and how desire feels, and just when it seems like Stephen might finally be intimate and happy, we watch as she shatters any chance of acceding to a normal future. If it is frustrating and disappointing to watch Stephen surrender *yet again*, it is important to consider that while Stephen relies on the trope of her continued suffering to perpetuate the drama of her submission (to normativity in this instance), by the time she chooses writing over Mary, the trope becomes a powerful affect within which her "own voice" can, for the first time, emerge. Although it is precisely her default affective register—as lonely, freakish, and despairing—that we, as readers, want eventual relief from, these feelings bear the trace of how her parents treated her; their anxiety, shame, and mourning are what she stubbornly, unto the end, refuses to let go of. Except that, in spite of the tragic, "parental" tone in which she frames it, Stephen's final scene depicts the first encounter with a body and a "voice" that is "her own" even as—through the use of anguished and melodramatic affect—it insists on the inextricability of "gender" from specific "inscribers" and the impossibility therefore, of ultimate freedom from psychic relationships that, having been "assigned" us, persist. From this perspective, the difficulty of "looking backward" involves acknowledging that, as Love has said, "grief is politics" and "politics is inseparable from history" (128); but, I would also suggest, that "gender" is historical and lived in relationships that continue, in the present. Gender is relational.

In a recent clinical engagement with the question of non-normative gender and sexuality, Brian Kloppenberg writes, "The psychoanalytic mode of thought must be understood as an interminable process. . . . Rather than seeing Freud's contributions as a stumbling block to greater theoretical nuance, readers of Freud . . . demonstrate the radical potential in the psychoanalytic mode of thought and therefore the ongoing importance of engaging with Freud in our contemporary explorations of what it is to be sexual and gendered."[28] By focusing on the psychic quality of the subject's experience, we are confronted with the possibility of bewildering antinomies between people's conscious feelings about "gender" and their lived experiences in relationship to complex others. Laplanche insists that "gender" is ultimately inextricable from specific "inscribers" and it is impossible, therefore, to obtain ultimate freedom from psychic relationships that, having been "assigned" us, persist. What is a possible agenda for critical theory that has the radical relational subject at its center? In order to sustain its transformative aims and amplify its conceptual reach, critical theory requires and deserves a complex formulation of subjectivity wherein the subject is not merely something Theory struggles to plug into existing ideas of capitalism and ideology—to explain *after* its other arguments about sociality are formulated—but instead constitutes a source of theoretical complexity that challenges our understanding of the subject's plasticity and resilience.

6 / Two Girls²: Sedgwick + Berlant, Relational and Queer

Queer Relationality?

To readers familiar with the *anti*-relational topoi of queer studies, it may seem necessary to justify this final chapter's inquiry into the topic of relationality. After all, wouldn't the field's proud antipathy toward relationality's familiar tropes testify to a widely held *dis*interest in what people do together, or what it means and why it matters? And yet, what are the stakes of queer*ing* subjectivity if sex-without-the-mess-of-otherness is all that's finally achieved? Besides, if we have learned with Laplanche that sexuality originates in *relation* to others, by a process of involuntary relating that we can neither master, coincide with, nor avoid, what kind of queerness imagines it can celebrate sexuality by dismissing its constitutive relationality? In their recent dialogue, *Sex, or the Unbearable*, Lauren Berlant and Lee Edelman undertake to theorize relationality as a separable sphere of experience by locating "sex" as one scene among many of "relations that overwhelm and anchor us"[1] and suggesting an approach to "the scene of relationality" as a category of encounters that "disturbs the presumption of sovereignty ... specifically, an encounter with the estrangement and intimacy of being in relation. Sex is exemplary in the way it powerfully induces such encounters, but such encounters exceed those experiences we recognize as sex" (viii). This avowal of "relationality" as a capacious term that includes, but is not reducible to, a certain kind of psycho-sexual encounter, offers a way into this chapter's exposition of the relationship between queerness and relationality, and specifically, what relationality has to do with self-transformation.

I begin by exploring how efforts in contemporary critical and literary theory to explain the complex relational experiences of psychic subjectivities can be traced back to an unreflective reliance on applied Lacanian psychoanalysis as its only and ultimate interpretive apparatus. The chapter ends by drawing on Laplanche's radical innovations in metapsychology to develop new narrative trajectories for how knowledge is, relationally, transmitted and transformative. At this chapter's center is my encounter with Mary Gaitskill's novel, *Two Girls, Fat and Thin*, and Lauren Berlant's essay on Gaitskill's novel of the same name, "Two Girls, Fat and Thin." And because I first discovered this text while Berlant was my teacher and I was her student, and because this is an essay on relationality, at the center of my critical encounter with Gaitskill is also my pedagogic encounter with Berlant.

Although the particular "girls" named by the dyad vary depending on whether it is Gaitskill's novel (Dorothy/Justine), Berlant's essay (Lauren/ Eve), or my chapter (Student/Teacher), in every iteration the expression "two girls" functions as a formulation of the relationship between two girls in the moment of some kind of learning. Although Gaitskill has a distinctive oeuvre in contemporary American literature as an author of sexually and psychologically subversive fiction, and Berlant is unique in her prominence as a leading influential critic in both queer and affect theory, *Two Girls* is unusual among Gaitskill's works for using each girl's different relationship to a transformative teacher as the context for drawing out whatever intimacy they already or eventually share, and Berlant's essay is not an intervention in Gaitskill's critical reception so much as an occasion to reflect on the relationship between trauma and history via her own intimacy with, and juxtaposition to, fellow queer/affect theorist Eve Kosofsky Sedgwick. That is, rather than being exemplary of each thinker's abiding formal or thematic interests, "two girls" has the status of being unusual in each thinker's repertoire. (Gaitskill has two protagonists who take turns narrating the story, instead of one, and Berlant, who avowedly resists the tropes of self-experience, threads her close reading through autobiography.) My choice of these "atypical" texts magnified the curiosity of my own critical agenda: After all, even though I might find a clever way to justify these object choices, there is, perhaps, the crude arithmetic embarrassment that by the time one counts my own trauma/history as well as my own pedagogic relation to Berlant, there are enough traumatized girls in any given sentence to feel uneasy and discouraged about the chances that critique can be anything other than a feat of extraordinary sublimation. In the name of high theory, I often found myself wondering: How many "two girls" is *too* many girls?

By this I mean that I was suspicious of my motives. After all, isn't it unequivocally the case that nothing quite screams Oedipal rivalry like a younger thinker writing critically about an older one? In fact, for months the ostensible obviousness of this rhetorical/interpersonal act deterred me from approaching these texts. All I could think was that in my endeavor to problematize existing models of pedagogic transformation, I challenged my own teacher's explanatory paradigm, and, in so doing, didn't my radical critique of anxious influence sink before it ever sailed? Harold Bloom has most forcefully linked these terms together when, in *The Anxiety of Influence* (1973), all relations between younger and older poets could be explicable as some version of the paternal drama and all creative difference as agonistic overthrowing. Maternalizing this dynamic hasn't done much to radically challenge the explanatory hegemony of Freud's metapsychological account. That is, even where attempts have been made to imagine a softer, daughterly push between women—insofar as it presumes the familiar psychoanalytic teleology of transformation— such attempts invariably retain the symbolic coordinates of an Oedipal showdown.

Naturally, I bristled at the reduction of critical thought to such primitive psychological gestures, as if the need to compete, defy, or overcome my teacher offered an appropriate explanation for my argument or object choices. I grew sometimes weary, sometimes hysterical, to notice how defensive my every self-justifications seemed (*there's no such thing as objectivity! critique is hardly the most efficient means of differentiation! difference is a tribute not a method of retaliation!*). It wasn't difficult to concede that I was probably squeamish about my ambition, and aggression, but even when I allowed that this was something I probably needed to work through, a theoretical problem nagged at me: What was the distinctiveness of pedagogic relationality if self-transformation was always and only a reaction to the parental bond? And then I realized: What kind of motivational paradigm situates the relationship *before* the psychic events it enables? Wasn't the incoherence of these tropes, and critical theory's uncritical deployment of them, precisely the object of this critique? By using an idea of paternity as the template for all development, the Freudian/Bloomian topos of transformation generates a confused model of psychic motivation that somehow treats all the contortions of *becoming* as a reaction against relating rather than emblematic of how the pedagogic form is itself *already* the response to a constellation of common, overlapping, questions. Enforcing linear causality belies the distinctiveness of transformational phenomena. As a result, equating each figure in the dyad with its ostensibly transparent chronological position arrantly and incongruously misplaces how the motivation to relate comes *from* the experience of having one's own knowledge challenged and provoked by its dynamic relation to the knowledge of another.

And so, what if intellectual filiation did not need, necessarily, to culminate in the declared supersession of someone else's thought but could become instead the occasion for elaborating impact and relation? I want my way of reading to be a practice in the *relating* I seek to describe. That said, *reading* and *relating* are not an opposition here. This chapter is an argument that uses style to put pressure on how kinship is conceptualized by staging teacher-student relationality as both a topic and an experience of relating. Berlant refers to the unique potential of performative theory when she writes, "Reimagining forms of relation entails imagining new genres of experience" (ix) and it is to further elaborate this connection between theoretical writing and relational engagement that my encounter with Berlant takes the form it does here. Throughout, I want what I'll be calling "resonance"—the kinetic force that registers relation—to appear legible yet apart from relationality's existing tropological forms. This is, I believe, the dehiscence that Berlant shows us Gaitskill enables, and that Berlant uses Lacan to stitch closed.

Reading Berlant Reading *Two Girls*

Lauren Berlant's essay, "Two Girls, Fat and Thin," about Mary Gaitskill's novel of the same name is a powerful account of the connection between imagining alternative relational modes that are not reducible to conventional plots of desire and belonging, and understanding psychic subjectivities as too functionally incoherent and structurally inconsistent to be assimilated into dominant paradigms of attachment, history and sociality.² The novel tells the story of two girls who, in different but formally similar ways, are each abused by those who are entrusted with loving them, embody their damaged psyches through an array of compulsive fixations, and in varying degrees of rage, lethargy, and disappointment negate psychic itineraries that promise either redemption or cure. Summarizing the book's psychic-affective landscape, Berlant writes:

> Justine's response to Dorothy is at first like Dorothy's to her—a desire to tell a hard story to a stranger to whom she feels averse, followed by confusion about that impulse lived as ambivalence toward the person who animates it. Far more impersonal than Dorothy, Justine

has a slower emotional metabolism (yet Dorothy is the fat one, Justine the thin), but eventually she returns to Dorothy, sensing that Dorothy knows something that Justine cannot bear to know on her own. This meeting and return frame the book. . . . We witness them growing up paralyzed by fear and at the same time launching into madnesses of thinking, reading, eating, masturbating, attaching, and fucking. . . . If she wants a good life, what's a girl, or two girls, to do? When does the doing matter? (29)

The two girls of the novel meet through a shared interest in Anna Granite, the once famous and hypnotic Ayn Rand–like leader of a social and intellectual movement/cult called Definitism. Dorothy was infatuated with Granite and had left college to work for her, and Justine is now writing an article about her. With the prospective article as the novel's organizing center, the story traces the awkward conversations between these two girls who, except for a common investment in Granite, are strangers to each other. The girls keep meeting to discuss Dorothy's firsthand experience of Granite as a teacher/leader and repeatedly find themselves instead, or in parallel, swapping stories about their lives. But rather than eventually maturing into a more typical or recognizable genre of relating, the intimacy between these girls extends without ever quite graduating into a "normal" form. Much like "fat" and "thin" of the novel's title, each girl seems to retain their essential size and shape throughout the novel as if to literalize that they never merge into a unit/couple, nor that either girl ever loses or gains any weight from having taken in the other. This homeostatic situation threatens to buckle under the pressure of the novel's end when Dorothy feels betrayed and enraged by the scathing article Justine has written on Definitism and goes to Justine's house to confront her, but instead interrupts a dangerous S/M encounter, scares the guy away, and rather than unleashing her meticulous diatribe, takes Justine's naked, wounded body into her arms. But then, instead of climax or a breakthrough, they rest together and fall asleep.

The novel's ending "is not a lesbian ending, exactly," Berlant writes, "since exhaustion is neither sex, love, nor object choice," but it is "not nothing, it's something else" (152). This is just one example of Berlant's indefatigable commitment to protect the possibility of perplexing subtlety in strange and sometimes bewildering personal and interpersonal moments from the critic's interpretive overreach. One way that Berlant navigates this critical project is by continually breathing air into dominant explanatory frameworks, coaxing her peers to try (at least once?) trading their attachment to certainty for thought-experiments with non-coherence. In one such characteristic moment, Berlant writes: "In this habit of representing the intentional subject, a manifest lack of self-cultivating attention can easily become recast as irresponsibility, shallowness, resistance, refusal, or incapacity; and habit itself can begin to look deeply overmeaningful, such that addiction, reaction formation, conventional gesture clusters, or just being different can be read as heroic placeholders for resistance to something, affirmation of something, or a transformative desire."³ For Berlant, it could never be critically responsible to merely impugn people for trying, in her words, to "stay afloat" in the world under conditions of precarity and near-chronic oppression, nor could the epistemological comfort of any simple anti-formalism explain with any generosity or ingenuity how a subject can be something *other* than "performatively sovereign," *not* "deeply overmeaningful" and whose ways of being may be something *else* than "heroic placeholders for resistance to something, affirmation of something, or a transformative desire." Berlant unrelentingly deshames the value (and necessity) of binding oneself to a life raft by insisting that any analysis involving what people do to survive must seek out language that strives to capture the infinite subtlety of experiential encounters. In this way, Berlant keeps showing that no matter how sophisticatedly posed, assailing attachment for being "ideological" leads too readily and inevitably to judging people's effort to manage their lives—and bolstering with it the ideological apparatus it seeks to critique. By disrupting the putative "straight" line from ideology to a person's complex self-experience, Berlant's writing relentlessly avoids precisely the vulgar Marxist/Foucauldian relationship to ideology that we observed in Butler's totalizing conflation of "gender" with the Law, making Berlant one of the most deft psychologists in queer studies today.

Perhaps because of the idiosyncratic way that the personal/psychological and social/ideological are inextricably interdependent in Berlant's analysis, her work exemplifies the field's most sophisticated attempt to articulate the kind of subject that is at once "historical" *and* "psychological." Taking into account the Marxist and Foucauldian assaults on the myth of sovereign "individuality," Berlant locates her own approach to subjectivity somewhere in between the extremes of naïve psychological realism, on the one hand, and posthumanist abolitions of the subject on the other. This sense of her "between-ness" is not incidental to how she elaborates her critical position; rather than through polemic or critique, Berlant's particular approach unfolds through staged juxtapositions to the "strong" positions of other critics. In "Two Girls," Berlant's "impersonality" emerges in contrast to Sedgwick's commitment to the "person," whereas in *Sex, or the Unbearable*, Berlant's belief in relational repair stands out in contradistinction to the hard edges of Edelman's anti-relationality. Therefore, Berlant's position "between" the extremes of rela-tionality/anti-relationality—*less* personal than Sedgwick, *more* relational than Edelman—makes her work among the closest that contemporary critical theory comes to using the close-reading of a text in order to endeavor a defense of what motivates people to do whatever weird and confusing things they do, in the paradoxical and inexplicable ways they do it.[4] Berlant's wariness of the "overmeaningful" and "performatively sovereign" subject challenges the way psychology is typically deployed, where "a manifest lack of self-cultivating attention can easily become recast as irresponsibility, shallowness, resistance, refusal, or incapacity."[5] In so doing, her work can be seen to complement and powerfully extend the range of queer and affect theory's critical mission to unhinge psycho-logical acts and identities from habituated tropes of a normativizing interpretive determinism. But what I mean to show in reading the two readings of Berlant's essay—her reading of Gaitskill's novel and her own relationship to Sedgwick—is that although Berlant's analytic practice is rigorously *less* deterministic than conventional mobilizations of theory, the version of psychoanalysis it uses renders it ultimately no less *relation-ally* determined. Put another way, the anti-"personal," "anti-meaningful" approach Berlant mobilizes as a defense of critical nuance leads to an impoverished conceptualization of subjectivity that uniformly fails to explain the psychological transformations that occur as a result of com-plex, intimate relationality. As an alternative to Berlant's applied Laca-nianism, I develop Laplanche's concept of "reactivation" to propose a theory of "textuality" that foregrounds relationality as the foundation of subjectivity.

I will be exploring how Berlant's essay simultaneously elaborates the superabundance of what connects people to one another and refuses to allow the specificity of those connections to matter. Throughout her tour de force dilation of the ways all four girls are brought into relation, Ber-lant's essay performs being transformed by particular others while at the same time insisting on transformation as the formal effect of non-relational encounters. Given her singular purchase on the way interiority and ideology are inextricably linked, Berlant wants to emphasize that relationships can be powerful without being over-determined by heter-onormative tropes of kinship. For example, the way Berlant describes meeting Sedgwick ("She gave a paper, and we talked about it. Years later, I gave one, and she listened to it. She wrote another book, and I read it") versus her account of being impacted by her ("For me, though, the luck of encountering her grandiosity . . . is of unsurpassable consequence") seems deliberately to choreograph *as* a tension how little you can "know" the other person versus how transformed by them you can become. De-dramatization as a stylistic device is a powerful antidote to the inflated narratives of true love and true selves, love that occurs at first sight and the kind that completes you. But whereas Gaitskill amplifies the girls' entanglement to intensify epistemological pressure, Berlant collapses indeterminacy and structuralism to abrogate the question of what brings and holds these girls together.

Applying Lacan and the "poetics of *méconnaisance*," Berlant turns each girl into a "placeholder" that "they take personally but that has, in a sense, nothing to do with anything substantive about each other, except insofar as each woman functions formally as an enigmatic opportunity for something transformative" ("Two Girls, Fat and Thin," 127).⁶ Indeed, only a paragraph earlier Berlant points out that the girls' names, Dorothy Never and Justine Shade, are "shades of *The Wizard of Oz*, *Pale Fire*, and *Justine*" and in the accompanying footnote, that the novel's literary history "requires a story of its own." But this reference to Nabokov and repetition of "shade" might signal more than just the novel's general literariness and indicate instead a more substantial connection between Gaitskill and Nabokov's fictional projects. It is, after all, with a passage from a different Nabokov text that Gaitskill's own novel begins: "All one could do was to glimpse, amid the haze and chimeras, something real ahead, just as persons endowed with unusual persistence of diurnal cerebration are able to perceive in their deepest sleep, somewhere beyond the throes of an entangled and inept nightmare, the ordered reality of the waking hour."⁷ We are reminded here that Nabokov's technical virtuosity is singularly focused on tracking his obsession with the occult underpinnings of human behavior. Not only is Nabokov's oeuvre distinguished for its experimental preoccupations with doppelgangers (a pair of Nabokovian "two girls" might really be "one"?) but this prefatory passage expressly establishes the provocative dissonance between what we see and what we follow.

Therefore, although Berlant's essay captures and recreates the rich panoply of relational dyads and dynamics, it does so in order to repeatedly hollow out the relational mechanisms of any meaningful content, and to systematically insist that what underlies relationality must be either determinable or "hav[e] nothing to do with anything substantive about each other" (127). This repudiation of "anything substantive" is an extreme alternative to exegetic density; the choice between a claustrophobic hermeneutics and a permissive one is an ultimatum that prefigures Berlant's conflation of biography with psychology in the context of a text that seems so deliberately and with such virtuosity to crank up the tension between "everygirl" and peculiar ones, oracular forces and the mundane. The Marxist observation that even generic types can have eccentric variations seems insufficiently able to explain the novel's experimental logic because, instead of recuperating agency, it dramatizes the powerlessness, awkwardness, and erotics with which people are moved toward others for reasons that are strong and yet just out of perceptual reach. Berlant's reading is exemplary of the limited critical imagination with which contemporary theory, and affect/queer theory specifically, approaches relationality. Although, as it pertains to these questions, I mostly treat affect/queer theory as a homogenous discourse, this chapter traces a fundamental difference between Sedgwick and Berlant that Berlant's use of "two girls" as a narrative frame both addresses and absorbs. Specifically, what I think this analysis will show is that in the name of resisting a kind of prestructuralist psychoanalytic determinism, relationality, as a mechanism, has been drained of any material and psychological force and diffused instead into an empty "happening" that can determine everything that transpires around it without ever being accessible or worthy of curiosity and definition.

Theorizing Relationality in Queer/Affect Theory

If any discourse has seemed interested and equipped to offer a corrective to the limitations of a conventional, and conventionally deterministic, psychoanalytic interpretive regime, affect theory has been the most promising—not least because it uses as its founding text the essay by Eve Sedgwick and Adam Frank, "Shame in the Cybernetic Fold: Reading Silvan Tomkins," in which Tomkins's research on "affect" is hailed as the much-needed alternative to critical theory's overly psychoanalytic, insufficiently nuanced paradigms of human need and action.[8] Indeed, among queer theorists, Sedgwick has arguably done the most to try unmooring sexuality studies from its "trieb"-centered Freudian base. In *Touching Feeling*, Sedgwick writes, "The post-Romantic 'power/knowledge' regime that Foucault analyzes, the one that structures and propagates the repressive hypothesis, follows the Freudian understanding that one physiological drive—sexuality, libido, desire—is the ultimate source, and hence in Foucault's word is seen to embody the 'truth,' of human motivation, identity, and emotion."[9] Using Tomkins's affect theory to dislodge the "one physiological drive," Sedgwick and Frank show that as a fierce critic of Freudian drive theory, Tomkins long ago insisted on untying the knots made by confusing biological needs with emotional ones.

As Tomkins writes, "In the concepts of orality, the hunger drive mechanism was confused with the dependency-communion complex, which from the beginning is more general than the need for food and the situation of being fed. In the concept of anality, the elimination drive mechanism had been confused with the contempt-shame humiliation complex. . . . While it is true that oral, anal, and sexual aspects of these complexes are deeply disturbing and central to the psychopathology of many individuals, aspects not emphasized by Freud are more disturbing and more central to the psychopathology of others."[10] Although Tomkins does not directly address "relating" as a distinctive psychological mechanism, one reason his work has the quality of a breakthrough is its reorientation away from the tendency to theorize the subject in isolation and toward its imbrication in affective states, the environment, and others.

Sedgwick's use of Tomkins to insist on a new and different motivational structure avowedly compels a reevaluation of dominant explanatory models. While this call for nuance is not aimed at relationality specifically, the critical exasperation with "over-meaningful" accounts of psychic action, and interpretive limitedness more generally, promises fresh attention to dimensions of experience that have until now been systematically neglected. In their introduction to *The Affect Theory Reader*, Melissa Gregg and Gregory J. Seigworth write:

> Almost all of the tried-and-true handholds and footholds for so much critical-cultural-philosophical inquiry and for theory—subject/object, representation and meaning, rationality, consciousness, time and space, inside/outside, human/nonhuman, identity, structure, background/foreground, and so forth—become decidedly less sure and more nonsequential. . . . Because affect emerges out of muddy, unmediated relatedness and not in some dialectical reconciliation of cleanly oppositional elements of primary units, it makes easy compartmentalisms give way to thresholds and tensions, blends and blurs.[11]

As the writing and thinking in this passage illustrates, affect theory is characterized by a language of sensation, of "thresholds and tensions, blends and blurs," that eludes dominant critical "compartmentalisms" and that in doing so insists upon the "muddy, unmediated relatedness" of belonging in the world. This is an incredibly powerful framework, or slipping out from under what with a capital "F" becomes a "framework's" noose, that testifies to the imaginative and pragmatic opportunities made possible by having "no single, generalizable theory of affect" (3).

Indeed, in keeping with its multidisciplinary resources and commitment to expanding the critical and perceptual range of our interpretive practices, affect theory has a robust theoretical apparatus for reconceptualizing the relational context. Maurice Merleau-Ponty's phenomenological philosophy exerts one of the most crucial influences in this discursive landscape. Not only did Merleau-Ponty seek to undermine Cartesian mind-body dualism by demonstrating that all knowledge was necessarily "embodied," but his work on perception and psychology further demonstrates that all knowledge is *not* representational. Teresa Brennan's "transmission of affect" is extraordinarily helpful in further elucidating the conceptual consequences of reorienting our dominant physiological-psychological divide. Brennan writes, "The taken-for-grantedness of the emotionally contained subject is a residual bastion of Eurocentrism in critical thinking" and what "the transmission of affect means [is] that we are not self-contained in terms of our energies. There is no secure distinction between the 'individual' and the 'environment.'"[12] This *in*secure distinction "between the 'individual' and the 'environment'" is so important for Brennan because it opens up a whole new language for tracking embodied experience; "rather than the generational line of inheritance (the vertical line of history), the transmission of affect, conceptually, presupposes a horizontal line of transmission" via "olfaction and the circulation of blood," hormones, facial expressions, touch. One major claim resulting from this project is that perception is not contingent on representation; or put another way, what we *sense* of our/another's affect or experience does not need to be represent*able* in order to be *perceptually* operative.

Although opening the door to materialism can often sound like it slams the door on language, one of my points in this essay is not that affect gets us away from discourse, but that affect theory diversifies our analytic tools by focusing on a world of forces and impacts that are not reducible to, or identical with, those thematized by the structuralist paradigm.[13] This intellectual development seemed to me like an especially promising innovation for theorizing subjectivity, and metapsychology generally, because it put back at the center of analysis a rigorous respect for the singular dimensions of experiential life that are necessary to elucidating why, for example, people become the people they do, and how that happened. I realize that "materialism" as it is typically mobilized in philosophical discourse refers to "real-world" concerns like capitalism or the ecological crisis rather than phenomena in a subject's psychological life, but one of this essay's organizing contentions is that a narrow conceptualization of materiality (one that derogates psychology to immateriality) or of subjectivity (one that does not consider the conditions for transformation to be material in nature or effect) limits the radical potential of realist philosophy to change how existence in the lifeworld is thought and lived.

Coextensive with my conviction that metapsychological questions are integral to any materialist philosophical system is my interest in literary criticism as a "practical psychology." By this I mean that because the exercise of close reading is charged with the task of interpreting human action as it occurs in narrative form, a psychology of the subject is never abstract, or incidental to, the explanatory power of hermeneutic engagement. Therefore, for example, rather than looking for a logical flaw in Lacan's theorization of subjectivity, I consider how an applied-Lacanian reading reveals what may be missing in Lacan's theoretical system. Throughout, I draw upon Laplanche's theoretical interventions to consider how the models of subjectivity currently in use mitigate any sustained critical awareness of psycho-sexuality as intrusive, exogenous and originating in the material "other." It follows from my avowedly idiosyncratic use of literary criticism that I do not begin with any established theory of the subject but rather read closely trying to find one.[14]

"Textuality" and Relationality

Dorothy's account of how she met Justine opens the novel: "I entered the strange world of Justine Shade via a message on the bulletin board in a Laundromat filled with bitterness and the hot breath of dryers. 'Writer interested in talking to followers of Anna Granite. Please call —.' It was written in rigorous, precise, feminine print on a modest card displayed amidst dozens of cards, garish Xeroxed sheets, newsprint, and ragged tongues of paper" (*Two Girls, Fat and Thin*, 11). "Textuality" is a literal feature of their relationship and is linked, from the novel's first words, with a dual sense of casualness and fate; an eleven-word ad "displayed amidst dozens of cards" hardly seems to augur a life-altering event, but then again, what are the chances that the writer *of* the "index card" and the writer *in* the index card will be read by someone who both reads index cards in laundromats and happens to be among the former "followers of Anna Granite." Dorothy draws out the connection between fortuity and accident by saying, somewhat crankily, "The owners of this laundry establishment seem to have an especially lax policy when it comes to the bulletin board, and upon it any nut can advertise himself." For a moment it doesn't matter that Dorothy happened upon the "modest card"; it only matters that she almost didn't. Bemoaning the clutter of idiosyncratic longing, Dorothy's indignation reflects her discomfort with offhanded characterizations of Granite and meaningfulness generally. However, whereas Dorothy is indignant and overwhelmed that intimacy is mediated by "index cards" and "bulletin boards," Berlant is buoyed to find that getting to know Sedgwick by reading each other's books is "one place where the impersonality of intimacy can be transacted without harm to anyone" (126).

Elaborating on Berlant's formulation, I consider how "textuality" is not only a pattern of interacting *through* texts but a model for relating to each other *as* texts. I develop the term "textuality" to provide a non-hermeneutic account of psychological engagement. Instead of using "textuality" as a paradigm for all interpretive activity (as some branches of hermeneutics have),[15] I suggest that relationality is amplified when we consider that interpretive reading is not the only way to engage a text. As Laplanche has masterfully shown, within Freud's metapsychology there is no logical explanation of how unconscious sexuality *originates*. For Freud, it seems good enough to say that sexuality becomes a "drive" somewhat supernaturally, by being either an inborn feature of every psychic system or the sudden but inevitable outgrowth of infant development. But as Laplanche has persuasively shown, Freud's conflation of "instinct" and "drive" leads to a deeply problematic misunderstanding of how enlarged sexuality works. Describing this theoretical problem, Laplanche writes, "Instinct is hereditary, fixed, and adaptive; it starts with somatic tension, has a 'specific action' and a satisfying object, and leads to a sustained relaxation of the tension. In contrast, drive in the pure sense would not be hereditary, nor necessarily adaptive. The model of source, aim, and adequate object cannot easily be applied to the drive. I have insisted more than once, notably in relation to the idea of 'source,' that if one can say with any rigor that the anus is the source of anal drive, then one must question with even greater rigor how one could ever maintain that the drive to see, voyeurism, aims at lowering something that one could call 'ocular tension.'"[16] We know that instinctual life is predetermined by biology and we also know that adult sexuality is a fact of psychological experience but, within psychoanalytic metapsychology, we have no way of understanding *how* we get *from* basic, hardwired instinctuality *to* enlarged, unconscious sexuality.

Laplanche shows that in the absence of a logical explanation for how "drive" originates, Freud resorted to Lamarckian ideas about the phylogenetic transmission of universal psychic fantasies. That is, unable to explain how certain powerful emotional experiences developed in the individual,

Freud relied on the idea that ancestral social events could bridge the gap between "ancient interpersonal experiences and the universal underlying features of internal psychic structure,"[17] and that, when it came to "drive" sexuality, every individual acquired erotic interests out of some mysterious *endogenous* process. This move—from external events to internal reactions—was always Freud's particular talent; as noted earlier, he distinguished psychoanalysis from the therapeutic endeavors of Charcot precisely in this way, making subjective experience more psychologically meaningful than any particular traumatic event. However, while this move was extraordinarily successful in shining a light on a vast range of internal experience, it nearly immediately resulted in a well-worn philosophical problem, which was how then to account for the role of the *outside* world, and of the *other* person? As the psychoanalysts Stephen Mitchell and Jay Greenberg have observed, classical drive/structure theories echo the "highly *individualistic, atomistic tradition* of Locke and Hobbes in British political philosophy"(30) wherein "man cannot live outside society, but society is in a fundamental sense inimical to his very nature and precludes the possibility for his deepest, fullest satisfactions."[18] While in the Anglo-American tradition, relational theory has ventured to remedy the psyche's atomism by dispensing with drive altogether and instead reorienting psychology toward the interpersonal context, Laplanche takes a different approach that retains sexuality as the primary object of psychoanalysis but fundamentally transforms our understanding of how it works.

To do this, Laplanche situates the emergence of "drive" in the communicative exchanges *between* the adult and child. Emphatically rejecting Freud's efforts to make "drive" the spontaneous outgrowth of instinctual life, Laplanche instead suggests that we view sexuality as the inevitable result of the mind's developmental process, which is fundamentally dependent on the other/adult person. The fact of this dependence is extremely important for Laplanche insofar as it establishes a *channel* for the exchange of material between adult and child. Why is it so important for a channel to exist? Because, as Laplanche will show, once you have a mechanism for transmitting information between an adult and a child, then you also have a way of explaining where "drive" sexuality originates—which is in the unconscious of the adult. According to Laplanche, *seduction* names the fact that in order to survive, the human infant depends upon the adult as a caretaker but that this caretaker, who is an adult, also has an unconscious of his own. While in and of itself this statement hardly seems that radical, what Laplanche goes on to describe is the impact—on the child—of encountering the adult's unconscious sexuality. Specifically, that when faced with the adult's sexuality, the infant sets about to "translate" what she is picking up on. Why? Because to the infant, experiencing the adult's unconscious sexuality is an *affective* event. Laplanche writes, "It is only because the adult's messages are compromised by his sexual unconscious that, secondarily, the child's attempts at symbolization are set in motion, where the child actively works on material that is *already* sexual."[19] Although Laplanche does not ever explicate how "translation" or "symbolization" work at a technical or biopsychical level, our contemporary understanding of affect enables us to fill in the blanks. That is, viewed in terms of affect, unconscious sexuality can be understood to be areas of the adult's psychic life that have not been worked on by language or symbolization, meaning they are raw and largely unprocessed. While the adult may be undisturbed by what he doesn't consciously feel, the child has a different experience. For the child, repeatedly confronting large batches of unprocessed affect prompts regulatory action, propelling the child to diminish the intensity of incoming affect by setting to work on the material, "translating" it into images, fantasies, symbols, and so on. It is precisely this process of "translation" that establishes "drive" sexuality in the child. Understood functionally, affect is therefore able to explain what no theoretical program could explain without it—the development of unconscious sexuality. Laplanche calls this sequence of events the "Fundamental Anthropological Situation," by which he means that it is "the truly universal relation *between a child* who has no genetically programmed unconscious ('genetically innocent') and *an adult* (not necessarily the mother) who, psychoanalysis tells us, is inhabited by an unconscious. It is a situation that is absolutely ineluctable, even if the infant has no parents, and even if he is . . . a clone!"[20]

Laplanche outlines a profound and original hypothesis about how what propels psychological *becoming* is simultaneously forceful and enigmatic, external and nowhere we could know. This depiction of how the subject is constituted by its necessary *response* to an-other's desire is crucial for what I call "questions" because it foregrounds how the forces that shape object-relating have to do with being compelled by "messages" that a subject bears but did not generate on his own. Even more importantly, Laplanche's paradigm of unconscious sexuality challenges the popularity of projection as the dominant mechanism of interpsychic communication by showing how one person's psychological effects on another person are never as straightforward as the drama of misrecognition suggests. That is, if we take seriously Laplanche's insistence on the other person being an "other" to himself, then it becomes practically impossible to declare, as Berlant does, that what I respond to in the other person is only ever what *I* put into him. The problem with reducing all the complexity of dynamic relationality to the linear plot of transference is that "everything is constructed from the center, all mechanisms are conceived with, as subject, the person in question."²¹ "Is it possible," Laplanche asks, "for us to succeed in this intellectual conversion, this unimaginable 'version'? to abandon the centrifugal arrow, free ourselves from the idea that every-thing is already in Pierre's pouch" in which we continue to imagine that "everything would be in the internal 'convenience store,' and would be reduced to the simplistic question of 'moving the inside to the outside'" (226). What if instead of this classical model, we began to understand that each person—having been a "translator" of his parent's unconscious "messages" since infancy—has a store of "questions" that are susceptible to reactivation by any new person he meets?

If having one's "questions" reactivated by someone else's "questions" sounds like science fiction, that isn't incidental to Nabokov's effort—through webs of fortuities that stretch realism's range—to complicate the representation of reality's operation. We can observe a similar project at work in Gaitskill's text in the form of Dorothy as someone whose hyper-vigilance about connections and deeper meanings often seems desper-ately superstitious and vaguely paranoid. For example, after discovering the fateful "index card," Dorothy says: "When I woke in the afternoon, I called 'writer' again. Again, no response. Instead of relief, I felt irritation. Why had this person put his/her number on a bulletin board if he/she didn't have a machine to take calls? . . . 'Writer' had sent a quivering through my quotidian existence, and now everything was significant" (15). Even though Dorothy's exaggerated responses seem like they would automatically undermine her narrative credibility, Gaitskill's text instead consistently frustrates and disorients the distinction between Dorothy's acuity and her self-deception. After finally reaching Justine and arranging their first interview, Dorothy says, "I invented possible scenarios daily, growing more and more excited by the impending intellectual adventure" (17). This sounds like the kind of inflated imaginative reverie we come to expect from Dorothy until suddenly Dorothy's description aligns exactly with the story the novel will tell: "My wildest invention, however, didn't prepare me for what actually happened. . . . I had thought of Anna Gran-ite as the summit of my life, the definitive, devastating climax—and yet perhaps she had only been the foreshadowing catalyst for the connection that occurred between me and Justine, the bridge without which our lives would have continued to run their spiritually parallel courses" (17). By positioning Dorothy as the indefatigable apostle of life's mysterious underpinnings (and not just the deluded counterpart to Justine's jagged skepticism), the novel appoints Dorothy as the occult's eccentric beholder, whose perspicacity accurately captures the strange-yet-ordained quality of transformation.

Transformation and Relating

Dorothy's vivid depictions of her encounter with Granite are especially striking for their contrast with the scripted, impatient manner she has for talking about anything else. Consider the juxtaposition between the matter-of-fact style in which she reports having "been forced to have an incestuous affair with my father, starting at age fourteen" (26) with her recollection of first discovering Granite: "I read Anna Granite and suddenly a whole different way of looking at life was presented to me. She showed me that human beings can live in strength and honor. . . . And then the rest was just . . . the sheer beauty of her ideas . . . she held up a vision for me, and her vision helped me through terrible times. I mean, by the time I discovered Granite, I had just about given up" (28). Unlike the other moments where Dorothy dutifully and begrudgingly itemizes her traumas, this description of Granite is the first time Dorothy sounds *narrative*. Whereas trying to answer the interview questions felt coarse and unintuitive—at one point Dorothy even says, "I regarded Justine with dislike and awaited her next prepackaged question" (32)—talking about Granite recreates the aura of romance and transformation.

In her descriptions of discovering Sedgwick, Berlant imitates Dorothy's narrative arc when she says, "Eve Sedgwick's work has changed sexuality's history and destiny. She is a referent, and there is a professional field with a jargon and things, and articles and books that summarize it. For me, though, the luck of encountering her grandiosity, her belief that it is good to disseminate the intelligent force of an attachment to a thing, a thought, a sensation, is of unsurpassable consequence" ("Two Girls, Fat and Thin," 122). When later in the essay Berlant offers an account of how it is that another person can effectuate such impactful transformation, the concept of "emancipatory form" is introduced to suggest that, "in the spectacularly alien capacity to absorb a person, to take her out of her old way of being whether or not she finds a place elsewhere," the "emancipatory form does not require a particular content but instead the capacity to be both surprised and confirmed by an attachment of which one knows little" (141). Non-specificity is an essential feature of the "emancipatory form" because what the subject experiences as transformative isn't anything "particular" about the object per se, but "in the spectacularly alien

capacity to absorb a person, to take her out of her old way of being."
Transformation is a version of absorption, and given the immense burden of Dorothy's traumatic past, it is no wonder that, according to Berlant, "the most thematic but not least dramatic instance of this double
movement is in Dorothy's encounter with Granite."

Privileging the formalism of a transformative event is crucial to understanding what people do to have and hold onto their optimism, but in the
commitment to "deshame fantasmatic attachments" there is a wholesale
flattening of relational forms into things that have value *despite* their
"particular content." Working against the critical tendency to devalue and
dismiss the subject's strategies for "staying afloat," Berlant's essay seeks to
redeem the silly or sentimental cathexis by demonstrating that fantasy-
based attachment is on a spectrum of projective need, not a symptom of
the proletariat's errancy. The twofold implication here is that fantasy is the
universal mechanism of everyone's object relations (everyone does it) and
it is the common ground for all different kinds of object relations (every
relationship is equally fantasmatic). An interpretive model that takes the
subject's self-alienation as presumptive opens up innumerable possibilities for being curious and compassionate about all that compels us
toward/away from each other and ourselves. But then what is the specificity of being transformed as a process of becoming-different? Here I think
we can begin to perceive a non-difference, in Berlant's account, between
"absorption" as a technique for managing anxiety and pain versus "relating" as the connection to an object that enables psychic change. In fact,
extrapolating from this conflation of absorption with relating, it is as
though all attachment becomes functionally identical to any other compulsion for managing distress. Can individuals use objects outside over-
determined circuits of meaning? This seems indisputable to me. And
where in doubt, Berlant's oeuvre resolutely shows that pleasure and relief
are not derived from necessarily "coherent" or "appropriate" activities.
But how can we make the leap from this observation to the notion that
there is no difference between being absorbed and being transformed
because an identical mechanism underlies both—a need getting met—
unless we consider transformation as somehow dissociable from psychic
relating?

Indeed, Berlant insists on severing the association between "particular content" and "emancipatory form" even as the novel and essay
proliferate evocative glimpses of barely symbolized, non-conscious, non-
representational "communication" between each set of girls. Dorothy
describes the power of Granite as "the first writer, ever" who "showed me
that human beings can live in strength and honor, not oppositional to it"

(27). Berlant replicates the rhythm of this scene when she says of Sedgwick's work, "To admit your surprising attachments, to trace your transformation over the course of a long (life) sentence, is sentience—that's
what I've learned" ("Two Girls, Fat and Thin," 122). Here and elsewhere,
scenes of learning refer to something *specific* about the object-as-teacher
that makes a given interchange transformative. And yet, when Berlant
conflates "absorption" and "relating" it is because "a poetics of misrecognition" redescribes all attachment as motivated by the projection upon
the object of a fantasmatic need. In his theory of the "mirror stage," Lacan
uses the child's experience of registering the disjunction between his
"unorganized jumble of sensations and impulses" and the reflection of a
"unified surface appearance similar to that of the child's far more capable,
coordinated, and powerful parents"²² to demonstrate the subject's foundational self-estrangement, the impossibility of aspiring to a True self and
the comedy of encountering, in every other, a self that is always already
mediated by fantasy. Using Lacan's formulation, Berlant writes that, "Misrecognition (*méconnaisance*) describes the psychic process by which fantasy recalibrates what we encounter so that we can imagine that something
or someone can fulfill our desire: its operation is central to the state of
cruel optimism. To misrecognize is not to err, but to project qualities onto
something so that we can love, hate, and manipulate it for having those
qualities—which it might or might not have" (122). The subject of this
scenario attempts to get what it needs and what it needs is, ultimately, to
manage confusion and get some relief. There can be a diversity of objects
who provide this and a multiplicity of means, but the need to "imagine
that something or someone can fulfill our desire" is the subject's most
elementary wish.

Berlant treats the "poetics of misrecognition" as an analytic formulation that, despite their slightly different critical investments, she and
Sedgwick both share. According to Berlant, "Sedgwick seeks to read every
word the subject writes (she believes in the author) to establish the avowed
and disavowed patterns of his or her desire, and then understands those
repetitions in terms of a story about sexuality that does not exist yet as a
convention or an identity. . . . The queer tendency of this method is to put
one's attachments back into play and into pleasure, into knowledge, into
worlds. It is to admit that they matter" (123). But "my world," Berlant
writes a few paragraphs later, "operates according to a proximate, but
different, fantasy of disappointment, optimism, aversion, and attachment than the one I attribute to Eve." Berlant avers that "this distinction
is not an opposition" because, "like Eve, I desire to angle knowledge
toward and from the places where it is (and we are) impossible. But

individuality—that monument of liberal fantasy, that site of commodity fetishism, that project of certain psychoanalytic desires, that sign of cultural and national modernity—is to me a contrary form. . . . There is an orientation toward interiority in much queer theory that brings me up short and makes me wonder: Must the project of queerness start 'inside' of the subject and spread out from there?" (125). To illustrate this point biographically, even though "in writing this way I am working against my own inclination," Berlant writes:

> My story, if I wrote it, would locate its optimism in a crowded scene too, but mine was dominated by a general environment not of thriving but of disappointment, contempt, and threat. I salvaged my capacity to attach to persons by reconceiving of both their violence and their love as impersonal. *This isn't about me.* This has had some unpleasant effects, as you might imagine. But it was also a way to protect my optimism. Selves seemed like ruthless personalizers. In contrast, to think of the world as organized around the impersonality of the structures and practices that conventionalize desire, intimacy, and even one's own personhood was to realize how uninevitable the experience of being personal, of having a personality, is. (125)

In what might otherwise be a heartbreaking glimpse of a terrifying childhood, Berlant insists instead that the subject's capacity to survive and the quality of her object-relating are not, necessarily, linked. This breach between attachment and personhood anticipates the disconnection between particular objects and impacted subjectivity that Berlant asserts is fundamental to every transformative relation. Moreover, by applying "this isn't about me" to object relating tout court, and transformative encounters especially, Berlant uses her interpretation of what transpires between two sets of fat and thin girls to prove that transformation is not about getting "personal"—because look at all the ways these women do not know or even care about each other—and subjectivity is not about being transformed—because motivation and the interiority it fabricates is a psychological and hermeneutic luxury for those who aren't simply desperately trying to "stay afloat."

What "staying afloat" shares with the "poetics of misrecognition" is a conceptualization of what constitutes the subject's basic needs. But this idea of the subject who relates by fantasmatically conforming the outside object to his internal needs depends upon the assertion that biological self-preservation and psychological growth are structurally and economically identical and moreover, that psychic development works the way eating does. Laplanche vigorously warns: "We must *refuse to believe*

TWO GIRLS^2 / 191

in the illusion that Freud proposes. From the hat of hunger, from a self-preservative instinct, Freud the illusionist claims to produce the rabbit of sexuality, as if by magic. This is only possible if sexuality has been hidden somewhere from the start."[23] While the experience of being fed and the mirror stage are different developmental moments, Laplanche identifies how both fables share the modeling of *all* psychic need on the mechanism of *alimentary* satisfaction. Because for Laplanche, the satisfaction of needs (milk) is always part of someone else's sexuality (breast), the notion that adult desire is autocentric, conscious, or necessarily even aligned with self-preservation belies the fact that there never was an object who was only or simply the provider of alimentary needs. Even the "provider" had a psychology that, while dispensing food, was also "enigmatic" and whose enigmas demanded the subject's "translation" and response. Therefore, whereas "self-preservation" (eating) works according to a principle of pleasure (satiety and the reduction of tension), the "drive" denotes a force that is "not goal-directed," "variable from one individual to the next," "determined by the individual's history," and that works according to a principle of excitation (increase in tension).[24] Because the drive "is bound to fantasy, which for its part is strictly personal," Berlant's insistence that desiring transformation is governed by the principle of "self-preservation" (survival) is incoherent to the extent that transformation is a product of the subject's fantasmatic life *as* constituted by relating to others. Transformation is not a basic need that can be efficiently met but a function of an idiosyncratic psyche pursuing *becoming*. Asking why an individual would attach to things that militate against flourishing presumes that somehow flourishing is dissociable from attachment. But while this construct makes sense within a Marxist frame, in a psychological one there is no way to separate what's in a subject's "interests" from the objects of attachment; the "interest" of the subject is survival and attachment is the means. "Cruel optimism" risks tautology by using psychological principles to redescribe a problematic those same principles presume.

Fat vs. Thin, Personal/Impersonal

Gaitskill uses this "fat/thin" distinction aesthetically and descriptively to denote the different psychic and environmental textures of each girl's experiential world, and in her essay Berlant elaborates this imagined juxtaposition by grafting onto "fat" and "thin" literal distinctions between her and Sedgwick (Sedgwick writes about being fat, Berlant talks about her asceticism) and conceptual ones, between personal and impersonal, biography and anti-biography, attachment and detachment. This over-arching categorization meditates on fat/thin as a difference of relational intensity that is concretely expressed in each girl's relationship to the ped-agogic object at the novel center: Dorothy is *over*-identified with Granite, imitative, infatuated, evangelical, while Justine is skeptical of Granite, journalistic, curious, interested in writing *about* her but not in becom-ing an actual acolyte. And so, although both "fat" and "thin" represent modes of impersonality, they each also figure for notably different rela-tional tendencies, such as: Dorothy/Sedgwick/Fat = voracious, entitled, outstretched vs. Justine/Berlant/Thin = aloof, apart, contained. (Insisting on relating and what my relating might mean, I think, though I'm skinny, we know whose company I'm in.) What is suggestive about Berlant's met-aphoric framing of relational styles in metabolic terms is that it consigns relationality to a spectrum of "greater" or "lesser" degrees of aggression (grandiosity) and demand (projection), the result of which is that Justine behaves fantasmatically and Dorothy tends to make-believe. However, the novel and essay contradict the classification she constructs: Not only are both girls compelled by Granite, even if Justine seems impassive and Dorothy feels cosmically ordained, but both the novel and the essay depend, for their existence, on thin girls trying to be intimate with what fat girls say they love.

The implications of this fat/thin distinction are not limited to analyses of each girl's fantasmatic range, but serve, in Berlant's essay, to characterize the different appetitive profiles of critical interpretation. Although the essay begins by sketching her and Sedgwick's "different, but proximate" fantasies of personhood, and Berlant assures us that this "distinction is not an opposition," the essay progresses by systematically collocating possible avenues to psychological meaning, then dispersing them onto an all-exterior landscape of un-interpretable sensation and non-comprehensible events. If the subject is only ever fumbling and stumbling and trying to survive with a bare minimum of optimism intact, then attributing behav-ior to interiority and interpreting what motivates sexual or "textual" desire already aspires to explain over-meaningfully; as if trying to understand the subject in psychological terms becomes itself a sign of critical greed. Or critics more wounded and austere would never even *be* that hungry.

Although Berlant's suggestion to be less hungry critics, or at least to train ourselves to evacuate whatever "meaning" we ingest, complemented the discourse's direction as one that focused its interpretive energies on adumbrating the "thresholds, tensions, blends and blurs" and rejecting the big "compartmentalisms" of subject/object, representation, memory, time/space, and so on—it also enabled psychoanalysis to retain its status as the absolute explanatory paradigm of human behavior by ratifying "transference" as the preeminent mechanism of object-relating. If, beyond insinuating that opposite body types attract because they are symbolically complementary, Berlant's essay cannot account for what brings these girls together, it is because when everyone is a "ruthless personalizer," what motivates contact is not much deeper than how well (or badly) the other serves one's own projective longings. This uncritical reduction of all relating to "transference" and projection preserves psychoanalysis's ideology of the autocentric subject and, in doing so, simplifies intimacy and transformation precisely where queer theory seemed uniquely poised to complicate it.

Since the concept's debut in Freud's early writings to the contemporary proliferation of diverse typologies, "transference" has become the ur-mechanism for how subjects experience each other as familiar objects. Initially, Freud defined "transference" as "new editions or facsimiles of the impulses and fantasies that are aroused and made conscious during the progress of the analysis; but they have this peculiarity . . . that they replace some earlier person by the person of the physician."[25] No matter what brand of transference it is (sexual, negative, Oedipal, narcissistic, and so on), certain key features are consistent: Temporality moves forward and/or backward, shuffling between present, past, and future tenses; the directionality of affect flows only from inside and toward outside, in varying permutations of projection and identification; fantasy and need are the main impulses for transporting affect between objects even if other mechanisms like the body or landscape function interactively as well. As we will see, it is impossible for transference to be used without invoking a specific ideology of affect whereby fantasy originates in *me* and gets projected onto *you*. The word "transference" itself, with the root verb "transfer" describing the movement of something in someone to someone/thing somewhere else, bears the trace of the concept's particular genealogy in classical Freudian psychoanalysis where transference represented the patient's affective "resistance" to the "talking cure." Although the term's antagonistic dynamics have been notably softened by the development of a "two-person" framework, I argue that no matter how brazenly contemporary clinicians insist on increasing the ratio between neutrality and the reality of an interpersonal context, the philosophical foundations of transference retain the infrastructure of a psychic subject whose experience originates in a monolithic historical past that gets reimposed on an otherwise innocent relational present.[26] Indeed, Sedgwick's mobilization of Tomkins's affect theory is directed at dethroning Freudian/Lacanian metapsychology at exactly the point where psychoanalytic formulations reduce subjectivity to a crude relational determinism and psychobiology. By showing that affects *motivate*, Sedgwick uses Tomkins to show that new possibilities emerge for interpreting the subject's experience. How, then, can we understand the totalizing reductiveness by which what happens between "two girls" becomes no more than a transferential event, the formal effect of the general wish each girl projects "for something transformative"?

As a critique of individuality—"that monument of liberal fantasy, that site of commodity fetishism, that project of certain psychoanalytic desires, that sign of cultural and national modernity"—Berlant's impersonality would seem, nearly automatically, to demand the dissolution of the auto-centric subject. However, by conflating all of psychology with (available/interior) consciousness, and flattening all relating into need-based projection, Berlant corroborates transference and its enforcement of psychoanalysis's most persistent and totalizing myths: that transformative relating is exogenous to the constitution of subjectivity. As an argument, Berlant's use of her relationship to Sedgwick, and Dorothy's relationship to Justine, to prove that relating does not need to be personal to be transformative, depends for its cogency on conflating biography with psychology, but they are not, after all, the same thing. In fact, it is precisely the tension *between* them that animates and challenges the critic's interpretive task. As such, while defending the subject's rights to incoherence is a vital hermeneutic precept, limiting the subject's psychological processes to originating "basic" needs and meeting them consolidates the subject's absolute, autarkic role. What about becoming-different as a form of relating irreducible to "getting by" or ontogenesis? After all, a girl whose compulsions we can't read and a girl whose compulsions have no meaning are two different things. Ruth Leys's seminal critique of affect theory's "anti-intentionalism"[27] echoes this chapter's observation that "a materialist theory that suspends considerations of meaning or intentionality in order to produce an account of the affects as inherently organic (indeed inherently mechanical) in nature"[28] is necessarily committed to an idea of emotions as "inherently objectless" so that, even though "I laugh when I am tickled," "I am not laughing *at you*." Laughing, but "not *at you*" helpfully demonstrates how affect theory's "anti-intentionalism" is practically contingent upon, and responsible for, a *non*-relational metapsychological framework. To extrapolate even further from these observations, I would suggest that the compatibility of Lacanian metapsychology with a Deleuzian ontology of immanence and non-representational theory occludes affect theory's *de*psychologization of relationality because linguistic structuralism effectively *materializes* psychic action into generalized "forms" that

are beyond personal, relational or concrete "content." I think it is a specific kind of formalism that is organized *against* the content of anything
"personal" about the object or relation that enables Berlant to claim that
what is transformative is the *self's* "impersonal," non-psychological
attachment to the object, not something—however imperceptible or non-
representational—that happens *between* them.

"Resonance" and Relationality

Perhaps the measure of how far affect theory moves us toward a new
vocabulary for describing relational experience while simultaneously cir-
cumscribing the theoretical range of what it will capably radicalize is evident in the different ways "resonance" can be understood. Berlant uses
"resonance" to characterize the sensation Dorothy and Justine experience
when they first meet: "At the time of their meeting, neither Justine nor
Dorothy has had a good conversation with anyone in many years. . . . Yet
from the moment of their initial phone call they resonate with each other,
a resonance that they take personally but that has, in a sense, nothing to
do with anything substantive about each other" (127). "Resonance" recurs
often in affect theory and in the phenomenological thought influenced
by Merleau-Ponty, offering, as it does, a term for signaling a "felt" occur-
rence that is not necessarily assimilable into linguistic representation or
more concrete signification. I want to suggest that in order for each girl
to function "formally" rather than "substantive[ly]" for each other, for
"formalism" to be juxtaposed to "content" in this way, we also have to
imagine that the "resonance that they take personally" can be physiological without being psychological, or, put another way, that in order to
be perceptual, meaning has to be perceptible, too. But Merleau-Ponty
uses "perceptual meaning" in a functionally similar way to Laplanche's
"psychic reality"—to denote an alternative logic of development that is
simultaneously constitutive of subjectivity *and* relationality, irreducible
to biological or linguistic reductionism, singular and not-me, singular
because *I* am where I respond to the *other*. If it is through the self's movement in relation to others that a self develops, then "resonance" is an
exemplary encounter with movement *as* being-moved that is not necessarily accessible to signification.

Therefore, whereas "resonance" within an applied Lacanian model
merely complements the affective topography of an ultimately transferential event, in a Laplanchian-inflected formulation of relational
encountering, "resonance" is how the impact of a transformative "textual" engagement becomes registered, non-meaningfully. This means that

we can "resonate" with an other even though we cannot know *what* or *why* or even *how*—only *that* we are resonant and, because our knowledge is embodied, because "textuality" lives in our gestures and glances, our resonance *means* even if we will never know *what* it means. This "resonance" that happens between subjectivities is not, then, a narrative moment where form exceeds or supersedes content, but a psycho-physiological instant that attunes me to my "textual" self, and to myself *as* "textual."

I have used "textuality" to refer to the *questions* (Laplanchian "messages") that propel transformative "relating" and "textual desire" to the need/wish to experience these questions *as* questions. What I want now to add to this formulation is the mechanism that links these two concepts, something Laplanche calls "reactivation":

> The translation of the enigmatic adult message doesn't happen all at once but *in two moments* . . . in the first moment, the message is simply inscribed or implanted, without being understood. It is as if maintained or held in position under a thin layer of consciousness, or *under the skin*. In a second moment the message is reactivated from within. It acts like an internal foreign body that must at all costs be mastered and integrated.[29]

The psychic mechanism Laplanche outlines makes it possible to imagine relationality as an experience of one's own "messages" being "reactivated" by the "messages" of another. What distinguishes this model from what Laplanche often refers to as the "trans-individual structures" of Lacanian "language," or the fantasmatic activity of Kleinian "projection," is that only a specific, concrete other whose "messages" *resonate* with my own can provoke the "reactivation" of my "untranslated" questions. This is the reality of the "message," i.e. of the "signifier as it is addressed by someone to someone." According to Laplanche, "to project, to introject, to identify, to disavow, to foreclose etc.—all the verbs used by analytic theory to describe psychical processes share the feature of having as subject the individual in question: *I* project, *I* disavow, *I* foreclose, etc. What has been scotomised . . . quite simply, is the discovery that *the process originally comes from the other*. Processes in which the individual takes an *active* part are all secondary in relation to the originary moment, which is that of a passivity: that of seduction."[30] It is no longer possible to think psychic life archeologically because development is mediated by the concrete "other," and what the child bears as "knowledge" is only ever *already* a product of how "enigmatic" content has been idiosyncratically "translated." With this, Laplanche offers a way out of "transference's" determinism because there is no unified or legible scene that could be wished-for or repeated—only implanted "messages" shot through with affect and signification that in their exigency compel us toward we know not what, or whom.

Two Girls, Relational and Queer

This chapter suggests that *Two Girls* is an exemplary dramatization of how relationality unfolds in non-hermeneutic, non-teleological, indeterminate ways, for not only is Dorothy's response to Justine's "index"-card call for "followers of Anna Granite" *literally* an answer to Justine's question about Granite, but Dorothy's relationship to Granite is something that, for whatever reason, Justine wants an occasion to live with (and through) for a while. Why else would Justine want to write about it? And even then, why interview ex-acolytes? This is not an attempt to deduce unconscious motivations but instead to insist we take seriously the conditions that bind any of the girls writing or being written about "two girls." This means that we cannot treat as narrative coincidence that these two girls are brought together on either side of Granite (a teacher) and Definitism (a movement compelled by the search for Truth), even if it looks as though the intimacy between someone detachedly curious and someone who cathects heroically is reducible merely to the structural drama of a thin girl experiencing proximity to a fat one. Because even when the manifold effects of this "comic *méconnaisance*" seem weird and queer and enigmatic, sadly, the motivational mechanisms that underlie it never are. For although putting each girl's desperate, justifiable need for a transformative object at the center of their encounter suggests that phenomenological rawness proves attachment has been stripped unsentimentally down to the bone, it only really strips attachment of the complexity that renders it any kind of relationship whatsoever.

While the biographical data we're given is at once too limited and conventional to explain their respective attraction to Definitism or each other, the novel seems decidedly more provocative as an exercise in rendering, as links, the possible knots of psychic entanglement that it could sketch but barely, if ever, begin to untangle. Therefore, insofar as "resonance" aims to describe the powerful, mostly nonlinguistic and nonrepresentational, relational current connecting psychic subjectivities to each other, I want to read the ending as the beginning the novel has been working its way to elaborating. The ending is therefore not only, "not nothing," but radical because it isn't any kind of ending at all but rather a singular moment of elaboration, where the "sonorous" sense of "resonance" "can only emerge little by little, and no doubt with difficulty," halting and halted in a holding embrace, where the force undergirding their "resonance" emerges and can glimpse something of what "resonance" would look like if it never had to assume a relational form. Whereas for Berlant, this ending resists categorization by being ambiguous, I want to read this ending as the concrete expression of a "resonance" these girls have experienced in relationship to each other *from the beginning*.

In her essay's countermanding conversion of all meaningfulness into abstraction, Berlant valorizes their inscrutable "falling asleep" by ignoring that Dorothy interrupts Justine during an S/M scene, which, in a novel this bracingly deliberate, we have to consider as being about more than just salvation from violence (they've each had so much of that already) and instead about the ways their complimentary, enigmatic "questions" dramatically intersect. For Justine, this final S/M scene marks an escalation of the danger/pleasure ratio she has been testing throughout the novel. While Dorothy spends the novel attempting to regulate her desire by idealizing then denigrating her objects, Justine tries outsmarting her detachment by finding a viable spot between terror and indifference. Although each girl is preoccupied privately and outside any dialogue they're explicitly having, the novel's trajectory plots them on parallel paths that converge when they experience their struggles in *relation* to each other. Of course, to every thin girl sureness looks big, and to every fat girl deprivation needs saving. But calling this a relational dynamic is not identical to a conventional love plot. We need terms for distinguishing relationality from structures of compulsory kinship—otherwise all attachment is effectively heterosexual and all relationality automatically non-queer.

What Do Teachers Have to Do with "Two Girls"?

I doubt it is incidental that pedagogy brings all these unlikely pairs of girls into each other's orbit. While at first, Dorothy and Justine each perform rituals of projective appetitiveness that can make their cathexis to Anna Granite seem like the desperate attachment of students onto the teacher-hero as empty form, as the novel progresses we observe the way they circle and evade each other as if they are each compelled to keep sharing *something*. This isn't what happens *to* two girls *in spite* of their history but what happens *between* them *because* of it. Indeed, not only is Gaitskill's novel a story of "two girls" who meet through a teacher, and not only is Berlant's essay an account of what she learned and "Professor Sedgwick" taught, but Berlant's essay itself begins, and ends, with a sentence—"history is what hurts"—from her *own* teacher's text. Although

Fredric Jameson is nowhere situated as her teacherly interlocutor, Berlant implicitly avows the essay's pedagogic context when, in addition to her opening riff, "history hurts, but not only" (121), she later adds: "Here is a stupidity of mine: 'History is what hurts,' that motto of *The Political Unconscious*, is a phrase that I love. It resonates as truth; it performs a truth-effect in me. But because it is in the genre of the maxim, I have never tried to understand it. That is one project of this essay" (126). Again there is "resonance"—this time between Berlant and something she loves of what her teacher has said. And *what* is that "phrase I love" without ever "try[ing] to understand it" but her own teacher's idea of history's relation to subjectivity, genre, and trauma, a theory of transformation and impact that she distills her own meditation on traumatized subjectivity *in relation to*?

For that matter, what is that sentence from Jameson she calls "a stupidity of mine" but precisely a knowledge that she just does not yet "understand" because before she has a chance to intervene, it "performs a truth-effect in me?" Berlant blames the sentence's formalism for obstructing her access to critical self-reflection: "Because it is in the genre of the maxim," she says, "I have never tried to understand it." But isn't it actually the "genre" of *pedagogy* that makes this motto feel so unavailable to critique? For if teacher-student relationality has no phenomenological integrity that can't eventually be reduced to the hysterical relay of impersonal projections, then endeavoring to elaborate one's own textual objects has no recourse to engage a material, specifiable other. Indeed, her account of "a phrase that I love" is surrounded at every turn by references to its mystical genealogy, as if attachment can be either sensible or magical, legible or stupid, desperate or depressive. But if pedagogy is the condition of Berlant's attempt to push against what she calls her "stupidity" while writing about someone else from whom she's learned, and pedagogy is the context of Dorothy's initial struggle to become a girl who is not her father's daughter, a project she begins with Granite and resumes in relation to another girl's learning, it may be because resonating with the question another person asks *is* the only way to reactivate "messages" that I *have*, but have no access to?

What I think this means is that teachers are not those we learn from by "overthrowing"—besides, rage against temporal difference seems far more like the aging father's problem than the younger son's. But rather, we learn from those who help us survive our *questions* by inviting us into their own. Since resonances are partial and non-meaningfully known, difference is constitutive of attachment, not its retributive form. As such, if the pedagogic relation is so essential to every iteration of "two girls" it

200 / TWO GIRLS²

is because pedagogy cannot be reduced to merely another non-specific psychic mechanism of survival-by-any-projective-means necessary. Relationality is not *only* what happens in the suspension and disorganization of genre—a formulation that ultimately reifies social categorization by locating potentiality in materiality's elusive "elsewhere." Relationality is *how* "textuality" becomes transmissible and transformed. While contemporary critical and literary theory proliferates generative and rich possibilities for how subjectivity can be non-symptomologically experienced and expressed, it maintains a distinctly more limited imagination about what happens between subjects who are not only structural placeholders for abstract psychic functions but concrete others carrying "enigmatic messages" that "resonate" and compel. Insofar as relationality requires a methodology that foregrounds between-ness epistemologically, we need a metapsychology that can wonder how strangers reach and turn away from each other, how *Two Girls* is about what happens *between* two girls, and how it is what's elaborated *between* girls that is potentially transformative for *each* girl. To the extent that "history" is not *only* what "hurts," it is in no small part because of whom we meet and what, because of who they are, we find transformable, and transformed, about ourselves.

ACKNOWLEDGMENTS

Upon completing an earlier version of this work, Lee Edelman asked if this was my "farewell letter" to the field. Although I wasn't entirely sure what he meant, I imagined it had something to do with my complaints about the limits of queer theory, as well as my interest in psychoanalysis as a clinical practice and not just theoretical paradigm. I would like to believe that critiquing my field, even comprehensively, does not automatically equate to saying "farewell" to it and that there is a place within the discourse for what I've tried to say. I want to thank my teachers for supporting me and for never demanding that I share their views. If cultivating independence is one effect of "negativity," it has been my favorite kind. I want to thank Lee for his inimitable ferocity and grace. I want to thank Lauren Berlant for introducing me to the world of queer theory in Chicago over a decade ago. Everything she said was new to me and it blew me away and I knew, at the time, that I had found a discourse I could be attached to, even if ambivalently (is there any other way to *be* attached?). I want to thank her for holding my hand, by which I mean saying that teachers aren't for holding hands but for pointing students in a possible direction. This approach fit so well with my own inclinations. I want to thank all of my teachers at the University of Chicago for teaching me how to turn my questions into academic projects. At Tufts, I want to specifically also thank Christina Sharpe and Joe Litvak who have been generous and challenging readers.

Writing between critical theory and psychoanalysis is a special place and I want to thank Katie Gentile for being such an energizing friend and comrade. Meeting Katie and Lisa Baraitser at a conference on affect theory several years ago was so inspiring because they believed there was a place in contemporary theory for more rigorous psychological thought. Jessica Benjamin has been a dear friend who listened to many of these ideas in their earliest forms. Her passion for bridging the divide between critical theory and psychoanalysis has been an endless source of conversation and argument.

I want to thank Patricia Clough for her generous comments on my essays over the years, and for being an example of someone who lives in two different worlds at once. I want to thank Mari Ruti for being an incomparable critic, whose investment in making theory "work" is inspiring and gives me hope.

I want to thank the organizers of the many conferences where I've presented portions of this work over the years. I also want to thank the editors of *Criticism, Postmodern Culture* and *Studies in Gender and Sexuality.*

Thank you to Richard Morrison for being a wonderful editor and guiding me through this process with spirit and support.

And to Jonathan, who makes everything possible.

Notes

Introduction. Homo Psyche: On Queer Theory and Erotophobia

1. Jean Laplanche, "Masochism and the General Theory of Seduction," *Essays on Otherness*, trans. John Fletcher (New York: Routledge, 1999), 198.

2. Eve Kosofsky Sedgwick, *Epistemology of the Closet* (Berkeley: University of California Press, 2008), 1.

3. Annamarie Jagose, *Queer Theory: An Introduction* (New York: New York University Press, 1996), 1.

4. Jack Halberstam, "Public Thinker: Jack Halberstam on Wildness, Anarchy, and Growing up Punk," interview by Damon Young, *Public Books*, March 26, 2019.

5. Michael Warner, "Queer and Then?: The End of Queer Theory?" *The Chronicle of Higher Education, The Chronicle Review*, January 1, 2012.

6. Janet Halley and Andrew Parker, eds., *After Sex? On Writing Since Queer Theory* (Durham: Duke University Press, 2011), 1

7. Heather Love, "Queer Critique, Queer Refusal," *The Great Refusal: Herbert Marcuse and Contemporary Social Movements*, ed. Andrew Lamas, Todd Wolfson, and Peter N. Funke (Philadelphia: Temple University Press, 2017), 119.

8. See E. Patrick Johnson and Mae G. Henderson, eds., *Black Queer Studies: A Critical Anthology* (Durham: Duke University Press, 2005); Christina Sharpe, *In the Wake: On Blackness and Being* (Durham: Duke University Press, 2016); E. Patrick Johnson, *No Tea, No Shade: New Writings in Black Queer Studies* (Durham: Duke University Press, 2016).

9. David L. Eng, Judith Halberstam, Jose Esteban Munoz, "What's Queer about Queer Studies Now?" *Social Text* 23, 84–85 (Fall/Winter 2005): 11.

10. Snediker writes, "One doesn't really shatter when one is fucked, despite Bersani's accounts of it as such; millions of persons who imagine their subjectivity as fairly cohesive and nonfictive do not necessarily feel melancholy, even if Butler claims melancholy as the cost of that cohesiveness. If these models of shattering and gender-melancholy seem less than practiceable (or survivable) in lived experience, they've

become ubiquitous in the no less lived (if differently lived) biosphere of the academy" (Michael D. Snediker, *Queer Optimism: Lyric Personhood and Other Felicitous Persuasions* [Minneapolis: University of Minnesota Press, 2009], 13).

11. Amy Allen and Mari Ruti, *Critical Theory Between Klein and Lacan: A Dialogue* (New York: Bloomsbury, 2019), x.

12. Robyn Wiegman and Elizabeth A. Wilson, "Introduction: Antinormativity's Queer Conventions," *differences* (May 2015): 1–25.

13. In one of the most pointed rebuttals, Jack Halberstam writes: "For those of you who are still wondering what the answer is to the question posed by this volume of differences in the first place, namely 'what is queer studies without antinormativity,' I think I have an answer for you—it is disciplinary, neoliberal, no stakes, straight thinking." See "Straight Eye for the Queer Theorist—A Review of Queer Theory Without Antinormativity," bullybloggers.wordpress.com, Sept 12, 2015.

14. Bruno Latour, "Why Has Critique Run Out of Steam? From Matters of Fact to Matters of Concern," *Critical Inquiry* 30, no. 2 (Winter 2004): 225–48; Elizabeth S. Anker and Rita Felski, eds., *Critique and Postcritique* (Durham: Duke University Press, 2017); Stephen Best and Sharon Marcus, "Surface Reading: An Introduction," *Representations* 108, no. 1 (Fall 2009); Heather Love, "Close but Not Deep: Literary Ethics and the Descriptive Turn," *New Literary History* 41, no. 2 (Spring 2010).

15. Heather Love, "Close but Not Deep"; Lisa Ruddick, "When Nothing Is Cool" in *The Future of Scholarly Writing*, ed. Angelika Bammer and Ruth-Ellen Boetcher Joeres (New York: Palgrave, 2015), 71–86.

16. See, for example, Sharon Patricia Holland, Jasbir Puar, Christina Sharpe, Amber Jamilla Musser, Laura Kipnis, Michael Warner, Sara Ahmed, Joseph Penney, Valerie Rohy.

17. Kadji Amin, *Disturbing Attachments: Genet, Modern Pederasty, and Queer History* (Durham: Duke University Press, 2017), 183.

18. Joseph J. Fischel, *Sex and Harm in the Age of Consent* (Minneapolis: University of Minnesota Press, 2016).

19. Heather Love, "Doing Being Deviant: Deviance Studies, Description, and the Queer Ordinary," *differences* 26, no. 1 (2015): 74–95, 87.

20. Adrian Johnston, *Time Driven: Metapsychology and the Splitting of the Drive* (Chicago: Northwestern University Press: 2005), 11.

21. Jean Laplanche, *Freud and the Sexual*, trans. John Fletcher, Jonathan House, and Nicholas Ray (New York: Unconscious in Translation, 2011), 93.

22. See Lynne Huffer, *Mad for Foucault: Rethinking the Foundations of Queer Theory* (New York: Columbia University Press, 2010) for the most comprehensive analysis of this divide in queer studies. See also, Melissa Gregg and Gregory J. Seigworth, eds. *The Affect Theory Reader* (Durham: Duke University Press, 2010) for an account of how affect studies formalizes a decisive move away from psychological explanations.

23. There are a number of feminist critics who have challenged Lacanian psychoanalysis in significant and substantial ways, but for the most part the versions of Freud and Lacan that circulate most widely apply the paradigms of these metapsychological thinkers without changing them at all. A recent book that stages a "dialogue" between Amy Allen and Mari Ruti, *Critical Theory Between Klein and Lacan*, tries to challenge the dominance of Freud and Lacan by introducing the work of Melanie Klein (in Allen's work) and a more relationally oriented and ethical Lacan (in Ruti's work).

24. Huffer, *Mad for Foucault*, 135.

25. Joel Whitebook, "Against Interiority: Freud's Struggle with Psychoanalysis," *The Cambridge Companion to Foucault,* Second Edition, ed. Gary Gutting (Cambridge: Cambridge University Press, 2003), 337.

26. Tim Dean, *Beyond Sexuality* (Chicago: University of Chicago Press, 2000).

27. Lana Lin, *Freud's Jaw and Other Lost Objects: Fractured Subjectivity in the Face of Cancer* (New York: Fordham University Press, 2017), 18.

28. Tim Dean and Christopher Lane, eds., *Homosexuality and Psychoanalysis* (Chicago: University of Chicago Press, 2001), 1.

29. Noreen Giffney and Eve Watson, *Clinical Encounters in Sexuality: Psychoanalytic Practice and Queer Theory* (Santa Barbara: Punctum, 2017), 1.

30. Dean and Christopher Lane, *Homosexuality and Psychoanalysis,* 22.

31. Giffney and Watson, *Clinical Encounters in Sexuality,* 28.

32. Hortense Spiller's essay "Mama's Baby, Papa's Maybe: An American Grammar Book" is a tour de force exploration of the problem with psychoanalysis. See also, Christopher Lane, ed., *The Psychoanalysis of Race* (New York: Columbia University Press, 1998).

33. Gilles Deleuze and Felix Guattari, *Anti-Oedipus,* trans. Robert Hurley, Mark Seem, and Helen R. Lane (London: Continuum, 2004).

34. For a concise account of their position and its weaknesses compared to Lacan, see Dean, *Beyond Sexuality,* especially Chapter 6.

35. Laplanche, *Freud and the Sexual,* 248.

36. Jean Laplanche, *Freud and the Sexual,* 247.

37. Amy Allen and Brian O'Connor, eds., *Transitional Subjects: Critical Theory and Object Relations* (New York: Columbia University Press, 2019), 5.

38. Amy Allen, *The Politics of Our Selves: Power, Autonomy, and Gender in Contemporary Critical Theory* (New York: Columbia University Press, 2008), 12.

39. For a comprehensive account of this argument, see Mari Ruti's *The Ethics of Opting Out: Queer Theory's Defiant Subjects* (New York: Columbia University Press, 2017).

40. Some recent work that is exemplary of this effort is Snediker's writing on Winnicott: Michael Snediker, "Out of Line, On Hold: D. W. Winnicott's Queer Sensibilities," in *Clinical Encounters in Sexuality: Psychoanalytic Practice and Queer Theory,* ed. Noreen Giffney and Eve Watson (Santa Barbara: Punctum, 2017); Amy Allen writes on Klein, and Amanda Anderson has recently written about needing more psychoanalytic paradigms.

41. Noelle McAfee, "Politics and the Fear of Breakdown" in *Transitional Subjects: Critical Theory and Object Relations,* ed. Amy Allen and Brian O'Conner (New York: Columbia University Press, 2019), 224.

42. Robert S. Wallerstein, ed., *The Common Ground of Psychoanalysis* (Northvale: Jason Aronson, 1992); Lewis Aron, Sue Grand, and Joyce Slochower, eds., *Decentering Relational Theory: A Comparative Critique* (New York: Routledge, 2018); Arnold M. Cooper, "American Psychoanalysis Today: A Plurality of Orthodoxies," *Journal of the American Academy of Psychoanalysis and Dynamic Psychiatry* 36, no. 2, 235–53, 2008.

43. Term attributed to Roy Schafer.

44. Laplanche has become increasingly popular in recent years. As a student of Lacan who is widely considered the most rigorous reader of Freud, Laplanche has recently become the focus of increased clinical and scholarly interest, as evidenced by the recent retranslation of Laplanche's seminal text, *New Foundations for Psychoanalysis* (New York: Unconscious in Translation, 2017) and a series of conference roundtables

and journal articles dedicated to introducing Laplanche's thought to an English-speaking audience.

45. This is part of a much longer argument within the field of psychoanalysis but it is part of a debate about the value of pluralism and also the absence of theories of motivation—see Drew Westen.

46. I write about this in my project on Laplanche; see *Exigent Psychoanalysis: The Interventions of Jean Laplanche* (London: Routledge, 2021). For a brilliant account of contemporary pluralism, see Cooper, "American Psychoanalysis Today: A Plurality of Orthodoxies," *Journal of the American Academy of Psychoanalysis and Dynamic Psychiatry* 36, no. 2, 235–53.

47. Jean Laplanche, *Essays on Otherness*, 60.

48. Jean Laplanche, *Freud and the Sexual*, 36.

49. Jean Laplanche, *Essays on Otherness*, 147.

50. Jean Laplanche, *Freud and the Sexual*, 142.

51. Laplanche uses the word "enlarged" to refer to the kind of sexuality that is not reducible to genital sexuality. The editors of *Freud and the Sexual* write, "Laplanche invents a neologism in French by transforming the German component adjective *Sexual*—into a free-standing noun, in pointed contrast with the standard French term *sexuel*. . . . This is an attempt to register terminologically the difference between the enlarged Freudian notion of sexuality (le sexual) and the common sense or traditional notiona of a genital sexuality (le sexuel). This terminological innovation can't really be captured in English as the German term Sexual coincides exactly with the spelling of the standard English term 'sexual,' rather than contrasting with it as in French. The translators have chosen to signal Laplanche's neologism by italicizing *sexual*—pronouncing with a long 'a': ahl," 1.

52. Jean Laplanche, *Essays on Otherness*, 53.

53. Sigmund Freud, *On the History of the Psycho-Analytic Movement*, Standard Edition 14: 7–66 (London: Hogarth Press, 1914).

54. Jean Laplanche, *Freud and the Sexual*, 1.

55. Affect Regulation Theory is a popular new subject in neurobiology and affective neuroscience, although it remains largely unintegrated into popular psychoanalysis.

56. Adrian Johnston and Catherine Malabou, *Self and Emotional Life: Philosophy, Psychoanalysis, and Neuroscience* (New York: Columbia University Press), 224.

57. Therefore, much in the tradition of Freud's early "wish fulfillment" theory wherein every symptom is interpretable as the result of a latent conflict between prohibition and desire, today's emphasis on the thematics of failure, backwardness, cruelty, damage, disturbance, death, and terror, inscribes a sexuality that is structurally indistinct from its symbolic mediations.

58. Eve Kosofsky Sedgwick, "Paranoid Reading and Reparative Reading, or, You're So Paranoid You Probably Think This Essay Is About You," *Touching Feeling: Affect, Pedagogy, Performativity* (Durham: Duke University Press: 2003).

59. I have written specifically about Sedgwick's relationship to psychoanalysis and critique in "The *Mis*diagnosis of Critique," *Criticism: A Quarterly for Literature and the Arts* 61, no. 2 (Spring 2019): 191–219.

60. Huffer, *Mad for Foucault*, 137.

61. See Michael Warner, *The Trouble with Normal; Sex, Politics, and the Ethics of Queer Life* (Cambridge: Harvard University Press, 1999), 38.

62. Janet Halley and Andrew Parker, *After Sex*, 1.

63. Leo Bersani, "Is the Rectum a Grave?" in *Is the Rectum A Grave?* (Chicago: University of Chicago Press, 2010), 1.

64. Mikko Tuhkanen, ed. *Leo Bersani: Queer Theory and Beyond* (Albany: SUNY Press, 2004), 1.

65. I am thinking of Lauren Berlant's frequent retort, "yeah, but then you get up and go to the fridge and get a banana." Michael Snediker similarly observes that, "one doesn't really shatter when one is fucked, despite Bersani's accounts of it as such" (*Queer Optimism*, 12).

66. I am thinking of Jose Munoz and J. Halberstam who challenge the implications of Bersani's link between queer sex and death. See especially, Jose Esteban Munoz, *Cruising Utopia: The Then and There of Queer Futurity* (New York: New York University Press, 2009).

67. Mikko Tuhkanen, "Monadological Psychoanalysis: Bersani, Laplanche, Beckett," in *Leo Bersani: Queer Theory and Beyond*, ed. Mikko Tuhkanen (Albany: SUNY Press, 2004).

68. Wiegman and Wilson, 2015; Ruti, 2017; Warner, 1999.

69. Joseph Fischel, *Sex and Harm*.

70. Wiegman and Wilson, "Introduction: Antinormativity's Queer Conventions," 4.

71. Heather Love, *Feeling Backward* (Cambridge: Harvard University Press, 2007), 100–1; Radclyffe Hall, *The Well of Loneliness* (New York: Anchor, 1990).

72. For an excellent analysis of Berlant's singular oeuvre, see Virginia Jackson's essay, "The Function of Criticism at the Present Time," *Los Angeles Review of Books*, April 12, 2015. Online.

73. Lauren Berlant, *Cruel Optimism* (Durham: Duke University Press, 2011), 10.

74. Lauren Berlant, "Two Girls, Fat and Thin," in *Cruel Optimism*, and Mary Gaitskill's novel, *Two Girls, Fat and Thin*. Berlant's essay was originally written for a festschrift honoring Sedgwick; see Stephen M. Barber and David L. Clark, eds. *Regarding Sedgwick: Essays on Queer Culture and Critical Theory* (New York and London: Routledge, 2002).

75. For an incisive account of the differences among Horkheimer, Adorno, and Marcuse on the question of ideology critique, see Daniel Held, *Introduction to Critical Theory: Horkheimer to Habermas* (Berkeley: University of California Press, 1980). It would be interesting to consider the "antihomophobic" agenda of queer studies as it relates to Horkheimer's thinking about "progressive" theory.

76. I begin some of this work in my essay on affect theory and Laplanche in "The Ideology of Transference: Laplanche and Affect Theory," *Studies in Gender and Sexuality* 19, no 2 (April-June 2018): 89–105.

77. In her book-length dialogue with Amy Allen, Mari Ruti uses "progressive theory" to "mean the kind of theory that has profited from the insights of French poststructuralism, Lacanian psychoanalysis, Foucauldian biopolitics, Agamben's notion of bare life, and other continental philosophical trends, frequently combining these trends with cultural studies, political critique, ethnic studies, postcolonial studies, deconstructive feminism, and queer theory" (ix).

78. Laplanche, *Freud and the Sexual*, 1.

79. There has been scant appraisals of this kind. One notable exception is a conference that took place at The New School for Social Research in New York City, November 12, 2016, called "The La-La Showdown: A Lacan-Laplanche Debate." The presentations were

reprinted in *Division Review: A Quarterly Psychoanalytic Forum*, no.17 (Fall 2017). Most of the presenters were Lacanians, as were the organizers of the conference and journal.

80. Amanda Anderson, *The Way We Argue Now: A Study in the Cultures of Theory* (Princeton: Princeton University Press, 2006). Anderson writes: "An insistence on the subjective, psychological, or irreducibly human elements of ostensibly impersonal or objective theories informs much of contemporary scholarship in the humanities" (134).

1. What "Theory" Knew: Sedgwick, Queerness, Hermeneutics

1. Garth Greenwell, "I wanted something 100% pornographic and 100% high art: the joy of writing about sex," *The Guardian*, May 8, 2020.

2. Lynne Huffer, *Mad for Foucault: Rethinking the Foundations of Queer Theory* (New York: Columbia University Press, 2010), 137.

3. Tim Dean and Christopher Lane, eds., *Homosexuality and Psychoanalysis* (Chicago: University of Chicago Press, 2001), 3.

4. See Joel Whitebook's "Against Interiority" in *The Cambridge Companion to Foucault*, Second Edition, ed. Gary Gutting (Cambridge University Press, 2003); Amy Allen, *The Politics of Our Selves: Politics, Autonomy, and Gender in Contemporary Critical Theory* (New York: Columbia University Press, 2008); John Caputo and Mark Yount, eds., *Foucault and the Critique of Institutions*, Penn State University Press, 1993); Michel Foucault, *Mental Illness and Psychology*, trans. Alan Sheridan (Berkeley: University of California Press, 2008).

5. In her recent books, Mari Ruti has also insisted on the need for queer theory to use a different "relational" Lacan; see *The Ethics of Opting Out* and *Critical Theory between Klein and Lacan*.

6. Tim Dean, *Beyond Sexuality* (Chicago: University of Chicago Press, 2000), 5.

7. Dean, *Beyond Sexuality*, 222.

8. Similarly, Teresa de Lauretis has extensively engaged Freud, Lacan, and Laplanche in an attempt to develop a model of queer desire that can be sustained by the existing psychoanalytic template, finding in Freud and Lacan a "drive" that, like queerness, "offers no programme, no ethical position, no polemic, only queer figures of passing in the uninhabited space between mind and matter." See *Freud's Drive: Psychoanalysis, Literature and Film* (New York: Palgrave Macmillan, 2008), 87, for de Lauretis's most recent engagement with these ideas.

9. For a more detailed exploration of the role of affect studies in illuminating this developmental paradigm, see my article, "The Ideology of Transference: Laplanche and Affect Theory," *Studies in Gender and Sexuality* 19, no. 2 (April–June 2018): 89–105.

In a recent debate about the alternatives to psychoanalytic subjectivity, Lee Edelman asks Huffer: "What would motivate desubjectivation, after all, and where would its energies emerge from if such an 'ahistorical' antagonism didn't inhabit and divide the subject?" Lee Edelman, "An Ethics of Desubjectivation?," *differences* (December 2016): 106–17.

10. Sedgwick's status as a pioneer of an emerging field is traced to the publication in 1985 of her path-breaking *Between Men: English Literature and Male Homosocial Desire* (New York: Columbia University Press, 2016), and in 1990, *Epistemology of the Closet* (Berkeley: University of California Press, 2008). See Wayne Koestenbaum, Forward to *Between Men: English Literature and Male Homosocial Desire* (New York: Columbia University Press, 2016). For a more extensive history of the field, see also, Heather Love's *Looking Backward: Loss and the Politics of Queer History* (Durham:

Duke University Press, 2007), and Robyn Wiegman's "Eve's Triangles: Queer Studies beside Itself," in *Reading Sedgwick*, ed. Lauren Berlant (Durham: Duke University Press, 2019).

11. Stephen M. Barber and David L. Clark, eds., *Regarding Sedgwick: Essays on Queer Culture and Critical Theory* (New York: Routledge, 2002), 3.

12. See Barber and Clark *Regarding Sedgwick*, and a recent collection of essays in *Reading Sedgwick*, ed. Lauren Berlant (Durham: Duke University Press, 2019); for a wonderful essay on Sedgwick's unique style of queer theoretical writing, see Ramzi Fawa, "An Open Mesh of Possibilities: The Necessity of Eve Sedgwick in Dark Times," in *Reading Sedgwick*.

13. Barber and Clark, *Regarding Sedgwick*, 31.

14. Annamarie Jagose, *Queer Theory: An Introduction* (New York: New York University Press, 1996), 3.

15. David Halperin, *Saint Foucault: Towards A Gay Hagiography* (Oxford: Oxford University Press, 1995), 62.

16. Michael Warner, ed., *Fear of a Queer Planet: Queer Politics and Social Theory* (Minneapolis: University of Minnesota Press, 1993), xiii.

17. Max Horkheimer, "Traditional and Critical Theory," *Critical Theory: Selected Essays*, trans. Matthew J. O'Connell (New York: Continuum, 2002), 207. For Habermas's articulation of the status of critical theory today, see also, Axel Honneth, "Social Dynamics of Disrespect: Situating Critical Theory Today," in *Habermas: A Critical Reader*, ed. Peter Dews, 320–37 (Oxford: Blackwell: Oxford, 1999). For a comprehensive genealogy of critical theory as a field of study, see David Held, *Introduction to Critical Theory: Horkheimer to Habermas* (Berkeley: University of California Press, 1980).

18. Carla Freccero, *Queer/Early/Modern* (Durham: Duke University Press, 2006), 20.

19. Elizabeth Freeman, *Time Binds: Queer Temporalities, Queer Histories* (Durham: Duke University Press, 2010), xiii.

20. Sedgwick, *Epistemology of the Closet*, 12.

21. Eve Kosofsky Sedgwick, *Tendencies* (Durham: Duke University Press, 1993), 9.

22. Eve Kosofsky Sedgwick, *The Weather in Proust*, ed. Jonathan Goldberg (Durham: Duke University Press, 2011), 199.

23. Eve Kosofsky Sedgwick, "Paranoid Reading and Reparative Reading, or, You're So Paranoid You Probably Think This Essay Is About You," in *Touching Feeling: Affect, Pedagogy, Performativity* (Durham: Duke University Press, 2003).

24. Eve Kosofsky Sedgwick and Adam Frank, *Shame and Its Sisters: A Silvan Tomkins Reader* (Durham: Duke University Press, 1995), 16, 17.

25. Lauren Berlant and Lee Edelman, *Sex, or the Unbearable?* (Durham: Duke University Press, 2014), 45.

26. Koestenbaum, Forward to *Between Men*, xv.

27. Sedgwick, *Tendencies*, xiv.

28. Sedgwick, "A Poem Is Being Written," *Tendencies*, 209.

29. Karin Sellberg, "Queer Patience: Sedgwick's Identity Narratives" in *Reading Sedgwick*, ed. Lauren Berlant (Durham: Duke University Press, 2019), 194.

30. Articulating a possible alternative to psychoanalytic subjectivity, Elizabeth Grosz has drawn on Deleuze, Bergson, and Simendon to develop an alternative model of desire that dislocates psychic interiority in favor of "a mode of surface contact" in which the erotic is first and foremost an experience of the body. This exciting body of experimental theory emphasizes the emancipatory potential of reorienting subjectivity

in movement and fluidity, instead of development and representation, but the wholesale transcendence of object relations as a vital site of "being" and "becoming" makes it difficult to work with as an analytic tool outside of the most general metaphysical claims.

31. Jean Laplanche, *The Temptation of Biology*, trans. Donald Nicholson-Smith (New York: Unconscious in Translation, 2015), 127.

32. Adrian Johnston, *Time Driven: Metapsychology and the Splitting of the Drive* (Chicago: Northwestern University Press: 2005), 11.

33. J. Laplanche and J-B. Pontalis, *The Language of Psycho-Analysis*, trans. Donald Nicholson-Smith (New York: Norton, 1973), 249.

34. In "Levels of Proof," Laplanche draws on Karl Popper in order to explain that what distinguishes the "scientific" from the "metaphysical" is that the "scientific is that which is susceptible to being falsified and indicates the paths of its possible falsification" (246). Laplanche evaluates the metapsychological status of psychoanalysis according to Popper's levels of proof and contends that there are "intermediate levels between what one might call 'psychoanalytic doctrine,' to use Freud's term, or general metapsychology, and something I shall shortly call the 'mytho-symbolic.' Between these two levels there are the intermediate levels of theories of conflict, of psychopathology, of symptoms, of *Witz*, etc., even the theory of dreams. Would a modification of the theory of dreams necessarily entail a falsification of the whole of metapsychology? I don't think so. You see that the idea of a theory that is ultimately supple and open to reworking, a theory containing on the one hand a relatively dense kernel and on the other hand statements that are not deduced from the general theory, is valid not only for psychoanalysis but for every science" (Jean Laplanche, *Freud and the Sexual*, trans. John Fletcher, Jonathan House, and Nicholas Ray [New York: Unconscious in Translation, 2011], 240).

35. Charles Brenner wrote a classic essay articulating the "classical" defense of this argument and Merton Gill and Philip Holzman wrote from the other position, which came to be called the "hermeneutic" position within psychoanalytic theorizing.

36. Jean Laplanche, "Interpretation between Determinism and Hermeneutics," in *Essays on Otherness*, ed. John Fletcher (New York: Routledge, 1999), 147.

37. Dany Nobus, "Undoing Psychoanalysis: Towards a Clinical and Conceptual *Metistopia*," in *Clinical Encounters in Sexuality: Psychoanalytic Practice and Queer Theory*, ed. Noreen Giffney and Eve Watson (Santa Barbara: Punctum, 2017), 353.

38. Nobus, "Undoing Psychoanalysis," 353.

2. The Genealogy of Sex: Bersani, Laplanche, and Self-Shattering Sexuality

1. See Michael Warner, *The Trouble with Normal; Sex, Politics, and the Ethics of Queer Life* (Cambridge: Harvard University Press, 1999), 38.

2. Janet Halley and Andrew Parker, *After Sex: On Writing Since Queer Theory* (Durham: Duke University Press, 2011), 1.

3. Leo Bersani, "Is the Rectum a Grave?" in *Is the Rectum a Grave?* (Chicago: University of Chicago Press, 2010), 1.

4. Mikko Tuhkanen, ed., *Leo Bersani: Queer Theory and Beyond* (Albany: SUNY Press, 2004), 1.

5. I am thinking of Lauren Berlant's retort, "Yeah, but then you get up and go to the fridge and get a banana." Michael Snediker similarly observes, "One doesn't really

shatter when one is fucked, despite Bersani's accounts of it as such" (*Queer Optimism: Lyric Personhood and Other Felicitous Persuasions* [Minneapolis: University of Minnesota Press, 2009], 12).

6. I am thinking of Jose Munoz and J. Halberstam who challenge the implications of Bersani's link between queer sex and death.

7. Mikko Tuhkanen, "Monadological Psychoanalysis: Bersani, Laplanche, Beckett," in *Leo Bersani: Queer Theory and Beyond*, ed. Mikko Tuhkanen (Albany: SUNY Press, 2004).

8. In *Baudelaire and Freud*, Bersani writes in a footnote, "From here on, my discussion differs in important ways from Laplanche's analyses (especially the view I take of the relation between 'nonsexual sadism' [step one] and primary masochism)" (Leo Bersani, *Baudelaire and Freud* [Berkeley: University of California Press, 1977], 79).

9. Tuhkanen, "Monadological Psychoanalysis," 142.

10. Leo Bersani, *Homos* (Cambridge: Harvard University Press, 1995).

11. To my reading, *Homos* offers Bersani's most sustained direct engagement with other thinkers in queer studies. Specifically, his chapter "The Gay Absence" addresses Wittig's project at more length and challenges prevailing intellectual and political trends in the field.

12. Leo Bersani, Preface to *Is the Rectum a Grave?* (Chicago: University of Chicago Press, 2010), ix.

13. Leo Bersani, "Fr-oucault and the End of Sex" in *Is the Rectum a Grave?* (Chicago: University of Chicago Press, 2010), 137.

14. Bersani, "Fr-oucault and the End of Sex," 133.

15. Leo Bersani, "Why Sex?" YouTube. *SPI: The Society for Psychoanalytic Inquiry*, YouTube, January 8, 2014.

16. Leo Bersani, *The Freudian Body: Psychoanalysis and Art* (New York: Columbia University Press, 1986), 38.

17. Jean Laplanche, *Life and Death in Psychoanalysis*, trans. Jeffrey Mehlman (Baltimore: Johns Hopkins University Press, 1970), 88.

18. Leo Bersani, *The Culture of Redemption* (Cambridge: Harvard University Press, 1990), 45.

19. Leo Bersani and Ulysse Dutoit, *Forms of Being: Cinema, Aesthetics, Subjectivity* (London: BFI, 2004), 177.

20. Bersani, *Homos*, 81.

21. Bersani, "The Gay Daddy," in *Homos*, 95.

22. Leo Bersani and Ulysse Dutoit, *Acts of Impoverishment: Beckett, Rothko, Resnais* (Cambridge: Harvard University Press, 1993), 142.

23. Adam Phillips, *Intimacies*, ed. Leo Bersani and Adam Phillips (Chicago: University of Chicago Press, 2008), 94.

24. Jean Laplanche, *The Temptation of Biology: Freud's Theories of Sexuality*, trans. Donald Nicholson-Smith (New York: Unconscious in Translation, 2015), 121.

25. Jean Laplanche, *Freud and the Sexual*, trans. John Fletcher (New York: Unconscious in Translation, 2011), 43.

26. Laplanche offers three versions of the answer to this question: "(1) an impoverished interpretation that proposes a mechanistic parallelism; (2) an interpretation that makes it into a process of emergence; (3) a contrary interpretation, made in terms of seduction" (*Freud and the Sexual*, 45).

27. Dominique Scarfone, *Laplanche: An Introduction*, trans. Dorothee Bonnigal-Katz (New York: Unconscious in Translation, 2015), 21; Laplanche further delineates a

difference between "sexual instinct" and "sexual drive" in order to show that instinctive sexuality is not identical with drive sexuality.

28. Jean Laplanche, *New Foundations for Psychoanalysis*, trans. Jonathan House (New York: Unconscious in Translation, 2016), 124.

29. Laplanche, *Freud and the Sexual*, 44.

30. I think affect theory is an indispensable resource for understanding the process Laplanche is describing and I work some of that out in "The Ideology of Transference: Laplanche and Affect Theory," *Studies in Gender and Sexuality* 19, no. 2 (April–June 2018): 89–105.

31. By "structuralist" I am not referring to Lacan and linguistic structuralism (although Laplanche's relationship to Lacan is an important and relevant subject in its own right), but to Laplanche's insistence that in order for psychoanalysis to develop as a science it must offer explanations that it can verify by its own speculative rigor and analysis.

32. Jean Laplanche, "Masochism and the General Theory of Seduction," in *Essays on Otherness*, trans. John Fletcher (New York: Routledge, 1999), 198.

33. Laplanche, *Temptation of Biology*, 87.

34. Tuhkanen, "Monadological Psychoanalysis," 147.

35. Bersani, *The Culture of Redemption*, 45.

36. See Laplanche's essay, "The Unfinished Copernican Revolution," in *Essays on Otherness*, trans. John Fletcher (New York: Routledge, 1999).

37. Laplanche, "Transference: Its Provocation by the Analyst," in *Essays on Otherness*, trans. John Fletcher (New York: Routledge, 1999), 254.

38. Leo Bersani and Ulysse Dutoit, *Caravaggio's Secrets* (Cambridge: MIT Press, 1998), 40.

39. Patrick ffrench, "Addressing Oneself: Bersani and the Form/Fold of Self-Relation," in *Leo Bersani: Queer Theory and Beyond*, ed. Mikko Tuhkanen (Albany: SUNY Press, 2014), 135.

40. Bersani, "The Gay Outlaw," in *Homos*, 149.

41. For a more sustained exposition of these ideas, see Bersani's recent elaboration of "impersonal narcissism" in *Intimacies*.

42. Mikko Tuhkanen, Introduction to *Leo Bersani: Queer Theory and Beyond* (Albany: SUNY Press, 2014), 9.

43. Laplanche, *Essays on Otherness*, 82.

3. Boundaries Are for Sissies: Violation in Jane Gallop and Henry James

1. Joseph Fischel, *Sex and Harm in the Age of Consent* (Minneapolis: University of Minnesota Press, 2016), 15.

2. Jane Gallop, *Feminist Accused of Sexual Harassment* (Durham: Duke University Press, 1997).

3. Some of the most engaged and popular responses to Gallop's text include: Elaine Showalter, "Good Girl, Bad Girl," *London Review of Books*, June 5, 1997; Laura Duhan Kaplan, "Feminist Accused of Sexual Harassment" (Review), *Philosophy and Literature* 22, no. 2 (October 1998): 521–23; Janet Malcolm, "It happened in Milwaukee," *New York Review of Books*, October 23, 1997; Roger Kimball, "The Distinguished Professor," *The New Criterion* 36, no. 5 (April 1997).

4. Eve Kosofsky Sedgwick consecrates this contiguity between reading Henry James and the methodology of queer interpretation as such when, in "The Beast in the

NOTES TO PAGES 87–98 / 213

Closet," the penultimate essay in *Epistemology of the Closet* in which she offers a close reading of "The Beast in the Jungle," Sedgwick codes John Marcher's ignorance of his own "secret" as a story about "the irredeemably self-ignorant man who embodies and enforces heterosexual compulsion." Toward the essay's end, Sedgwick further wonders whether the relationship of May Bertram to John Marcher is not, at last, unlike the connection between a queer theorist and a closeted man.

5. Laura Kipnis, *Unwanted Advances: Sexual Paranoia Comes to Campus* (New York: Harper, 2017), 7.

6. For a recent exploration of feminism in the time of #MeToo, see "Sexual Politics, Sexual Panics," *differences* 30, no. 1 (May 2019).

7. Robyn Wiegman and Elizabeth A. Wilson, "Introduction: Antinormativity's Queer Conventions," *differences* (May 2019).

8. See James Kincaid's *Erotic Innocence* (Durham: Duke University Press, 1998). Kincaid identifies as "gothic" the stories we tell about childhood sexual abuse and focuses on the work this is doing for the consumer of these stories. Kincaid writes: "The stark moral drama offered by our child-molesting stories does suggest the possibility of scapegoating, or at least of a cover narrative camouflaging needs so dark and urgent we want neither to face them nor to give them up" (11). See also, Lee Edelman's *No Future* for a comprehensive analysis of the way normative ideology deploys the "child" to secure its homophobic agenda.

9. Lee Edelman, *No Future: Queer Theory and the Death Drive* (Durham: Duke University Press, 2004).

10. Ellis Hanson, "Teaching Shame," in *Gay Shame*, ed David M. Halperin and Valerie Traub (Chicago: University of Chicago Press, , 2009), 145. See also George E. Haggerty and Bonnie Zimmerman, eds., *Professions of Desire* (New York: MLA, 1995).

11. Jane Gallop and Lauren Berlant, "Loose Lips," Interview in *Our Monica, Ourselves: The Clinton Affair and the National Interest*, ed. Lauren Berlant and Lisa Duggan (New York: New York University Press, 2001); see also page 12.

12. Some more famous examples include *What Maisie Knew* and *The Turn of the Screw*.

13. Michel Foucault, "Friendship As a Way of Life" (Interview) in *Foucault Live: Collected Interviews, 1961–1984*, ed. Sylvere Lotringer, trans. Lysa Hochroth and John Johnston (New York: Semiotext(e), 1996), 309.

14. Michael Moon, *A Small Boy and Others: Imitation and Initiation in American Culture from Henry James to Andy Warhol* (Durham: Duke University Press, 1998). Moon writes about "The Pupil," but his focus is on sexuality, and particularly the relationship between Morgan's mother and Pemberton, the tutor; Bell focuses exclusively on the thematics of money.

15. Millicent Bell, "The Unmentionable Subject in 'The Pupil'" in *The Cambridge Companion to Henry James* (Cambridge: Cambridge University Press, 1998), 139.

16. Shoshana Felman, "Turning the Screw of Interpretation" in *The Turn of the Screw: A Norton Critical Edition*, Second Edition, ed. Deborah Esch and Jonathan Warren (New York: Norton, 1999), 217.

17. Sharon Cameron, *Thinking in Henry James* (Chicago: University of Chicago Press, 1989), 2.

18. Kevin Ohi, *Henry James and the Queerness of Style* (Minneapolis: University of Minnesota Press, 2011), 2.

19. Michael Anesko offers a comprehensive history of the critical reception of James, *Monopolizing the Master: Henry James and the Politics of Modern Literary*

Scholarship (Stanford: Stanford University Press, 2012). Also, as it has already been widely noted in the critical literature, much of recent criticism is an attempt to counter the effects of Leon Edel whose multi-volume biography of James and monopolistic control of his private letters enabled him to claim that James was assuredly celibate his entire life. In his recent biographical/literary study, *Portrait of a Novel*, Michael Gorra writes of the speculation around James's sexuality: "Other young men on a European tour found that the Continent offered them the chance for a safely anonymous sexual life. . . . James would have had such opportunities, but we will never learn if he took them . . . about some parts of his own life we must accept a sense of bafflement. He has never been convincingly linked to another person, and his precise mixture of self-knowledge and self-control, of repression and sublimation, remains a formula that we do not know" (Michael Gorra, *Portrait of a Novel: Henry James and the Making of an American Masterpiece* [New York: Liveright, 2013].) In her memoir, *Henry James at Work*, James's longtime secretary, Theodora Bosanquet, writes: "Many men whose prime business is the art of writing find rest and refreshment in other occupations. They marry or they keep dogs, they play golf or bridge, they study Sanskrit or collect postage stamps. Except for a period of ownership of a dachshund, Henry James did none of these things. He lived a life consecrated to the service of a jealous, insatiable, and supremely rewarding goddess, and all his activities had essential reference to that service" (Theodora Bosanquet, *Henry James at Work* [Ann Arbor: University of Michigan Press, 2007]).

20. Kevin Ohi, *Innocence and Rapture: The Erotic Child in Pater, Wilde, James, and Nabokov* (New York: Palgrave Macmillan, 2005), 5.

21. James Kincaid draws attention to this requisite acknowledgement that sexual "abuse" is "real" but also points out why this insistence forecloses more rigorous analysis of the dynamics underlying this "epidemic." See Kincaid, *Erotic Innocence.*

22. Gallop, *Feminist Accused*, 1.

23. Jane Gallop, *The Daughter's Seduction: Feminism and Psychoanalysis* (Ithaca, N.Y.: Cornell University Press, 1992), xii; for an analysis of Gallop's relation to feminism as it pertains to *Feminist Accused*, see Kirstin Campbell, "The Pedagogical in the Political: Reconfiguring Pedagogical Mastery" in *Pedagogical Desire: Authority, Seduction, Transference, and the Question of Ethics*, ed. Jan Jagodzinski, 75–90 (Bergin & Garvey, 2002).

24. Gallop and Berlant, "Loose Lips," Interview in *Our Monica, Ourselves*, 264; for more of Gallop's thinking about this period, see also, Gallop, *Living with His Camera* (Durham: Duke University Press, 2003).

25. Michel Foucault, "The Ethics of the Concern for Self as a Practice of Freedom" in *Foucault Live: Collected Interviews, 1961–1984*, ed. Sylvere Lotringer, trans. Lysa Hochroth and John Johnston (New York: Semiotext(e) 1996), 433.

26. Jean Laplanche, *Freud and the Sexual*, trans. John Fletcher, Jonathan House, and Nicholas Ray (New York: Unconscious in Translation, 2011), 69.

27. Henry James, "Preface to *What Maisie Knew*" in *The Art of the Novel: Critical Prefaces of Henry James* (Chicago: University of Chicago Press, 2011).

28. Jean Strouse, *Alice James: A Biography* (New York: New York Review of Books, 1980), 17.

29. Henry James, *A Small Boy and Others: A Critical Edition*, ed. Peter Collister (Charlottesville: University of Virginia Press, 2011), 24.

30. James's primary letter-writing relationships include Isabella Stewart Gardner, Edith Wharton, Hendrik Andersen, Howard Sturgis, Hugh Walpole, and Jocelyn Persse.

31. Henry James and William James, "Letter, August 2" in *Selected Letters*, ed. Ignas K. Skrupskelis and Elizabeth M. Berkeley, 380–81 (Charlottesville: University of Virginia Press, 1997).

32. Henry James and William James, "Letter, August 4," in *Selected Letters*, 381–85.

33. Fischel, *Sex and Harm in the Age of Consent*, 14.

4. Adults Only: Lee Edelman's *No Future* and the Limits of Queer Critique

1. This essay is dedicated to Lee Edelman, my teacher.

2. Kadji Amin, *Disturbing Attachments: Genet, Modern Pederasty, and Queer History* (Durham: Duke University Press, 2017), 180.

3. Michael Warner, *The Trouble with Normal: Sex, Politics, and the Ethics of Queer Life* (Cambridge: Harvard University Press, 1999), 3.

4. Maggie Nelson, *The Argonauts* (Minneapolis: Graywolf Press, 2015), 13.

5. Robyn Wiegman and Elizabeth A. Wilson, "Introduction: Antinormativity's Queer Conventions," *differences* (May 2015): 1–25.

6. See Heather Love, "Queer Critique, Queer Refusal," in *The Great Refusal: Herbert Marcuse and Contemporary Social Movements*, ed. Andrew Lamas, Todd Wolfson, and Peter Funke (Philadelphia: Temple University Press: 2017).

7. Elizabeth Anker and Rita Felski, eds., *Critique and Postcritique* (Durham: Duke University Press, 2017), 15.

8. Mari Ruti, *The Ethics of Opting Out: Queer Theory's Defiant Subjects* (New York: Columbia University Press, 2017), 9.

9. Michael D. Snediker, *Queer Optimism: Lyric Personhood and Other Felicitous Persuasions* (Minneapolis: University of Minnesota Press, 2009).

10. Rita Felski, *The Limits of Critique* (Chicago: University of Chicago Press, 2015), 135. Felski's text provides an extensive and engaged recent history of the development of "critique" in the academy today. See also, Anker and Felski, *Critique and Postcritique*.

11. Felski, *Limits of Critique*, 10.

12. Lee Edelman, *No Future: Queer Theory and the Death Drive* (Durham: Duke University Press, 2004), 6.

13. Lauren Berlant and Lee Edelman, *Sex, or the Unbearable* (Durham: Duke University Press, 2014), 100.

14. See also Tim Dean's critique of Edelman's conflation of the structural/unconscious and empirical/cultural registers: "An Impossible Embrace: Queerness, Futurity, and the Death Drive," in *A Time for the Humanities: Futurity and the Limits of Autonomy*, ed. James J. Bono, Tim Dean, and Ewa Plonowska Ziarek (New York: Fordham University Press, 2008); for an exploration of the "child" as a figure in queer thought that uses prevailing psychoanalytic ideas to link queer theory to early childhood, see Kathryn Bond Stockton, *The Queer Child: Or Growing up Sideways in the Twentieth Century* (Durham: Duke University Press, 2009).

15. In one early example, Edelman writes: "Far from partaking of this narrative movement toward a viable political future, far from perpetuating the fantasy of meaning's eventual realization, the queer comes to figure the bar to every realization of futurity, the resistance, internal to the social, to every social structure or form" (5).

16. Jacques Derrida, *Of Grammatology*, trans. Gayatri Chakravorty Spivak (Baltimore: Johns Hopkins University Press, 1994), 7.

17. Jonathan Culler makes note of Derrida's different treatment of contemporary and historical thinkers in order to demonstrate that although the metaphysics of presence cannot be unilaterally avoided, there are different degrees of rigor that can be applied to one's own thought in order to work through their own terminology and categorizations. Referring to Derrida's treatment of fellow philosophers, Culler writes: "They are engaged in a critique of knowledge, truth, objectivity, presence, and at the same time are producing impressive analyses of cultural products and human activities. Their awareness of the problem of their own discourse, which claims knowledge at the same time as it calls knowledge into question, is in a sense beside the point. This awareness, Derrida suggests, should issue in a rigorous questioning of their own categories which will serve to displace those categories." *Structuralism and Since: From Levi Strauss to Derrida*, ed. John Sturrock (Oxford: Oxford University Press, 1979), 175.

18. See Jean-Michel Rabate, "Lacan's Return to Freud," in *The Cambridge Companion to Lacan*, ed. Jean-Michel Rabate (Cambridge: Cambridge University Press, 2003), 1–24; see also, Ed Pluth, Lorenzo Chiesa, Dylan Evans, Dany Nobus, Elisabeth Roudinesco, Adrian Johnston.

19. Dany Nobus, "Life and Death in the Glass: A New Look at the Mirror Stage," in *Key Concepts of Lacanian Psychoanalysis*, ed. Dany Nobus (Other Press, 1999), 117.

20. Bruce Fink, *The Lacanian Subject: Between Language and Jouissance* (Princeton: Princeton University, 1995), 68.

21. For a critique of "negation" in contemporary philosophy and an exploration of its "affirmationist" consequences, see Benjamin Noys, *The Persistence of the Negative: A Critique of Contemporary Continental Theory* (Edinburgh: Edinburgh University Press, 2012).

22. Robert L. Cesario, Lee Edelman, Judith Halberstam, Jose Esteban Munoz, Tim Dean, "The Antisocial Thesis in Queer Theory," *PMLA Forum: Conference Debates* 121, no. 3 (2006): 819–28; Mari Ruti, "Why There Is Always a Future in the Future," *Angelaki* (April 2008): 113–26; Nina Power, "Non-Reproductive Futurism: Ranciere's rational equality against Edelman's body apolitic," *borderlands* 8, no. 2 (2009): 1–16; Chris Coffman, "The Sinthomosexual's Failed Challenge to (Hetero)sexual Difference," *Culture, Theory and Critique* 54, no. 1 (2013): 1–30; Karin Lesnik-Oberstein, "Childhood, queer theory, and feminism," *Feminist Theory* 11, no. 3 (2010): 309–21; James Bliss, "Hope Against Hope: Queer Negativity, Black Feminist Theorizing, and Reproduction without Futurity," *Mosaic* (March 2015): 83–99; Tim Dean, "Sex and the Aesthetics of Existence," *PMLA* (March 2010): 387–92.

23. Jacques Lacan, *The Ethics of Psychoanalysis 1959–1960*, The Seminar of Jacques Lacan Book VII, trans. Jacques-Alain Miller (New York: Norton, 1997); Jacques Lacan, *The Sinthome*, The Seminar of Jacques Lacan, Book XXIII, trans. A. R. Price (Polity, 2016).

24. Jacques Lacan, *The Four Fundamental Concepts of Psychoanalysis*, The Seminar of Jacques Lacan, Book XI, trans. Jacques-Alain Miller (New York: Norton, 1978).

25. Jacques Lacan, *Freud's Papers on Technique, 1953–1954*, The Seminar of Jacques Lacan, Book I, trans. John Forrester, ed. Jacques-Alain Miller (New York: Norton, 1988).

26. Theodor Adorno, *Letters to Walter Benjamin*, Aesthetics and Politics (Verso, 2007), 123.

27. Adrian Johnston, *Time Driven: Metapsychology and the Splitting of the Drive* (Chicago: Northwestern University Press, 2005), xxii.

28. Tim Dean, "An Impossible Embrace," 127; see also, Tim Dean, *Beyond Sexuality* (Chicago: University of Chicago Press, 2000). Michael Snediker develops a critique of Edelman's *No Future* as an "apogee of queer pessimism" and focuses on Edelman's language as well as argument in order to show that "the ubiquity of 'always' and 'every,' in Edelman's argument is stunning, and both contrary to Lacan's insistence on particularity, and indicative of *No Future*'s coerciveness" (24). Snediker links this absoluteness to a problematic attachment to negativity: "Always this, always this, always that. This absoluteness, meant to rally and provoke, recalls Sedgwick's incredulous reading of Frederic Jameson's ukase, 'Always historicize.' . . . The axiomatic thrust of Edelman's 'always' makes the world so irrevocably one thing. But still: why does rejection of a primary attachment to futurity (regardless of what this futurity always does or doesn't do) necessarily require the embodiment of negativity?" (*Queer Optimism*, 24).

29. Further in this passage, Dean characterizes this "style" by saying it "often remains unclear whether the reader is witnessing the results of ventriloquism or spirit possession. As Edelman formulates his argument regarding conservative perspectives on queerness, his campy hybrid of fundamentalist rhetoric and Lacanian jargon conjures a spectacle of Slavoj Zizek demonically taking possession of the body of Jerry Falwell" (126). Edelman has responded to attacks on his style and made the point that such critiques are not innocent of their own political and homophobic agendas. See specifically, Edelman's response to Halberstam in PMLA forum. See also, Edelman's discussion of "style" in the Preface to *Homographesis* (Routledge, 1994).

30. Teresa de Lauretis has responded to Edelman's *No Future* by critiquing his use of Lacan and calls instead for a reformulation of the "death drive" that brings to bear Laplanche's critique of the "death drive" in Freud and Lacan. Teresa de Lauretis, *Freud's Drive: Psychoanalysis, Literature and Film* (New York: Palgrave, 2010); see also, Teresa de Lauretis, "Queer Texts, Bad Habits, and the Issue of a Future," *GLQ* 17, no. 2 (2011): 243–63.

31. Wiegman and Wilson observe that Edelman does not cite Foucault at all in *No Future* and link this to his general disregard for working with (or answering to) the analysis of power that Foucault provides; Dean also points out the absence of Foucault in Edelman's work, as have others.

32. Margaret S. Mahler, Fred Pine, Anni Bergman, *The Psychological Birth of the Human Infant* (Basic, 2000). In one of my favorite illustrations of the function of "no" in child development, a clinical colleague tells the story of her two-year-old son taking a bath and her announcing to him that there were five minutes left before he needed to get up. He responded, "No! Two minutes!" an indication that although he didn't understand time (two was less than five), he needed to assert his autonomy nevertheless.

33. Jean Laplanche, *Freud and the Sexual*, trans. John Fletcher (New York: Unconscious in Translation, 2011), 43.

34. Laplanche offers three versions of the answer to this question: "(1) an impoverished interpretation that proposes a mechanistic parallelism; (2) an interpretation that makes it into a process of emergence; (3) a contrary interpretation, made in terms of seduction" (45).

35. I think affect theory, as it has been developed within neurobiology and regulation theory, to be an indispensable resource for understanding the process Laplanche is

describing, and I work some of that out in my paper on Laplanche and affect theory, "The Ideology of Transference: Laplanche and Affect Theory," *Studies in Gender and Sexuality* 19, no. 2 (April–June 2018): 89–105.

36. It would be interesting to think in this connection of Lacan's seminar, "Love of one's neighbor" where he explains how the commandment to "love one's neighbor" is articulated as an attempt to counter the hatred one reflexively feels toward one's neighbor, as when he writes, "my neighbor's jouissance, his harmful, malignant jouissance, is that which poses a problem for my love" (187). Jacques Lacan, *The Seminar of Jacques Lacan: The Ethics of Psychoanalysis, 1959–1960*, trans. Dennis Porter (New York: Norton, 1992).

37. Jacques Lacan, "The Subversion of the Subject and the Dialectic of Desire in the Freudian Unconscious," *Ecrits*, trans. Bruce Fink (New York: Norton, 2006); Dany Nobus, "Life and Death in the Glass," 122; Nobus explains in a footnote that Alan Sheridan has translated *futur antérieur* as "future perfect tense" (fn.137).

5. Psychology as Ideology-Lite: Butler, and the Trouble with Gender Theory

1. Seyla Benhabib, *Situating the Self: Gender, Community and Postmodernism in Contemporary Ethics* (New Haven: Yale University Press, 2013).

2. Wendy Brown, *States of Injury: Power and Freedom in Late Modernity* (Princeton: Princeton University Press, 1995), 37.

3. For an excellent history of the field's emergence, see Annamarie Jagose, *Queer Theory: An Introduction* (New York: New York University Press, 1996).

4. Wendy Brown, *Edgework: Critical Essays on Knowledge and Politics* (Princeton: Princeton University Press, 2005), 111.

5. Judith Butler, "Against Proper Objects," *Feminism Meets Queer Theory*, ed. Elizabeth Weed and Naomi Schor (Bloomington: Indiana University Press, 1997), 2.

6. Brown, *Edgework*, 114. Brown writes: "This is not the right naming of our problem" and is, in fact, a "symptom of a condition in which women's studies has not simply lost its revolutionary impulse but has turned against this impulse, against its desire to have done with these objects" (114).

7. Amy Allen, *The Politics of Our Selves: Power, Autonomy, and Gender in Contemporary Critical Theory* (New York: Columbia University Press, 2007), 12.

8. Lois McNay, *Gender and Agency* (Cambridge, UK: Polity Press, 2000), 5.

9. Mari Ruti, *The Ethics of Opting Out* (New York: Columbia University Press, 2017), 59.

10. Focusing on Jasbir Puar's *Terrorist Assemblages* (Durham: Duke University Press, 2007), Ruti writes: "Puar's allegiance to the Deleuzian-Guattaruan ideal of the utter pulverization of subjectivity leads her to elevate the suicide bomber—whose 'identity' is, literally, blown to pieces—to an icon of a 'queer assemblage,' to assert that 'self-annihilation is the ultimate form of resistance' (2007, 216). . . . Indeed, by presenting the suicide bomber as a queer figure, Puar takes the queer rhetoric of opting out to a level that some might hesitate to embrace, for it is not merely unitary identities, narratives of progress, and other targets of posthumanist critique that get blown up with the body of the terrorist but also, arguably, any viable conception of queerness as anything but an all-purpose placeholder for whatever is destructive" (32–33).

11. Shannon Winnubst, *Way Too Cool: Selling Out Race and Ethics* (New York: Columbia University Press, 2015), 6.

12. Judith Butler, *The Psychic Life of Power: Theories in Subjection* (Stanford: Stanford University Press, 1997).

13. Heather Love, *Feeling Backward* (Cambridge: Harvard University Press, 2007), 100–1; Radclyffe Hall, *The Well of Loneliness* (Anchor, 1990).

14. Laura Doan and Jay Prosser, eds., *Palatable Poison: Critical Perspectives on The Well of Loneliness* (New York: Columbia University Press, 2001).

15. Doan and Prosser, *Palatable Poison*, 14. The heading of this section is from Terry Castle's, "Afterword: It Was Good, Good, Good" in Doan and Prosser (394–402).

16. Doan and Prosser, *Palatable Poison*, 2001), 17; Esther Newton, "The Mythic Mannish Lesbian: Radclyffe Hall and the New Woman," *Signs* 9, no. 4, The Lesbian Issue (Summer 1984): 557–75.

17. Teresa de Lauretis, "The Lure of the Mannish Lesbian: The Fantasy of Castration and the Signification of Desire," in *The Practice of Love: Lesbian Sexuality and Perverse Desire* (Bloomington: Indiana University Press, 1994).

18. Judith Halberstam, *Female Masculinity* (Durham: Duke University Press, 1998).

19. Jay Prosser, *Second Skins: The Body Narratives of Transsexuality* (New York: Columbia University Press, 1998).

20. Jean Laplanche, *Freud and the Sexual*, trans. John Fletcher (New York: Unconscious in Translation, 2011), note on p. 1; The editors of *Freud and the Sexual* explain that, "This is an attempt to register terminologically the difference between the enlarged Freudian notion of sexuality (*le sexual*) and the common sense or traditional notion of genital sexuality (*le sexuel*). This terminological innovation can't really be captured in English as the German term '*sexual*' coincides exactly with the spelling of the standard English term 'sexual,' rather than contrasting with it in French."

21. Laplanche, "Gender, Sex, and the Sexual," in *Freud and the Sexual*, 173.

22. Laplanche, "Gender, Sex, and the Sexual," 174.

23. Judith Butler, *Gender Trouble* (New York: Routledge, 1990), 86.

24. Monique Wittig, *The Straight Mind and Other Essays* (Beacon Press, 1992), 20; Prosser, *Second Skins*.

25. Greg Boucher writes, "Butler's rhetoric, I suggest, resonates with psychoanalytic terminology, but without any theoretical correspondence. She constantly conflates the elementary psychoanalytic distinction between the repression of unconscious desire and the resistance conducted by the ego, generating a generalized politico-psychological 'resistance.' This should warn us that her relation to Freudian theory is one of syncretic appropriations through selective citation, rather than a theoretical synthesis" (142). *The Charmed Circle of Ideology* (re.press, 2008).

26. See Butler's article, "Melancholy Gender—Refused Identification," *Psychoanalytic Dialogues* 5, no. 2 (1995): 165–80; *Bodies That Matter: On the Discursive Limits of Sex* (New York: Routledge, 2011); I found Prosser especially helpful for a phenomenal close reading of Butler's confusion between gender and sex.

27. Winnubst, *Way Too Cool*, 61.

28. Brian Kloppenberg, "The Psychoanalytic Mode of Thought and Its Application to the Non-Normative Analysis of Sexuality and Gender," *Journal of the American Psychoanalytic Association* 64, no. 1 (January 27, 2016): 133–59.

6. Two Girls[2]: Sedgwick + Berlant, Relational and Queer

1. Lauren Berlant and Lee Edelman, *Sex, or the Unbearable* (Durham: Duke University Press, 2014), vii.

2. Lauren Berlant, "Two Girls, Fat and Thin," in *Cruel Optimism* (Durham: Duke University Press, 2011), and Mary Gaitskill's Novel, *Two Girls, Fat and Thin* (New York: Simon and Schuster, 1998). Berlant's essay was originally written for a festschrift honoring Sedgwick. See Stephen M. Barber and David L. Clark, eds. *Regarding Sedgwick: Essays on Queer Culture and Critical Theory* (New York: Routledge, 2002).

3. Lauren Berlant, "Slow Death," in *Cruel Optimism* (Durham: Duke University Press, 2011), 99.

4. Virginia Jackson describes Berlant as a "critic's critic" and offers a compelling account of what makes Berlant's oeuvre unique at the present moment. Virginia Jackson, "The Function of Criticism at the Present Time," *Los Angeles Review of Books*, April 12, 2015.

5. Berlant, "Slow Death," *Cruel Optimism*, 99.

6. Berlant's formulation relies upon Leo Bersani's radical transformation of sexuality from a mechanism of self-knowledge into a site of ego-"shattering," which he later calls "impersonal narcissism." Bersani writes, "Might there be forms of self-divestiture not grounded in a teleology (or a theology) of the suppression of the ego and, ultimately, the sacrifice of the self?" (56). Adam Phillips elaborates the transformative power of "impersonal narcissism" when he explains, "The psychoanalyst becomes intimate with someone by not taking what they say personally." Leo Bersani and Adam Phillips, *Intimacies* (Chicago: University of Chicago Press, 2008).

7. Gaitskill, *Two Girls, Fat and Thin*, 10.

8. Eve Kosofsky Sedgwick and Adam Frank, eds. *Shame and Its Sisters: A Silvan Tomkins Reader* (Durham: Duke University Press, 1995).

9. Eve Kosofsky Sedgwick, *Touching Feeling: Affect, Pedagogy, Performativity* (Durham: Duke University Press, 2003), 18.

10. Sedgwick and Frank, *Shame and Its Sisters*, 34.

11. Melissa Gregg and Gregory J. Seigworth, eds., *The Affect Theory Reader* (Durham: Duke University Press, 2010), 4; see also, Introduction to *The Affective Turn: Theorizing the Social*, ed. Patricia Ticineto Clough and Jean Halley (Durham: Duke University Press, 2007).

12. Teresa Brennan, *The Transmission of Affect* (Ithaca, N.Y.: Cornell University Press, 2004), 2–6. The development of affect theory belongs to a broader moment in philosophy that, often exuberantly, avows its disinterest in representation's familiar limits and instead calls for stretching perception beyond the linguistic/symbolic frame. As Levi Bryant, Nick Srnicek, and Graham Harman write in "Towards a Speculative Philosophy," "Even while disdaining the traditional idealist position that all that exists is some variation of mind or spirit, continental philosophy has fallen into an equally anti-realist stance in the form of what Meillassoux calls 'correlationism'—the 'idea according to which we only ever have access to the correlation between thinking and being, and never to either term considered apart from the other.' This position tacitly holds that we can aim our thoughts at being, exist as beings-in-the-world, or have phenomenal experiences of the world, yet we can never consistently speak about a realm independent of thought or language" (*The Speculative Turn: Continental Materialism and Realism*, ed. Levi Bryant, Nick Srnicek, and Graham Harman [re.press, 2011], 4). Variously called Speculative Realism, Object-Oriented-Ontology, New Materialism,

Transcendental Materialism, and Non-Philosophy, these related developments share the wish to "distance themselves from the linguistic paradigm."

13. As my use of Laplanche and "textuality" will show, affect does not invalidate the grip of language on the formation of subjectivity and sociality but alerts us to the need to put what we know about signification in relation to other things we know about affective transmission, nonhuman lifeworlds, brain synapses, and so on.

14. This methodology is an essential feature of my project's commitment to speculative psychology. I am using "speculative" in the sense defined by Tom Sparrow, which builds upon work in Speculative Realism and related philosophy. Sparrow writes: "The proliferation of speculative philosophy in recent years may be unnerving to some. Is this the return of dogmatic, ungrounded, free-floating knowledge claims? Has the Kantian lesson withered away, leaving us just where we were before the 1780s? In a less alarmist tone, the speculative turn is not a rejection of the critical philosophy but 'a recognition' of [its] inherent limitations. Speculation in this sense aims 'beyond' the critical and linguistic turns. As such, it recuperates the pre-critical sense of 'speculation' as a concern with the Absolute, while also taking into account the undeniable progress that is due to the labor of critique [Brassier]." *The End of Phenomenology: Metaphysics and the New Realism* (Edinburgh: Edinburgh University Press, 2014), 19.

15. Shaun Gallagher, *Hermeneutics and Education*. (Albany: SUNY Press, 1992), 8. I am thinking of Paul Ricoeur, whose focus on a "hermeneutics of selfhood" outlines how the subject emerges through interpretation; see *The Conflict of Interpretations: Essays on Hermeneutics* (Evanston: Northwestern University Press, 2007). We could think of Roland Barthes's oeuvre as expanding our ideas of what a text can refer to and varieties of ways we can engage a text; see *S/Z: An Essay*, trans. Richard Miller (New York: Hill and Wang: 1970); *The Pleasure of the Text*, trans. Richard Miller (New York: Hill and Wang, 1975).

16. Jean Laplanche, *Freud and the Sexual*, trans. John Fletcher, Jonathan House, and Nicholas Ray (New York: Unconscious in Translation, 2011), 12.

17. Malcom Owen Slavin and Daniel Kriegman, *The Adaptive Design of the Human Psyche: Psychoanalysis, Evolutionary Biology, and the Therapeutic Process* (New York: Guilford Press, 1992), 36.

18. Jay R. Greenberg and Stephen A. Mitchell, *Object Relations in Psychoanalytic Theory* (Cambridge: Harvard University Press, 1983), 402.

19. Laplanche, *Freud and the Sexual*, 47.

20. Laplanche, *Freud and the Sexual*, 48.

21. Jean Laplanche, *Essays on Otherness*, ed. and trans. John Fletcher (New York: Routledge, 1999), 225.

22. Jacques Lacan, *Ecrits*, trans. Bruce Fink (New York: Norton, 2006), 13.

23. Laplanche, *Essays on Otherness*, 69.

24. Jean Laplanche, *The Temptation of Biology: Freud's Theories of Sexuality*, trans. Donald Nicholson-Smith (New York: Unconscious in Translation, 2015), 121.

25. Sigmund Freud, "Fragment of the analysis of a case of Hysteria" (3–124), The Standard Edition, Volume VII (1905), ed. and trans. James Strachey (London: Hogarth Press), 116.

26. Gila Ashtor, "The Ideology of Transference: Laplanche and Affect Theory," *Studies in Gender and Sexuality* 19, no. 2 (April–June 2018): 89–105.

27. Specifically, I am thinking of work by Walter Benjamin, Gilles Deleuze, Michel de Certeau, Brian Massumi, and Nigel Thrift, which studies performativity and bodily

practices in the everyday rather than focus on representation and meaning. In his seminal *Non-Representational Theory*, Thrift writes "non-representational theory is resolutely anti-biographical and pre-individual. It trades in modes of perception which are not subject-based." *Non-Representational Theory: Space, Politics, Affect* (New York: Routledge), 7.

28. Ruth Leys, "The Turn to Affect: A Critique," *Critical Inquiry* 37, no. 3 (Spring 2011), 463.

29. Laplanche, *Freud and the Sexual*, 208.

30. Jean Laplanche, "Implantation, Intromission," in *Essays on Otherness*, 136.

Works Cited

Adorno, Theodor. *Letters to Walter Benjamin.* Aesthetics and Politics. New York: Verso, 2007.

Allen, Amy. *The Politics of Our Selves: Power, Autonomy, and Gender in Contemporary Critical Theory.* New York: Columbia University Press, 2007.

Allen, Amy, and Brian O'Connor, eds. *Transitional Subjects: Critical Theory and Object Relations.* New York: Columbia University Press, 2019.

Allen, Amy, and Mari Ruti. *Critical Theory Between Klein and Lacan: A Dialogue.* New York: Bloomsbury, 2019.

Amin, Kadji, *Disturbing Attachments: Genet, Modern Pederasty, and Queer History.* Durham: Duke University Press, 2017.

Anderson, Amanda. *The Way We Argue Now: A Study in the Cultures of Theory.* Princeton: Princeton University Press, 2006.

Anker, Elizabeth S., and Rita Felski, eds. *Critique and Postcritique.* Durham: Duke University Press, 2017.

Ashtor, Gila. "The Ideology of Transference: Laplanche and Affect Theory." *Studies in Gender and Sexuality* 19, no. 2 (April–June 2018): 89–105.

———. "The *Mis*diagnosis of Critique." *Criticism: A Quarterly for Literature and the Arts* 61, no. 2 (Spring 2019): 191–219.

———. "Transgressive Textuality: Transference and the Ideology of Affect—A Laplanchian Critique." (Forthcoming, *Studies in Gender and Sexuality*).

Barber, Stephen M., and David L. Clark, eds. *Regarding Sedgwick: Essays on Queer Culture and Critical Theory.* New York: Routledge, 2002.

Barthes, Roland. *The Pleasure of the Text.* Translated by Richard Miller. New York: Hill and Wang, 1975.

———. *S/Z: An Essay.* Translated by Richard Miller. New York: Hill and Wang, 1970.

Benhabib, Seyla. *Situating the Self: Gender, Community and Postmodernism in Contemporary Ethics*. New Haven: Yale University Press, 2013.

Berlant, Lauren. "After Eve, in honor of Eve Kosofsky Sedgwick." http://super-valentthought.com/2010/03/18/after-eve-in-honor-of-eve-kosofsky-sedgwick/. Accessed February 12, 2014.

———. *The Anatomy of National Fantasy: Hawthorne, Utopia, and Everyday Life*. Chicago: University of Chicago Press, 1991.

———, ed. *Compassion*. New York: Routledge, 2004.

———. *Cruel Optimism*. Durham: Duke University Press, 2011.

———. *The Female Complaint: The Unfinished Business of Sentimentality in American Culture*: Durham, Duke University Press, 2008.

———, ed. *Intimacy*. Chicago: University of Chicago Press, 2000.

———. *The Queen of America Goes to Washington City: Essays on Sex and Citizenship*. Durham: Duke University Press, 1997.

———, ed. *Reading Sedgwick*. Durham: Duke University Press, 2019.

———. "The Subject of True Feeling: Pain, Privacy, and Politics." In *Left Legalism/Left Critique*. Edited by Wendy Brown and Janet Halley. Durham: Duke University Press, 2002.

———. "Two Girls, Fat and Thin." In *Cruel Optimism*. Durham: Duke University Press, 2011.

Berlant, Lauren, and Jane Gallop. "Loose Lips." In *Our Monica, Ourselves: The Clinton Affair and the National Interest*. Edited by Lauren Berlant and Lisa Duggan. New York: New York University Press, 2001.

Berlant, Lauren, and Lee Edelman. *Sex, or the Unbearable?* Durham: Duke University Press, 2014.

Bersani, Leo. *Baudelaire and Freud*. Berkeley: University of California Press, 1977.

———. *The Culture of Redemption*. Cambridge: Harvard University Press, 1990.

———. *The Freudian Body: Psychoanalysis and Art*. New York: Columbia University Press, 1986.

———. *Homos*. Cambridge: Harvard University Press, 1995.

———. *Is the Rectum A Grave?* Chicago: University of Chicago Press, 2010.

———. "Why Sex?" *SPI: The Society for Psychoanalytic Inquiry*. YouTube. Published: January 8, 2014.

Bersani, Leo, and Adam Phillips. *Intimacies*. Chicago: University of Chicago Press, 2008.

Bersani, Leo, and Ulysse Dutoit. *Acts of Impoverishment: Beckett, Rothko, Resnais*. Cambridge: Harvard University Press, 1993.

———. *Caravaggio's Secrets*. Cambridge: MIT Press, 1998.

———. *Forms of Being: Cinema, Aesthetics, Subjectivity*. British Film Institute, 2004.

Best, Stephen, and Sharon Marcus. "Surface Reading: An Introduction." *Representations* 108, no. 1 (Fall 2009).

Bliss, James. "Hope Against Hope: Queer Negativity, Black Feminist Theorizing, and Reproduction without Futurity." *Mosaic* (March 2015).

Bloom, Harold. *The Anxiety of Influence: A Theory of Poetry*. Second Edition. New York: Oxford University Press, 1997.

Bosanquet, Theodora. *Henry James at Work*. Ann Arbor: University of Michigan Press, 2007.

Boucher, Greg. *The Charmed Circle of Ideology: A Critique of Laclau and Mouffe, Butler and Zizek*. Melbourne: re.press, 2008.

Brennan, Teresa. *The Transmission of Affect*. Ithaca, N.Y.: Cornell University Press, 2004.

Britzman, Deborah P. *After-Education: Anna Freud, Melanie Klein, and Psychoanalytic Histories of Learning*. Albany: SUNY Press, 2003.

———. *Lost Subjects, Contested Objects: Toward a Psychoanalytic Inquiry of Learning*. Albany: SUNY Press, 1998.

Brown, Wendy. *Edgework: Critical Essays on Knowledge and Politics*. Princeton: Princeton University Press, 2005.

———. *States of Injury: Power and Freedom in Late Modernity*. Princeton: Princeton University Press, 1995.

Bryant, Levi, Nick Srnicek, and Graham Harman. "Towards a Speculative Philosophy." *The Speculative Turn: Continental Materialism and Realism*. Edited by Levi Bryant, Nick Srnicek, and Graham Harman. Melbourne: re. press, 2011.

Butler, Judith. *Bodies That Matter: On the Discursive Limits of Sex*. New York: Routledge, 2011

———. *Gender Trouble*. New York: Routledge: 1990.

———. "Melancholy Gender—Refused Identification." *Psychoanalytic Dialogues* 5, no. 2 (1995): 165–80.

———. *The Psychic Life of Power: Theories in Subjection*. Stanford: Stanford University Press, 1997.

Caruth, Cathy. *Unclaimed Experience: Trauma, Narrative, and History*. Baltimore: Johns Hopkins University Press, 1996.

Castle, Terry. "Afterword: It Was Good, Good, Good." In *Palatable Poison: Critical Perspectives on The Well of Loneliness*, edited by Laura Doan and Jay Prosser, 394–402. New York: Columbia University Press, 2001.

Cesario, Robert L., Lee Edelman, Judith Halberstam, Jose Esteban Munoz, Tim Dean. "The Antisocial Thesis in Queer Theory." *PMLA Forum: Conference Debates* 121, no. 3 (2006).

Clough, Patricia Ticineto, and Jean Halley, eds. *The Affective Turn: Theorizing the Social*. Durham: Duke University Press, 2007.

Coffman, Chris. "The Sinthomosexual's Failed Challenge to (Hetero)sexual Difference." *Culture, Theory and Critique* 54, no. 1 (2013).

Cooper, Arnold. "Changes in Psychoanalytic Ideas: Transference Interpretation." In *Essential Papers on Transference*, edited by Aaron H. Esman, 511–28. New York: New York University Press, 1990.

Corbett, Ken. "The Transforming Nexus: Psychoanalysis, Social Theory, and Queer Childhood." In *Clinical Encounters in Sexuality: Psychoanalytic*

Practice and Queer Theory, edited by Noreen Giffney and Eve Watson. Santa Barbara: Punctum Books, 2017.

Cvetkovich, Ann. *Depression: A Public Feeling.* Durham: Duke University Press, 2012.

Dean, Tim. *Beyond Sexuality.* Chicago: University of Chicago Press, 2000.

———. "An Impossible Embrace: Queerness, Futurity and the Death Drive." In *A Time for the Humanities: Futurity and the Limits of Autonomy*, edited by James J. Bono, Tim Dean, Ewa Plonowska Ziarek. New York: Fordham University Press, 2008.

———. "Sex and the Aesthetics of Existence." *PMLA* (March 2010).

Dean, Tim, and Christopher Lane, eds. *Homosexuality and Psychoanalysis.* Chicago: University of Chicago Press, 2001.

de Lauretis, Teresa. *Freud's Drive: Psychoanalysis, Literature and Film.* New York: Palgrave, 2010.

———. "The Lure of the Mannish Lesbian: The Fantasy of Castration and the Signification of Desire." In *The Practice of Love: Lesbian Sexuality and Perverse Desire.* Bloomington: Indiana University Press, 1994.

———. "Queer Texts, Bad Habits, and the Issue of a Future." GLQ 17, no. 2 (2011).

De Man, Paul. *Blindness and Insight: Essays in the Rhetoric of Contemporary Criticism.* Minneapolis: University of Minnesota Press, 1983.

———. *Resistance to Theory.* Minneapolis: University of Minnesota Press, 1986.

Derrida, Jacques. *Of Grammatology.* Translated by Gayatri Chakravorty Spivak. Baltimore: Johns Hopkins University Press, 1994. Reprint

Doan, Laura and Jay Prosser, eds. *Palatable Poison: Critical Perspectives on The Well of Loneliness.* New York: Columbia University Press, 2001.

Edelman, Lee. "An Ethics of Desubjectivation?" *differences* (December 2016): 106–17.

———. *Homographesis: Essays in Gay Literary and Cultural Theory.* New York: Routledge, 1994.

———. "Learning Nothing: *Bad Education*," *differences* (May 2017).

———. *No Future: Queer Theory and the Death Drive.* Durham: Duke University Press, 2004.

Eng, David L., Judith Halberstam, Jose Esteban Munoz. "What's Queer about Queer Studies Now?" *Social Text* (Fall/Winter 2005): 84–85.

Evans, Dylan. *An Introductory Dictionary of Lacanian Psychoanalysis.* New York: Routledge, 1996.

Felski, Rita. *The Limits of Critique.* Chicago: University of Chicago Press, 2010.

ffrench, Patrick. "Addressing Oneself: Bersani and the Form/Fold of Self-Relation." In *Leo Bersani: Queer Theory and Beyond*, edited by Mikko Tuhkanen. Albany: SUNY Press, 2014.

Fink, Bruce. *The Lacanian Subject: Between Language and Jouissance.* Princeton: Princeton University Press, 1995.

Fischel, Joseph J. *Sex and Harm in the Age of Consent.* Minneapolis: University of Minnesota Press, 2016.

Foucault, Michel. *History of Sexuality. Volume One.* Translated by Robert Hurley. New York: Vintage Books, 1990.

Freccero, Carla. *Queer/Early/Modern.* Durham: Duke University Press, 2006.

Freeman, Elizabeth. *Time Binds: Queer Temporalities, Queer Histories.* Durham: Duke University Press, 2010.

Freud, Sigmund. "Fragment of the analysis of a case of Hysteria." In *The Standard Edition*, Volume VII (1905). Edited and translated by James Strachey. London: Hogarth Press.

Gaitskill, Mary. *Bad Behavior.* New York: Simon and Schuster, 1998.

———. *Because They Wanted To.* New York: Simon and Schuster, 1997.

———. *Don't Cry.* New York: Simon and Schuster, 2009.

———. *The Mare.* New York: Pantheon, 2015.

———. *Two Girls, Fat and Thin.* New York: Simon and Schuster, 1998.

———. *Veronica.* New York: Simon and Schuster, 2005.

Gallagher, Shaun. *Hermeneutics and Education.* Albany: SUNY Press, 1992.

Gallop, Jane. *Feminist Accused.* Durham: Duke University Press, 1997.

Giffney, Noreen, and Eve Watson, eds. *Clinical Encounters in Sexuality: Psychoanalytic Practice and Queer Theory.* Santa Barbara: Punctum Books, 2017.

Gorra, Michael. *Portrait of a Novel: Henry James and the Making of an American Masterpiece.* New York: Liveright, 2013.

Greenberg, Jay R., and Stephen A. Mitchell. *Object Relations in Psychoanalytic Theory.* Cambridge: Harvard University Press, 1983.

Greenwell, Garth. "'I wanted something 100% pornographic and 100% high art': the joy of writing about sex." *The Guardian.* May 8, 2020.

Gregg, Melissa, and Gregory J. Seigworth, eds. *The Affect Theory Reader.* Durham: Duke University Press, 2010.

Haggerty, George E. and Bonnie Zimmerman, eds. *Professions of Desire.* New York: MLA, 1995.

Halberstam, Jack. "Public Thinker: Jack Halberstam on Wildness, Anarchy, and Growing up Punk." Interview with Damon R. Young. *Public Books*, March 26, 2019.

———. "Straight Eye for the Queer Theorist—A Review of Queer Theory Without Antinormativity." bullybloggers.wordpress.com. Sept 12, 2015.

Halberstam, Judith. *Female Masculinity.* Durham: Duke University Press, 1998.

———. *The Queer Art of Failure.* Durham: Duke University Press, 2011.

Hall, Radclyffe. *The Well of Loneliness.* New York: Anchor Books, 1990.

Halley, Janet, and Andrew Parker, eds. *After Sex? On Writing Since Queer Theory.* Durham: Duke University Press, 2011.

Halperin, David M. *How to Be Gay.* Cambridge: Harvard University Press, 2012.

———. *Saint Foucault: Towards A Gay Hagiography.* New York: Oxford University Press, 1995.

Hanson, Ellis. "Teaching Shame." In *Gay Shame.* Edited by David M. Halperin and Valerie Traub. Chicago: Chicago University Press, 2009.

Held, Daniel, *Introduction to Critical Theory: Horkheimer to Habermas*, Berkeley: University of California Press, 1980.

Honneth, Axel. "Social Dynamics of Disrespect: Situating Critical Theory Today." In *Habermas: A Critical Reader*, edited by Peter Dews. Oxford: Blackwell, 1999.

Horkheimer, Max. "Traditional and Critical Theory." In *Critical Theory: Selected Essays*, translated by Matthew J. O'Connell. New York: Continuum, 2002.

Huffer, Lynne. *Mad for Foucault: Rethinking the Foundations of Queer Theory.* New York: Columbia University Press, 2010.

Jackson, Virginia. "The Function of Criticism at the Present Time." *Los Angeles Review of Books* (April 12, 2015).

Jagose, Annamarie. *Queer Theory: An Introduction.* New York: New York University Press, 1996.

James, Ian. *The New French Philosophy.* Cambridge, UK: Polity Press, 2012.

Jameson, Fredric. *Late Marxism: Adorno or the Persistence of the Dialectic.* London: Verso Books, 1990.

———. *Representing Capital: A Rereading of Volume One.* London: Verso Books, 2011.

Johnson, E. Patrick. *No Tea, No Shade: New Writings in Black Queer Studies.* Durham: Duke University Press, 2016.

Johnson, E. Patrick, and Mae G. Henderson, eds. *Black Queer Studies: A Critical Anthology.* Durham: Duke University Press, 2005.

Johnston, Adrian. *Time Driven: Metapsychology and the Splitting of the Drive.* Chicago: Northwestern University Press, 2005.

Johnston, Adrian, and Catherine Malabou. *Self and Emotional Life: Philosophy, Psychoanalysis, and Neuroscience.* New York: Columbia University Press, 2013.

Kincaid, James R. *Erotic Innocence: The Culture of Child Molesting.* Durham: Duke University Press, 1998.

Kloppenberg, Brian. "The Psychoanalytic Mode of Thought and Its Application to the Non-Normative Analysis of Sexuality and Gender." *Journal of the American Psychoanalytic Association* 64, no. 1 (January 27, 2016): 133–59.

Koestenbaum, Wayne. Forward to *Between Men: English Literature and Male Homosocial Desire.* New York: Columbia University Press, 2016.

Lacan, Jacques. *Anxiety: The Seminar of Jacques Lacan. Book X.* Translated by A. R. Prince. Edited by Jacques-Alain Miller. Cambridge, UK: Polity Press, 2014.

———. *Ecrits.* Translated by Bruce Fink. New York: Norton, 2006.

———. *The Ethics of Psychoanalysis. Book VII: 1959–1960.* Edited by Jacques-Alain Miller. Translated by Dennis Porter. New York: Norton, 1997.

———. *The Four Fundamental Concepts of Psychoanalysis*, The Seminar of Jacques Lacan Book XI. Edited by Jacques-Alain Miller. Translated by Alan Sheridan. New York: Norton, 1978.

———. *Freud's Papers on Technique, 1953–1954*, The Seminar of Jacques Lacan: Book I. Translated by John Forrester. Edited by Jacques-Alain Miller. New York: Norton, 1988.

———. "The Mirror Stage as Formative of the I Function as Revealed in Psycho-analytic Experience" (1949). In *Ecrits*. Translated by Bruce Fink. New York: Norton, 2006.

———. *On the Names-of-the-Father*. Translated by Bruce Fink. Cambridge, UK: Polity Press, 2013.

———. *The Sinthome*, The Seminar of Jacques Lacan Book XXIII. Translated by A. R. Price. Cambridge, UK: Polity Press, 2016.

———. "The Subversion of the Subject and the Dialectic of Desire in the Freudian Unconscious." *Ecrits*. Translated by Bruce Fink. New York: Norton 2006.

Lane, Christopher, ed. *The Psychoanalysis of Race*. New York: Columbia University Press, 1998.

Laplanche, Jean. "The Drive and Its Source-Object." *Essays in Otherness*. Edited by John Fletcher. London: Routledge, 1999.

———. *Essays on Otherness*. Edited by John Fletcher. New York: Routledge, 1999.

———. *Freud and the Sexual*. Translated by John Fletcher, Jonathan House, and Nicholas Ray. New York: Unconscious in Translation, 2011.

———. "Gender, Sex, and the Sexual." Translated by Susan Fairfield. *Studies in Gender and Sexuality* 8, no. 2 (2007): 201–19.

———. "Interpretation between Determinism and Hermeneutics." In *Essays on Otherness*. Edited by John Fletcher. London: Routledge, 1999.

———. *Life and Death in Psychoanalysis*. Translated by Jeffrey Mehlman. Baltimore: Johns Hopkins University Press, 1970.

———. *New Foundations for Psychoanalysis*. Translated by Jonathan House. New York: Unconscious in Translation, 2016.

———. "Sexuality and Attachment." In *Freud and the Sexual*, translated by John Fletcher, Jonathan House, and Nicholas Ray. New York: Unconscious in Translation, 2011.

———. *The Temptation of Biology: Freud's Theories of Sexuality*. Translated by Donald Nicholson-Smith. New York: Unconscious in Translation, 2015.

Laplanche, Jean, and J-B. Pontalis. *The Language of Psycho-Analysis*. Translated by Donald Nicholson-Smith. New York: Norton, 1973

Latour, Bruno. "Why Has Critique Run Out of Steam? From Matters of Fact to Matters of Concern." *Critical Inquiry* 30, no. 2 (Winter 2004): 225–48.

Lesnik-Oberstein, Karin. "Childhood, queer theory, and feminism." *Feminist Theory* 11, no. 3 (2010).

Leys, Ruth. "The Turn to Affect: A Critique." *Critical Inquiry* 37 (Spring 2011): 434–72.

Love, Heather. "Close but Not Deep: Literary Ethics and the Descriptive Turn." *New Literary History* 41, no. 2 (Spring 2010).

———. *Feeling Backward: Loss and the Politics of Queer History*. Cambridge: Harvard University Press, 2007.

———. "Queer Critique, Queer Refusal." In *The Great Refusal: Herbert Marcuse and Contemporary Social Movements*, edited by Andrew Lamas, Todd

Wolfson, and Peter N. Funke, 118–31. Philadelphia: Temple University Press, 2017.

McNay, Lois. *Gender and Agency*. Cambridge, UK: Polity Press, 2000.

Mahler, Margaret S., Fred Pine, and Anni Bergman. *The Psychological Birth of the Human Infant*. New York: Basic Books, 2000.

Merleau-Ponty, Maurice. *Phenomenology of Perception*. Translated by C. Smith. New York: Routledge, 1962.

Mitchell, Stephen. *Influence and Autonomy in Psychoanalysis*. New York: Routledge, 1997.

———. *Relationality: From Attachment to Intersubjectivity*. New York: Routledge, 2000.

Munoz, Jose Esteban, *Cruising Utopia: The Then and There of Queer Futurity*. New York: New York University Press, 2009.

Nelson, Maggie. *The Argonauts*. Minneapolis: Graywolf Press, 2015.

Newton, Esther. "The Mythic Mannish Lesbian: Radclyffe Hall and the New Woman." In *Palatable Poison: Critical Perspectives on "The Well of Loneliness*," edited by Laura Doan and Jay Prosser. New York: Columbia University Press, 2001.

Nobus, Dany. "Life and Death in the Glass: A New Look at the Mirror Stage." In *Key Concepts of Lacanian Psychoanalysis*, edited by Dany Nobus. Other Press, 1999.

———. "Undoing Psychoanalysis: Towards a Clinical and Conceptual Metistopia." In *Clinical Encounters in Sexuality: Psychoanalytic Practice and Queer Theory*, edited by Noreen Giffney and Eve Watson. Santa Barbara: Punctum, 2017.

Noys, Benjamin. *The Persistence of the Negative: A Critique of Contemporary Continental Theory*. Edinburgh: Edinburgh University Press, 2012.

Ohi, Kevin. *Innocence and Rapture: The Erotic Child in Pater, Wilde, James, and Nabokov*. New York: Palgrave Macmillan, 2005.

Power, Nina. "Non-Reproductive Futurism: Ranciere's rational equality against Edelman's body apolitic." *borderlands* 8 no. 2 (2009).

Prosser, Jay. *Second Skins: The Body Narratives of Transsexuality*. New York: Columbia University Press, 1998.

Rabate, Jean-Michel. "Lacan's Return to Freud." In *The Cambridge Companion to Lacan*, edited by Jean-Michel Rabate. Cambridge: Cambridge University Press, 2003.

Ricoeur, Paul. *The Conflict of Interpretations: Essays on Hermeneutics*. Chicago: Northwestern University Press, 2007.

Ruddick, Lisa. "When Nothing Is Cool." In *The Future of Scholarly Writing*, edited by Angelika Bammer and Ruth-Ellen Boetcher Joeres, 71–86. New York: Palgrave, 2015.

Ruti, Mari. *The Ethics of Opting Out: Queer Theory's Defiant Subjects*. New York: Columbia University Press, 2017.

———. "Why There Is Always a Future in the Future." *Angelaki* (April 2008).

Samuels, Robert. "From Freud to Lacan." In *Reading Seminars I and II: Lacan's Return to Freud*, edited by Bruce Fink, translated by Jacques-Alain Miller, 302. Albany: SUNY Press, 1996.

Scarfone, Dominique. *Laplanche: An Introduction*. Translated by Dorothee Bonnigal-Katz. New York: Unconscious in Translation, 2015.

Sedgwick, Eve Kosofsky. *Between Men: English Literature and Male Homosocial Desire*. New York: Columbia University Press, 2016.

———. *Epistemology of the Closet*. Berkeley: University of California Press, 2008.

———. "Paranoid Reading and Reparative Reading, Or, You're So Paranoid You Probably Think This Essay Is About You." In *Touching Feeling: Affect, Pedagogy, Performativity*. Durham: Duke University Press, 2003.

———. "Teaching/Depression." *The Scholar and Feminist Online* 4, no.2 (Spring 2006).

———. *Tendencies*. Durham: Duke University Press, 1993.

———. *Touching Feeling: Affect, Pedagogy, Performativity*. Durham: Duke University Press, 2003.

———. *The Weather in Proust*. Edited by Jonathan Goldberg. Durham: Duke University Press, 2011.

Sedgwick, Eve Kosofsky, and Adam Frank, eds. *Shame and Its Sisters: A Silvan Tomkins Reader*. Durham: Duke University Press, 1995.

Sellberg, Karin. "Queer Patience: Sedgwick's Identity Narratives." In *Reading Sedgwick*, edited by Lauren Berlant. Durham: Duke University Press, 2019.

Sharpe, Christina. *In the Wake: On Blackness and Being*. Durham: Duke University Press, 2016.

Slavin, Malcolm Owen, and Daniel Kriegman. *The Adaptive Design of the Human Psyche: Psychoanalysis, Evolutionary Biology, and the Therapeutic Process*. New York: Guilford Press, 1992.

Snediker, Michael D. *Queer Optimism: Lyric Personhood and Other Felicitous Persuasions*. Minneapolis: University of Minnesota Press, 2009.

Sparrow, Tom. *The End of Phenomenology: Metaphysics and the New Realism*. Edinburgh: Edinburgh University Press, 2014.

Spillers, Hortense J. *Black, White and in Color: Essays on American Literature and Culture*. Chicago: University of Chicago Press, 2003.

Stockton, Kathryn Bond. *The Queer Child: Or Growing Up Sideways in the Twentieth Century*. Durham: Duke University Press, 2009.

Tomkins, Silvan. *Exploring Affect: The Selected Writings of Silvan S. Tomkins*. Edited by E. Virginia Demos. Cambridge: Cambridge University Press, 1995.

———. *Shame and Its Sisters: A Silvan Tomkins Reader*. Edited by Eve Kosofsky Sedgwick and Adam Frank. Durham: Duke University Press, 1995.

Tuhkanen, Mikko, ed. *Leo Bersani: Queer Theory and Beyond*. Albany: SUNY Press, 2004.

———. "Monadological Psychoanalysis: Bersani, Laplanche, Beckett." In *Leo Bersani: Queer Theory and Beyond*, edited by Mikko Tuhkanen. Albany: SUNY Press, 2004.

Warner, Michael, ed. *Fear of A Queer Planet: Queer Politics and Social Theory*, Minneapolis: University of Minnesota Press, 1993.

———. "Queer and Then?: The End of Queer Theory?" *The Chronicle of Higher Education: The Chronicle Review*. January 1, 2012.

———. *The Trouble with Normal: Sex, Politics, and the Ethics of Queer Life*. Cambridge: Harvard University Press, 1999.

Whitebook, Joel. "Against Interiority: Foucault's Struggle with Psychoanalysis." In *The Cambridge Companion to Foucault: Second Edition*, edited by Gary Gutting. Cambridge: Cambridge University Press, 2003.

Wiegman, Robyn, and Elizabeth A. Wilson, "Introduction: Antinormativity's Queer Conventions." *differences* (May 2015): 1–25.

Winnubst, Shannon. *Way Too Cool: Selling Out Race and Ethics*. New York: Columbia University Press, 2015.

Wittig, Monique. *The Straight Mind and Other Essays*. Boston: Beacon Press, 1992.

Index

Barber, Stephen, 39
Baudelaire and Freud (Bersani), 68
becoming, psychological, 63, 74, 140, 173,
    185, 188, 194
Bell, Millicent, 91–92, 97–98
Benhabib, Seyla, 141–42
Berlant, Lauren, 8, 28–29, 102, 183; on desire,
    174, 176, 189, 192, 194; on fat and thin,
    191–95; on misrecognition, 29, 189–90;
    on queer relationality, 171; Sedgwick and,
    177–78, 179, 187, 189, 190, 198; on stupid-
    ity of mine, 199; works, 124, 172–74. *See
    also* reading Berlant reading *Two Girls*
Bersani, Leo: on ego, 80–81, 83–84; on
    Foucault, 65–67; on Freud, 66–67;
    on genealogy of sex, 65–67, 68, 71; on
    infantile sexuality, 68–70; on Laplanche,
    77–80, 81; on new relational modes,
    65–67, 70–71, 81; as reluctant queer the-
    orist, 65–67; on sex, 8, 22–24, 62, 63–65,
    211n8; on sex and masochism, 68–72; on
    sexuality, 62–65, 84, 210n5; on shattering
    as self-affirmation, 80–84; Tuhkanen on,
    63–64, 79–83; works, 66, 68, 70, 81–82,
    83, 211n11
Between Men (Sedgwick), 38, 52
bind affect, to representation, 75–76, 105–6,
    138, 161
bisexuality, 11
Bloom, Harold, 173
Borromean knot, 133
boundaries: antinormativity relating to,
    85, 87–89; appropriate *versus* inappro-
    priate, 24; not for faint of heart, 111–15;
    queerness and vulnerability, 85–87, 118;
    queer = sexual outlaw, 100–104; reading
    Henry James, 97–100; rereading James,
    106–11; of sex offenders as new queers,
    24, 87–90; sexual, 25; a small boy and
    others relating to, 90–97; violence of
    relationality, 104–6
bourgeois morality, 38
Brennan, Teresa, 181, 220n12
Brown, Wendy, 142–44
Butler, Judith, 219n25; on gender, 8, 11,
    26–27, 66, 163–66, 176; psychic narra-
    tives of, 148–51; works, 26, 144, 145, 147,
    148, 165, 166
Butlerian performativity, 147, 148, 176–77

Cameron, Sharon, 97–98
Caravaggio's Secrets (Bersani), 81–82
Cartesian coup, 35

Cartesian rationalism, 37, 181
Castle, Terry, 169
castration theory, 58
centering, 15, 80, 161
central consciousness, 98, 106–7
centrality: of homophobic oppression,
    44–45; of pleasure, 53
child: children and, 126–27; figural, 129, 138,
    139; politics = Imaginary, 129; uncon-
    scious sexuality relating to, 138–39,
    184–85, 218n36. *See also* adult-child
    relationship
childhood, 98–99
children, 117, 126; Anti-Child = Queer Sub-
    ject, 26; desire of, 138; fuck-off to, 89, 116,
    127, 131, 134; sexuality of, 24, 88, 213n8;
    sexual theories of, 57–61, 123, 210n34;
    unconscious sexuality relating to,
    138–39, 160–61, 184–85. *See also* sexual
    theories of children
children, innocence of: asymmetrical sexual
    development and, 25; fantasy of, 25–27,
    86, 100
Clark, David, 39
Clinical Encounters in Sexuality (Giffney
    and Watson), 35
cloacal theory, 58
coextensivity, 38
coming out, of lesbians, 53–54
comparative psychoanalyses, 14
consciousness, 34, 97; central, 98,
    106–7; Jamesian, 106–11, 114; non-
    consciousness, 106; self-consciousness,
    128; unconsciousness, 18, 19
consensual amorous relations, 101
Copernicus, 15, 16, 17, 18–19, 30–31, 80
critical and queer, metapsychology relating
    to, 9–14, 127
critical race theory analyses, 6, 11–12
critical theory, psychoanalyses and, 12–13
critical thought, queer, 1
critical turn: post-critical turn, 5; self-
    critical turn, 1–9, 20
criticism, of *The Well of Loneliness*, 151–58
critique, 121–23
cultural engagement, 148
cultural prohibition, on homosexuality,
    164–65
Culture of Redemption (Bersani), 66, 70

Daughter's Seduction, The (Gallop), 101–2
Dean, Tim, on Edelman, 123, 127, 133–35,
    217nn28–29

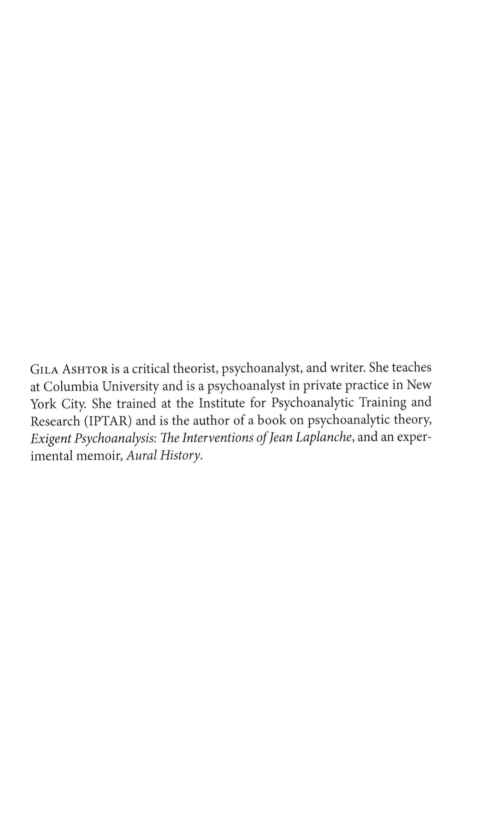

GILA ASHTOR is a critical theorist, psychoanalyst, and writer. She teaches at Columbia University and is a psychoanalyst in private practice in New York City. She trained at the Institute for Psychoanalytic Training and Research (IPTAR) and is the author of a book on psychoanalytic theory, *Exigent Psychoanalysis: The Interventions of Jean Laplanche*, and an experimental memoir, *Aural History*.

Printed and bound by CPI Group (UK) Ltd, Croydon, CR0 4YY

09/06/2025

14685660-0001